D1579542

Aberdeenshire Library and Information Service
www.aberdeenshire.gov.uk/libraries
Renewals Hotline 01224 661511

TUHABONYE, Gilbert

The running
man

Gilbert Tuhabonye is a world-class fitness, running coach and celebrity in his home town of Austin, Texas, where he lives with his wife and daughters.

Gary Brozek is a former senior editor at Guru/ Penguin and lives in Colorado.

THE RUNNING MAN

How the voice in my heart
helped me survive genocide and
realise my Olympic dream

Gilbert Tuhabonye

JOHN BLAKE

www.blake.co.uk

First published in paperback in 2008

ISBN: 978-1-84454-564-3

British Library Cataloguing-in-Publication Data:

A catalogue record for this book is available from the British Library.

Design by www.envydesign.co.uk

Printed in the UK by CPI William Clowes Ltd, Beccles, NR34 7TL

1 3 5 7 9 10 8 6 4 2

Papers used by John Blake Publishing are natural, recyclable products made from wood grown in sustainable forests. The manufacturing processes conform to the environmental regulations of the country of origin.

Every attempt has been made to contact the relevant copyright-holders, but some were unobtainable. We would be grateful if the appropriate people could contact us.

To all the victims of war – especially to the survivors of the
Burundi genocide. May God grant you peace in your heart,
hope, forgiveness, and the courage to go on.

It is easy to light a fire and difficult to extinguish it.

— BURUNDI PROVERB

ACKNOWLEDGEMENTS

Thanks be to God for giving me another chance to live, and for all the blessings you have bestowed upon me.

I would also like to thank all my family members – those in Burundi as well as in the United States of America. Thanks especially to my wonderful wife, Triphine, who has been supportive and encouraging from the beginning. I wouldn't have been able to accomplish nearly as much if I didn't have such an understanding and patient wife.

Thanks to all the coaches who nurtured my love and passion for running: Adolphe Rukenkanya, Ron, Abdi Bile, Kwizera Dieudonne, Jon Murray, Michel Lafont, and Paul Carrozza.

Thanks, too, to all of my teachers in Burundi and in the United States.

I am also indebted to many individuals and organisations that helped me get to where I am today . . .

In Burundi: I thank Renee Ndacayaba and Evrard Giswaswa for their enduring friendship. My cousins Bernard Manirakiza and Adolphe Hatungimana, thank you for being there for me in my time of need when I was in the hospital. Thanks to Alois

Nizigama, who – when I was left without any clothes – gave me my first Mizuno outfit to encourage me to run again and then helped me to find a scholarship in the United States. Thanks as well to Cox and Houghton, who sponsored my ticket to America. I also thank Leonald Nduwayo and the Burundi Federation, Deo Ndikumana, and Stany Niyonkuru.

In Georgia: thanks to Jim Manhattan and the La Grange Training Centre, La Grange College, and my host families Bob and Susan Carlay and James and Cindy of La Grange. Thanks also to my Savannah host family, Allen and Cynthia Boston, and the Savannah International Training Centre.

In Abilene: I wish to thank Abilene Christian University; Mr. and Mrs. Michael Winegeart; my daughter Emma's godparents, Judy and Doug Eichost; Emma and Jim Gibson and their friends, who sponsored my wedding; Graham and Dinah Gutting; and the Holy Family Catholic Church for sponsoring my return visit to Burundi in 1999.

In Florida: a special thank-you to Richard Lapschick for affording me the opportunity to visit the White Hourse to meet President Bill Clinton and also for sponsoring me on my trip home to Burundi.

In Austin: I am indebted to Paul Carrozza for being my mentor in everything from running to life – I don't know where I would be without you. I would like to give thanks to Aida and John Dieck and their friends for believing in me and for wanting to share my story, John Elissa Jackson and Robin and Melody Gatling for embracing Emma into their lives and for their spiritual support, Governor Rick Perry for inspiring and motivating me, John Conley for his race support, Mac Allen for his legal guidance, and Susan Dell for her kind words and encouragement. Thanks also to the RunTex family for their kinship. Gilbert's Gazelles Training Group, thanks for your enthusiasm, commitment, and camaraderie. To Drs. David Gordon, Stacy Miller, and Paul Casmedes for their support on my way to a great smile. I would also like to thank Michael Hall, Wyatt McSpadden, and the *Texas Monthly* staff for their hard work and commitment to sharing my story with the rest of the world. Last but not least, I thank the greater Austin community for the support they have given me over the years.

In Dallas: thanks to Bob Morgan and Cecilia Sauceda. A special thanks to TBB Media for all the hard work they put in to make this book happen. Tina Jacobson and her crew worked day and night to help me tell my story to the rest of the world.

Grateful acknowledgement is made to my sponsors who helped me train and travel in my mission to qualify for the 2004 Olympics: SBC, St. David's Health Care, Medronic, Paul and Shelia Carrozza and the RunTex Foundation, The Hicks Family Foundation 8, Aida and John Dieck, Jennifer and Brad Greenblum, Elissa and John Jackson, Camille and Thomas Tracy, Tamra and John Gorman, John McHale and Chris Mattson, Romano and Marisa Richetta, David and Pam Terrison, Brent Hardway and Phase 2 Consulting, Catherine and Bill Miller, Ed and Katy Chafizdeh, Wendy and Matthew Rogers, Lew and Jeannie Little, Michelle and Paul Tucker, Nancy and Jean Piere Bulhon, HEB, Jeffrey and Andrea Mitchel, Lucy and John Needham, Plains Capital Bank, Kim and Johnny Monsour, Susan and Geoff Armstrong, Julie and Pat Oles, Jerry and Rebecca Landauer, Ben and Julie Crenshaw, Terry and Tina Jacobson, Bill McDonald and Lake Austin Massage, and Peter Kroon.

If I just concentrated on my breathing, I could make the pain disappear. Sweat ran down my face and stung my eyes. The relentless heat and scorching wind parched my throat, and my tongue rasped across cracked, dry lips. The sound of my rapidly beating heart drummed in my ears, reducing my footsteps on the cinders to white noise. I just had to endure this pain for a while longer and I would be free. If I could just float above it, let my disembodied legs do what God had blessed them to do, I would survive this pain, break through to the other side, find the ecstasy of release that kept me pushing long past the point when my mind said surrender.

I love running with an abiding passion, but I wanted this workout to be over. I had many more things on my mind than the four-hundred- and eight-hundred-metre intervals we were running. I had studied a lot during my lunch hour, had prepared myself the best I could for the chemistry and biology examinations I faced the next day. Though I was a good student, I have never liked tests. For that reason, on the afternoon of the 20th October, 1993, I did not have a good workout.

The chemistry exam weighed most heavily on my mind. Molality. Gram molecular weight. Solute. 6.0527×10^{23}. ATP. These concepts paraded through my head as I ran. More so, the image of my chemistry teacher, Mr. Firmat Niyonkenguruka, kept piercing my consciousness. Over the summer, he had been appointed headmaster, and for a while I'd considered transferring to a different school. I'd loved and respected the man he replaced, Mr. Manase Ntibazonkiza, and had considered him a father. I wanted to finish my secondary education with him.

1

When I spoke to Mr. Ntibazonkiza in August, after hearing the announcement on state radio that he'd been appointed headmaster at a troubled school in Mwaro, he'd tried to calm my fears. He knew I was upset about his leaving, and he knew why, of all possible teachers to be appointed headmaster, Mr. Niyonkenguruka was my last choice. I had always excelled in chemistry and the sciences, but I had failed Mr. Niyonkenguruka's chemistry class the previous year. I had wanted to dispute my earlier marks because I felt Mr. Niyonkenguruka had graded me unfairly. Fortunately, during repêchage, the two-week period of remediation during the summer, I had managed to bring up my grade sufficiently to pass the class. Though I was popular with my peers and the other teachers at Lycée Kibimba, Mr. Niyonkenguruka did not like me. I understand this is the universal lament of students who fail a particular teacher's class, but I truly felt he bore some grudge against me.

The lone Hutu among the faculty, Mr. Niyonkenguruka was not popular, and he seldom participated in any of the school's activities. We students talked more about his clothes than about his pedagogical techniques – he never wore a suit and tie as our other teachers did, and he came to school clad in the same pair of pants each day. Sometimes I wondered if he was jealous of the attention I received as a champion runner and a student representative on the school's board, if perhaps he felt I didn't deserve the many perks I enjoyed as a result of my status among faculty and peers. In fact, one of his first acts when I returned to campus in August of that year was to strip me of the privilege of being a library monitor. For the past two years I had possessed the key to the library and was responsible for locking it up at night. This had afforded me unlimited access to the one truly quiet study area on the *campus. I missed being able to spend hours alone, long after I had checked in on the lower-school boys' dormitory and turned out the lights. I would study and dream of the scholarship offers I'd received to go to the United States to run. Tulane University, Boise State – these names rolled off my tongue like exotic ports of call.*

Maybe Mr. Niyonkenguruka's decision to strip me of this privilege was part of a plot to prevent me from realising my dream. Unless I passed his class, I would have to repeat year thirteen of my schooling. I wouldn't be able to take the national exam that would earn me a coveted spot at the university. What frightened me most was that this one man held my future in his hands.

Trying not to think about that possibility was difficult, but I had two more four-hundred-metre repeats to complete. I had no way of knowing it then, but just hours after that workout, a far more insidious plot was about to be set into motion, and the evil Mr. Niyonkenguruka of the chemistry classroom would seem positively benign compared with what he would become the very next day.

During dinner in the dormitory, I laughed and joked with classmates, but a part of me was far away, reciting definitions. As much as I would have liked to fully surrender to the merriment, I could think only of life at a school in the United States. Pass the national exam, and I would have an opportunity no one in my family had ever had before. Fail, and I would face another year in secondary school, while my friends and rivals advanced. My mother and father had sacrificed much to send me 150 miles from my home village of Fuku to this Protestant boarding school in Kibimba.

Just so you know I'm not perfect, that night, like any other student anywhere, I wished that God would intervene on my behalf, so that somehow, some way, the tests would be postponed. That evening, as I supervised and assisted the other students in cleaning up the cafeteria after dinner, I said a silent prayer, asking God to help me. I had no way of knowing that God would answer my prayer but that He had a far sterner test in store for me and my classmates.

Later that evening, I went to the seventh-graders' dorm room and made sure all the boys were in bed. I'd been supervising them since the start of the school year. Some of the more brazen boys were laughing and joking, but for the most part they were as silent as the cows I used to herd, and nearly as smart and odorous. I walked into the older boys' dormitory where I slept and was comforted by the familiar sights and sounds. We slept together in one large room, barracks-style, with bunk beds and standing lockers for our possessions. I had been living there for more than seven years, and I never questioned the routine. Just as, prior to that school year, I had never questioned the fact that I, a member of the Tutsi ethnic minority, slept with a Hutu on either side of me. In the past, they had just been my classmates and nothing more.

The summer's presidential election had called into question everything I had once believed about my country and the relationship between the majority Hutus and my group, the Tutsis. For the first time since 1960, when the first free elections were held in Burundi, a Hutu was in power. I wasn't troubled by the election results as much as I was by the tenor of the electioneering and the violence that preceded it. You could not travel anywhere without seeing the green-and-white banners of FRODEBU. The Front for Democracy in Burundi was a powerful Hutu party, and my friends Desire, Viatole, Denny, and Marcel – Hutus all – had told me that we Tutsis were going to see what life would be like now that we were no longer in power. I had always been an optimist and enjoyed good relationships with Hutus, so I dismissed their comments as the idle bragging of the victor. I also didn't put much stock in politics, though when I returned to school in August following the June elections, politics had been on everyone's minds and lips.

For most of 1993 the country had been torn by violence. In February Rwandan militants, supportive of the Hutu cause, crossed the border and began protesting against the Tutsi officials. This was an ethnic issue, so loyalties were to one's clan and tribe and not one's country – the one blood, the other an imposed artifice. These militants joined up with Hutus from Burundi and began a systematic elimination of Tutsi candidates that resulted in even more violence when Tutsis retaliated. Rwanda's President Habyarimana was likely behind the agitation. Like Burundi, Rwanda has a dominant Hutu population, but he was the first Hutu president and it was clear he wanted Burundi to also be run by a Hutu. Given what we know of what took place in Rwanda, the state-sponsored genocide there, can there be any doubt as to what the intentions were in Burundi? Tutsis were fighting, not just for their political lives but for their literal lives. In July, in the wake of the June elections that put Hutus in power in unprecedented numbers, Tutsi leaders sponsored a military coup, which failed.

By late October the fears of many Tutsis had proved unfounded, but I'd felt a subtle shift in my relationships with Hutu classmates. The school's population was the inverse of the general population: Nearly 80 percent of the students and faculty were Tutsis. Tutsis have a tradition of securing an education. For that reason, we have dominated government and education positions – a sore point among the less-educated majority.

Mr. Niyonkenguraka's appointment as headmaster had

fuelled my anxiety. He was a Hutu teacher, he was from the same region as the Hutu president, Melchior Ndadaye, and the rumor circulating was that his appointment had been politically motivated. But once the school year started, I pushed my worries aside, repeating to myself the admonition Mr. Ntibazonkiza had left me with the last time we spoke: Focus, Gilbert. Keep your mind on your studies. Don't be concerned with all these other matters.

I had also consoled myself by believing that my classmates considered me more than just a Tutsi or one of the herd of underachievers. Shortly after the lights went out, I got some good-natured teasing from my friends, Hutu and Tutsi alike, to remind me of the high regard they held me in. Teasing was good. Being ignored was bad.

After living and studying together for so long, we had come to know one another's strengths and weaknesses well. "Gilbert, perhaps the sun will not rise tomorrow," called my friend Josiah. "Then you will be spared."

"That would be a very good thing indeed," chimed in another voice.

"No, no. Gilbert will not like that. Then Gilbert will worry that his family will have to milk the cows in the dark. He will have to go home so they will know the right end."

This last remark came from a Hutu boy who ran on a relay along with me. It is well known that my people have traditionally kept livestock, while Hutus farmed. Raising and selling animals generally made one more prosperous, and my people have always been better off financially than the Hutus, enabling us to afford private education. Of course, that night I thought none of these thoughts. I simply tried to craft a teasing rejoinder. "They will have no problem. I have sent them a photograph of your face for them to study in case of just such an emergency."

The rest of the boys joined in a hooting chorus accompanied by a drumbeat of heels against mattresses.

A moment later, I felt a soft thump on the top of my head from a pillow tossed at me. I tucked it beneath my head. "Thank you. I will sleep much better now." I wished that that were true. In fact, my mind was buzzing. The Krebs cycle. Pyruvic acid. CO_2. Actyl CoA. 3 $NADH^+$. It was all blurring in my mind. I would have to review it all again. Long after the comforting sounds of my fellow students settled into a rhythmic chorus of sleeping and snoring, I lay awake studying by candlelight.

The next morning, when I awoke, I did what was customary for me. I turned on the radio at my bedside. The resulting silence was the first indication that this day was not going to go as planned. I am, in some ways, superstitious. Like many athletes, I like order and routine. When that order is disturbed, when my routine is interrupted, I find myself thinking thoughts that I should not. Distractions aren't good. And that morning, with two big tests ahead of me, I wasn't happy to have the batteries in my radio go dead. Listening to the radio helped me relax. Instead of music, I heard nothing. No static. No music. No news. I noticed the light illuminating the dial. At first I thought the sunlight was playing tricks on my eyes, but when I put the radio beneath my sheet, I saw the dial's dim glow. I didn't have time to consider this further; I pulled out my biology and chemistry notebooks and went about reviewing the material one more time.

Even before I got to my first class, I heard the febrile voices of my classmates. Kirundi, our native language, is beautiful. It has a musical, lilting quality. Though I speak French and English and a *bit of Swahili, I prefer Kirundi. Somehow, to me, the sounds of the words add a meaning English and French lack. Nearly every morning before classes started, my classmates and I, like teenagers everywhere, would gather and exchange teasing taunts. The more adventurous would flirt, and the preening males and females would flatter one another. It was amazing to me then how imaginatively we all managed to dress ourselves in spite of our uniforms – blue pants and white shirts for the males, blue skirts and white blouses for the females.*

That morning, however, the tone of the collective conversation was very different. Instead of the usual melody, voices drummed a frantic, urgent, staccato tempo. Rumours were flying. Someone reported that the radio station had gone off the air overnight. This confirmed my suspicion that my batteries were in good order – but suggested that the country was not. In Burundi, when the national radio station goes off the air, that usually signals one thing – a coup. The government controls the radio broadcasts, and if there was no radio, that might mean there was no government. If the rumours were true and the government had been over-thrown, whichever insurgent group had led the attack on President Ndadaye would know to seize control of the media. They would not want word to spread; if it did, the president's supporters could rise to his defence.

During the brief pauses between the students' outbursts, I noticed something else very unusual. Kibimba is a relatively large city; normally at this hour it bustled with noise and traffic. In particular, the main artery that led to Bujumbura, the capital, was heavily trafficked. I walked to the edge of the campus. Lycée Kibimba sat on a hilltop, and from that vantage point, I could see the highway ribboning across the countryside. A few cars tried to thread their way through a mass of pedestrians. They were all heading toward the capital, and soon the cars were swallowed up by that mass of humanity.

Looking east, I saw that the winding route to the school was sparsely populated. I stood staring in disbelief as first one, then another, then a third tree toppled to the ground. For a moment I was overcome by vertigo. I thought that perhaps I hadn't rehydrated properly after yesterday's workout, and I hadn't eaten yet, but at that moment my stomach twisted into a knot, and eating was the last thing on my mind. I'd awakened that morning needing to see something familiar, to fit into the pattern I had come to depend on during the last seven years. Instead, all had seemed to change overnight. It struck me then that whoever had chopped down those trees had chosen the most strategic locations for their obstacles. The road that wound up to Kibimba was narrow and twisting, and now with the trees blocking the tightest curves, no vehicle could get around them. The road had no shoulder, just a steep drop-off.

I turned back to the mass of students milling about. Where was my teammate Severin, the Hutu who ran along with me on the four-hundred-metre relay? I knew he lived in town, but he should have been here. Taking a quick mental inventory, I realised that few if any of the Hutu students were on campus. To be honest, as hard as I tried not to pay attention to the rhetoric about my own Tutsi people and the Hutus, it was unavoidable. You cannot grow up hearing about the laziness of another people and not, in some obvious and less obvious ways, believe it to be true. The Tutsis were more prosperous than the Hutus, mostly due to our willingness to tough our way through the demanding French-modelled school system. Though the two groups had intermarried for generations, we could usually tell without knowing a name who was a Hutu and who was a Tutsi.

It wasn't easy, and we could often be mistaken, but generally we knew by looking. Tutsis are tall and thin, with narrow noses. Hutus are shorter and more muscular, with broader noses. That day, those distinctions would matter more to me than they ever had before.

For most of my life, my home region had been free of the ethnic violence that had plagued Burundi for decades. I'd lost two uncles in 1972 to the conflict, but I'd abided by my grandmother's wishes. She'd preached unity, and we'd lived and worked side by side with Hutus our whole lives. I did not want to think that my grandmother and the rest of my family had been wrong, or that the lessons I'd learned at our Catholic church in Fuku and at this school built by Quaker missionaries as a place of peace, the relationships I had forged, could all be wrong or futile.

I'd been so fortunate for so long. I loved Burundi. Poised on the brink of a nearly limitless future, I felt my country had served me well. Now, trying to quell the riot in my mind and in my gut, I couldn't help but wonder if perhaps I had been studying the wrong subjects all these years. As I strode across the school yard, I said an Our Father and hoped that He would truly be able to deliver us from evil.

CHAPTER ONE

DELIVER US FROM EVIL

I f you were to read the history of Burundi in a schoolbook, it would tell a story very different from the story of my early years. You would read words like *war-torn, genocide, impoverished,* and *sanctions.* Despite all the violence and unrest that has plagued the country since it first achieved independence in 1962, for me, growing up on its southern hillsides and deep valleys, Burundi was truly a paradise. Beneath its lush triple canopy of forest and jungle foliage and from its rich volcanic soil, my family has made its home for generations. Like many Tutsi families, we grew our crops and raised our cows on land our ancestors settled after coming from the more arid south and what is today Ethiopia and Somalia. If you know anything about life in those places, then you can understand why most Burundians, Tutsi and Hutu alike, have such a deep love of and fierce loyalty to their fertile adopted homeland.

I do not know all of my family's history. I do know that my great-grandfather was a somewhat influential person during colonisation, when Burundi was under the influence of the Belgians, who ruled it, as part of Rwanda-Urundi, under a

League of Nations mandate granted in 1923 after it was no longer a part of German East Africa. While under colonial rule, the people of Burundi still had their own loose form of independent governance, and a good friend of my great-grandfather was responsible for the administration and distribution of land to the native people. This man, whose name my grandmother, Pauline Banyankanizi, had forgotten by the time she was telling me the stories of my family's early days on our land, granted my great-grandfather the equivalent of a deed or title to hundreds of acres on the hillsides of what is known as Fuku Mountain. Since written titles and deeds and a court system to administer them and settle land disputes were forbidden under colonial rule, that amounted to an understanding among the Tutsis that the land we cleared and cultivated was ours by the mandate of our labour as much as anything else. My great-grandfather chose this hilly land for many reasons, not the least of which was, as any military strategy book will tell you, that high ground is easy to defend.

He picked one mountaintop for himself, and he and each of his three brothers built a settlement there. More land was cleared for planting and grazing, and with each successive generation the land was passed down to the male children. For that reason, I grew up surrounded by family, and while we lived in separate dwellings (at first huts and later houses), we cared for one another's land when necessary and socialised constantly. My grandfather Simeone Ndayirukiye died when I was very young, and so my grandmother Pauline served as the head of our family. In the highlands of Burundi, I was isolated from the outside world and protected from its more violent elements.

By the time I was born, my father, Sabiyumva (the oldest son), and his seven siblings all worked our land. Our huts were gathered in an oval cluster, compound-style. While individual families had small gardens, we shared and worked together our largest plots of land. We got along well with our neighbours who lived on adjacent hillsides. While we considered ourselves a community and lived in a kind of village, we had no central buildings and only a few footpaths connecting our homes; what connected us was our bloodline.

Burundi itself lies on a high plateau rising from the shores of Lake Tanganyika, which serves as much of the western border with the Democratic Republic of Congo. Our property rose to nearly 5,500 feet above sea level, keeping it relatively cool compared with the steamy heat of the Lake Tanganyika region and other parts of the country.

Is it any wonder that this cool, fertile land should be the subject of so many disputes? Who wouldn't fight for control of a place as beautiful and life-sustaining as this, a place where people from many tribes and clans settled in order to feed themselves? Like most African people, Burundians have many loyalties: to their country, to their ethnic group, to their clan, and to their family. While I was born a Tutsi in Comina Songa (the rough equivalent of Songa County) in the province of Bururi in the country of Burundi, the story has more chapters than that. The Tutsis are a Bantu people – people who speak a Bantu language – and my family is part of the Batsinga tribe and the Abasafu clan. Those names tell you much about my family: *Batsinga* means "strong" and *Abasafu* means "those people who like to own cows." In our culture we do not have surnames; your individual name is meant to convey something of your personality, your history, or the circumstances of your birth.

To name a thing gives you great power over it, and for that reason, when I was born in April 1974, my mother named me

Tuhabonyemana, which means "child of God." (Later in life, when I gained some fame as a runner, I would drop the "mana" from my name because the radio announcers and the officials at the meets found it easier to say that way.) Though my mother was not as strictly religious as my grandmother or others in the family, I suppose she had several reasons for selecting this name. The months and years leading up to my birth were difficult ones – when it seemed as though a series of plagues visited us.

My parents had their first child, my oldest sister, Beatrice, shortly after independence in 1962. My brother, Dieudonné Irabandutira, was born in 1966. In the eight years between his birth and mine, much happened in our family. Perhaps most important, in 1972 a civil war erupted, and thousands of Hutus, and two of my uncles, were killed. The violence was a result of decades-long and complex conflicts going all the way back to 1966, when King Mwambutsa IV (a Tutsi) was deposed. He had reigned for fifty years, before his son Charles, aided by the army, overthrew him and suspended the constitution. Charles ruled as Ntare V, and his reign was considerably shorter than his father's. Captain Michel Micombero ousted Ntare V that same year and declared Burundi a republic. Micombero was also a Tutsi; thus his main rivals were the majority Hutus. But in 1972 the Hutus killed Ntare V, fearing that he would return to power and end the republic. In retaliation, the Tutsi military exacted revenge on the Hutus for having killed one of their own, regardless of what they felt about Ntare V previously. War ensued, and in the succeeding years, thousands and thousands of Burundians lost their lives as a Hutu rebellion was quashed. By the time I was born, this violence had for the most part ended; in Comina Songa particularly, things had been quiet.

For the two years prior to my birth, the entire country was

gripped by a devastating drought, a problem no one in my family had ever experienced in for as long as we'd been in Burundi. This was followed by an invasion of crickets, which further ruined the crops. Finally, shortly before I was born, my mother broke her ankle. In the United States, this would not be a major crisis, but we did not have access to a doctor or a hospital. In addition, though she was pregnant and hobbled by her ankle, my mother still had to keep the household and the farm running. Beatrice was a great help to her, but the burdens a mother in Burundi must bear are considerable.

The other name I was given, a kind of nickname, tells a great deal about me. Today, if you were to go back to Mount Fuku and ask people about Gilbert, you might get a few puzzled looks. If instead you asked the people of my community about Tumagu, you would be greeted with wide smiles and excited storytellers clamouring to tell you more about me. *Tumagu* is a difficult word to translate. Essentially, it means "energetic" and "constantly alert." And according to my family, as a little boy I was constantly in motion. My mother tells me that from the time I took my first steps, I was eager to run. They would put my excess of energy to work as soon as I was able, and I would never lose my love of running. In an agricultural region like Comina Songa, that meant activity from sunup to sundown.

We lived in a fairly large home made of wood from the eucalyptus trees dotting the property; by the time I was born, we had prospered enough to be able to afford a thatched grass roof. This was a great comfort, particularly during the rainy season. Without it, our compacted-dirt floors would have turned to mud; with it, our house remained remarkably clean and relatively dust-free. The house had four rooms – a central space that also was used for cooking, a room for my parents, and two rooms that the children shared. My brother, Dieudonné, and I shared a bed, and Beatrice and my younger sister, Francine Kagorore, who was born two years after me, slept together. With no electricity or running water, we always had work to do in order to cook or clean. My great-grandfather had been smart in selecting the site for his settlement, for he knew of a natural spring at the bottom of the mountain. Each day, one of us was responsible for heading down the mountain to fetch water. Some of my earliest memories are of walking beside my mother holding her hand as we navigated the steep and rutted path from our house to the spring and back.

Later, when I was able, I would run up and down that hill until I nearly wore myself out. From the time I was old enough to walk, I wanted to be able to carry the container on my head just like my mother did. When I was finally entrusted with the task, running with the heavy jug on my head became a challenge I had to master. This despite my mother's admonition that if my exuberance led to any spills and a broken jug, she would take a switch to my backside, spelling the end of my days as a runner.

I also wanted to be able to help my father and Dieudonné chop down trees for cooking fuel. Every day we devoted some time to this task. The eucalyptus trees were relatively small, and after we chopped them into lengths, we'd let them sit for a few days to dry out. Even now, though I am thousands of miles away, there are mornings when I wake up and can see the smudge of smoke rising from the fire pit and smell the piercing scent of the fragrant wood burning like incense.

My family had worked hard to clear the land and made terraces to separate crops and use as much of the property as possible for growing and grazing. Like most in Burundi, we were subsistence farmers and planted cyclically. Much of our life was governed by the seasons. Our main crops were corn, sorghum, sweet potato, white potato, beans, and peas. We moved our cows from one pasture to the next, never allowing them to overgraze, and remained constantly vigilant to make certain they didn't eat crops intended for our consumption. More important, we had to keep them out of our neighbours' fields.

Corn, which required the most water, was grown in the valley closest to the water. Besides the spring we used for drinking water, the Muhorera River ambled through our valley, and in the dry season, from mid-June through the end of September, we used its water to irrigate our crops. Generally we planted during the dry season and harvested at the beginning of the rainy season. From January to April the river did a lot more than amble – it frequently roared. Flooding was a major problem then, but because so much of the surrounding countryside was still wild with jungle, forest, or various forms of underbrush, we never had to be concerned about mudslides or erosion. We welcomed the rains, and saw them as just another benevolent force in our lives.

As I grew up, nature and its cycles were ingrained in me. Even if I didn't have a calendar, I eventually knew when it was time to plant the corn and potatoes. More important, I knew when it was time to harvest. I realise now that we didn't have much in terms of quantity or variety, but nearly everything we ate was fresh. My mouth still waters when I think of the eggs I used to eat; I brought them in to be cooked still warm in my hand from the hens, and I would gulp them down with fresh milk still warm from the cow. Three varieties of bananas – one for cooking, one for eating raw, and one for making beer (more on that later) – grew wild and in abundance just outside the clearing, as did fresh avocados, plantains, oranges, and a few other tropical fruits.

The few things we couldn't produce ourselves, like sugar and palm oil, my father would travel to the nearby village, some five miles from our house, to buy or trade for. Along with farming, my father had a small commercial enterprise in the village, selling goods his brother had delivered from the capital city, Bujumbura, where he lived. My uncle Eliphaz Batungwanayo had made himself into a great success as owner of a clothing shop and through his involvement in transportation, and he was to play a critical role in my life as a mentor and surrogate father.

Because I grew up surrounded mostly by family, I had no one else to compare my circumstances with. It seemed to me everyone in the world was reasonably well fed and clothed. It wasn't until I got older and I travelled with my grandmother to the Catholic church in the town of Rumeza that I realised this was not the case. Burundi was once home solely to the Twa, or Pygmy, people. Now just 1 percent of the population, they are primarily a nomadic, displaced group, and I frequently saw them in the village begging. Sometimes they would come onto our land and ask for food, and no matter what the level of our own supplies, my mother made certain we gave them something to eat. The first time I saw a Twa family, I was a bit frightened. My mother and I were walking the five miles to church when I saw them out of the corner of my eye. I must have been only about three or four years old, but I could sense that there was something different about these people. It wasn't only their height – under five feet – but their clothes as well. In my family, we wore a combination of Western and African clothing, and my mother was meticulous in making certain we kept it as neat and clean as possible. Like the Twa, we seldom wore shoes, and at that point in my life I had never had a pair and wouldn't for a few more years. The Twa family I saw wore little more than rags or what looked like animal skins. Most wore clothes made from trees. My grandmother explained to me some of the other differences between these people and our own, just as she had about the Hutus and Tutsis. I don't think there was ever a time when I didn't understand the distinctions among the three main ethnic groups in my homeland, but they had seldom seemed important.

Our area was home to both Tutsis and Hutus, and for the most part we lived very peacefully together. As a young boy, I could easily identify who was a Tutsi and who was a Hutu, probably in the same way a white American can make an educated guess as to who is an Italian American and who an Irish American. We base these suppositions on the broadest of generalities. For the most part, other than recognising what group someone belonged to, our unconscious assumptions didn't go very far. These distinctions between Hutu, Tutsi, and, to a lesser extent, Twa were a natural part of our lives, as reflexive in many ways as breathing, and similarly devoid of conscious thought.

Even though two of my father's brothers had been killed by Hutus before I was born, we held no resentment against them. In fact, I grew up hearing about how it was a Hutu man who came and informed my grandmother of the death of three of her sons. This Hutu man also assisted my family in the burial. Later, once we had grown more prosperous, we also employed several Hutus to help work on our land. As far as we were concerned, the differences between Hutus and Tutsis were superficial and not political. While ethnic violence occurred elsewhere in the country, the state of Bururi generally remained free of it.

If one element in our lives clearly marked us as different from the Hutus and also dominated our daily lives, it was keeping cows. Tutsis kept cows far more often and in far greater numbers than the Hutus did. And among our family, the raising of cows was of principal importance to us. The fresh milk we drank was a delight beyond compare. As far as I'm concerned, unless you have experienced the joy of drinking milk from a cow that is purely fed on fresh, chemical-free grasses, you have not had milk at all, just a poor substitute.

The joys of drinking their milk and the value the cows accrued for us – we used their manure to fertilise our crops – was nearly offset by the amount of work it took to tend to them. While women did much of the work on the crops, the men of our family were primarily responsible for tending the cows. You may be picturing the lumbering, rather docile animals you see peacefully grazing in the West's dairy lands, but the African cow is another beast altogether. Our cows possessed enormous horns that make the Texas longhorns I frequently see in my adopted home seem petite by comparison. And they knew how to use them. The same is true of their hooves. I had to learn that lesson the hard way, but it's a lesson I will never forget. It wasn't until I was nearly school age that I was entrusted to work with the cows, but previously my father attempted to teach me all he could about these large and powerful animals.

For the most part, my daily routine before I attended school varied little. I would wake up and either get the water for breakfast myself or go with my mother or an older sibling to fetch it. Beatrice was twelve years older than me, but she was not in school. She had attended the same primary school I would eventually attend in Rumeza, but she was an indifferent student who was bored easily and withered in the face of the strict discipline meted out by the teachers. As she later told me, why would she want to go somewhere to be constantly told what to do and whipped when she made a mistake? She much preferred the simpler and safer pleasures of working around the house and on our land. She and my mother were very close as a result, often acting more like sisters than mother and daughter. She didn't have the ambition that my brother and I shared, and to be fair, it was neither expected nor encouraged that she aspire to anything other than being a wife and mother, cooking, cleaning, and tending the crops.

I don't know if I fully understood this at the time, but I was fortunate to have a sister who was so much older than me. Had it just been Dieudonné and me, my life would have been much more difficult – if for no other reason than that assisting my mother with that one simple task of bringing water up the hillside was so arduous and unrelenting. I can't imagine how hard life would have been if I'd had to take on additional responsibilities. Much to my mother's and sister's credit, when Dieudonné or I wasn't able to fetch the water, they never complained about having to do it themselves.

Life for the women in my family was never easy; and the only times they didn't work all day was when they were sick. If one of the women was too sick to work, or pregnant or nursing, the others would help out. Our extended family was very much like a commune in that regard, and though parents were chiefly responsible for rearing their own children, my aunts and uncles were never afraid to discipline me, feed me, or instruct me. And they all set a fine example for me with their diligence and unswerving devotion to the land. To put it mildly, we were no strangers to hard work.

When I was very young I was of course eager to do what I saw my older siblings doing, so carrying the water was an honour to be treasured. However, the clay vessel we used was very heavy and very valuable. I was gradually worked up to the task by my mother and Beatrice, and the day I finally got to go unaided down the mountain to the spring I don't know what was filled fuller – my heart with pride or the container with water. I do know a good bit of each spilled on the long trek back home. Of course, I soon saw water carrying for what it was – a mundane, repetitive, but necessary part of our daily lives.

As head of the family, my grandmother Pauline Banyankanizi was the one who decided on which day we would plant the corn and when we would cultivate the soil. We seldom worked alone. Whenever it was time to work our land, we all got together and did as Grandma Pauline said. Eventually, my extended family grew to include more than thirty people, which was good because, though we never measured it, I imagine we had at least a hundred acres of land to work.

The labour was backbreaking – we had no modern farm machinery like you see in the West. We plowed with harrows pulled by our cows, sowed seeds by hand, and harvested the same way. The one saving grace was that we worked together. And anytime we worked as a group, we would sing. No memory of my growing up would be complete without the soundtrack of my family's voices raised in song. In our culture, songs teach lessons and tell stories. We learn melodies and some lyrics, but most often as you grow older and develop a sense for it, you learn to improvise your own words to tell the stories you want to tell.

If I were to translate a song for you, the words would not convey the rich meaning held in our hearts. For example, someone might sing a song that begins, "A man may till his fields when the sun is high. He has his many cows to aid him." The words fall flat on the page, but if you were to hear the voice, the syncopation, and understand that many of the musical elements date back hundreds of years to our ancestors, you would stop interpreting with your brain and let the music transform your soul. I loved to sing and to listen to my elders singing. As I got older, I attained a reputation as a good singer myself and someone who could improvise lyrics well. I can still feel those songs in my heart.

Another great joy of my life, and one of the things I miss most about my life in Burundi, is drinking my mother's sorghum beer. Like most people from my region, I drank beer from the time I was weaned from my mother's milk, but we drank it not for its alcohol content but for its great taste and high nutritional value. The production of sorghum beer was an enormous undertaking, so we didn't have it all the time. For any special occasion – Christmas or some other family get-togethers – we had beer, and I would fantasise about it for days when I knew my mother was planning – and especially when she was starting – the next batch.

Sorghum is one of the most important crops in Africa, and worldwide it is the second-most harvested grain after rice. A tropical, Old World grass, it is ideally suited for Africa's climate. Far more drought-resistant than corn, it doesn't require a lot of irrigation, and it can also survive immersion in water; thus we could plant it near or during rainy season and extend our land's productivity throughout the year. Still, there were times when we had no fresh foods to harvest, but since we could mill sorghum and corn into flours, we were able to store food for the lean weeks and months of rain. Like most African farms, we used no pesticides, inorganic fertilisers, and hybrid plant varie-ties, so our yields were fairly small – less than a ton per hectare (about 2.5 acres). But we were growing crops mostly for our own consumption and not for sale or trade. Later, when I studied agricultural science in secondary school and at university, I would read about these "poor" and "inefficient yields" and I would wish the professors and the authors of the textbooks and articles I read could have tasted our poor and inefficient sorghum beer.

Most people who truly love beer know that as far back as the ancient Egyptian times, humankind has had beer, and Africans have brewed fermented beverages for centuries. Besides being a rich source of carbohydrates and a varying amount of alcohol, depending upon how long it is allowed to ferment, it also provided us significant nutrition. I understand that today some sorghum beer is commercially available in various parts of southern Africa, including South Africa. It can be bottled but is most often packaged in cartons or plastic jugs. The most famous brand in Burundi is Vitalo, and it was the sponsor of my favourite football team, Vitalo Dynamique.

Before I got involved in organised sports and attended school, being in motion was always something I enjoyed as much as sorghum beer. Without cars, we went everywhere on foot. What few roads Songa Commune had were unpaved, and Burundi had no railroad. I did not travel by bus until I left home to go to secondary school. For the most part, our legs, hearts, and lungs were our automobiles and engines, powering us wherever we wanted to go. And I always wanted to be moving. My mother had to constantly remind me to sit still and eat. I must have had a very high metabolism even then, since I was an extremely thin child.

Just from the work I did daily I was becoming a strong boy. And when it came time to relax on rainy days, I would spend the time playing dominoes, card games, or *urubugu*, but what I really wanted to do was to be outside with my cousins and friends playing football or running. Like typical boys, we were extremely competitive, and though we didn't organise actual track meets, our games of tag and our ability to attack quickly and flee set apart the fleet from the slow. The currency we used to judge our standing was running speed, and my slight build and long legs gave me a natural advantage over others and earned me status. Even if I hadn't been among the fastest in our group, I would have loved running. The simple act of putting one foot in front of the other in rapid succession pleased me in ways I find difficult to explain. And for me running had a utilitarian value most Americans can't appreciate. Running fast aided me in countless ways. I could ignore the cows and get involved in a conversation or a game with friends for some time, then when I spotted the cows moving where I didn't want them to go, I could sprint ahead of them, get them turned around, and sprint back to whatever I was doing before. I could dawdle and delay going to school, then run to get there just before the bells rang.

Additionally, before I started school, I didn't have many friends other than my cousins, but I still found many ways to amuse myself – even if I was alone. Running was something I could do anytime, anywhere. I spent countless hours combining my two favourite activities into one – as I ran along I sang. I loved to run to the top of one of our hills. Once there, I would sing and hear my voice come back to me. Sometimes I would hear someone else join in from a nearby plot of land, and I used to imagine the song being carried along from one person to another before it went around the world and returned to me.

One of my other favourite things to do was to slide down the grassy hillsides on a banana leaf. This was especially fun early in the morning when the dew was still on the ground. For that reason, I often volunteered to get the morning water, despite the drudgery of the task. I would jump out of bed, grab the water jug, and head partway down the hill until I was out of sight of my mother and father. Then I would stash the jug just off the path and double back through the underbrush to find the best banana tree that I could find, the one with the largest leaves. They were big enough that I could sit on them, and after using my feet to push off, I'd hold on to the leaf's stem and steer myself down the hill a hundred metres or so. Of course, what went down had to go back up, so I would scramble back up the hill, the leaf trailing behind me like a kite. I was thrilled by the speed, the colours flashing past me, the cool wind whipping my face. I would get in as many rides as I could before I'd sense too much time had passed and my mother would be waiting for me and the water. Then I would sprint down the hill, balancing the water jug on my head, to make up for lost time. Just barely in control of myself as I ran, I loved the sense of gravity pulling me down the hill. It was as if my slapping feet and churning legs had disconnected from the rest of my body, and my head and chest were chasing after them. I loved the sound of the air rushing past my ears and the feeling that I could somehow escape the earth's boundary. I'd even double-time it up the path to home, mixing in a few bursts of running, all to eliminate any suspicions about my whereabouts. A bit of water would slosh out, but my mother had always told me not to fill the jug too high. I was also careful to never appear too out of breath or too sweaty, tricks that would pay dividends for me later in my track career. Believe me, when you are four or five years old, and you're more than five thousand feet above sea level and doing a series of sprints uphill every morning, then lugging several gallons of water on your head back up that hill, your legs and your heart soon grow very strong.

Only once did I come close to getting caught for spending time banana-leaf sledding. The leaves weren't nearly as durable as plastic or the metal runners of a true sled, and we lived in a rocky area, so I wore through the leaf pretty quickly and then through the seat of my short pants as well. Once when I was in school and thus wearing my uniform shorts to fetch the water, my mother noticed the holes in my seat. She held me by the crook of the elbow and turned me sideways so she could inspect my rear. After she turned me back around, she shook her head, pursed her lips, and furrowed her brow. I could tell she was wondering what I could have been doing to have worn down the fabric so quickly. I shrugged and tried to look innocent. I don't think she would have ever thought to ask if I had been banana-leaf sledding. She simply asked my father to get me another pair of shorts from Rumeza to replace the worn-out pair.

Since my brother was in school for much of the year, I was curious about where he went and what he did there. Because he was eight years older, by the time I was walking he was ten or eleven and had little time for me. Eventually, when he entered the sixth grade in 1979, he was sent away to a school in Bujumbura and I saw him even less frequently. When he did come home for breaks or for the summer, I was even more curious about what he did while he was gone. He would show me some of his books from the secondary school he attended, and he would tell me he was learning to count to ten in French and many other things. I desperately wanted to learn to read like he could and to learn a new language. Most of all, I wanted to better understand the world around me. My parents were so busy keeping us alive and thriving that they didn't have time to answer all the questions running through my head. If my father showed me how to mend the intricately woven fence surrounding our house, I didn't dare ask him why it was so important that we fence in our house when our nearest neighbors were all family members. Only later would I learn that unlike those in the United States, our fence was meant to keep things out rather than to keep them in. Fortunately for us, we did not need to worry too much about human intruders, just wildlife.

I eventually came to understand that my father was very well respected and, to a degree, feared in our provincial community. He was a powerfully built man, and all the hard work he had done made him thickly muscled, with pronounced cords of veins lining his forearms. He was also a very direct and forthright man whose few words carried weight. He laughed and smiled easily, but when his expression grew serious, his demeanor could freeze you in your tracks. I'd seen that happen a few times when he was around other men, and I learned that my father was not a man you would cross without paying a price. Whenever I was with him and I saw the respect others accorded him, I felt not fear but pride. My father was an imposing physical presence, but he was also unfailingly honest and just in his dealings with others. I'd like to think his morals and ethics earned him my community's respect. I have no reason to believe otherwise, since I never saw my father act violent. To others he might have appeared stern and serious, but I remember his high-pitched and frequent laughter, which was so different from the deep tenor tones of his speaking voice. He was a great storyteller, and I can understand why the other men would want to spend time with him and why he was so frequently away from home.

My father was the one to mete out punishment in our house – my mother was good for an angry warning that she would spank me but little else. I spent most of my time with my mother, and her stated and implied threat that *"your father"* would be unhappy with something I had done was often enough to convince me I should mend my ways. Unfortunately, it took some severe spankings to truly bring out my best behavior. I was slow to learn that threats and consequences were related in uncomfortable ways – try as my hindquarters might to get my brain to understand that important bit of cause and effect. I wasn't a wilful child – I was just easily seduced by the bounty of pleasures our rural existence offered. For all our labours, life was remarkably carefree – or at least that is how it seems to me in retrospect.

One of the other things I learned was it was good to be a male in Burundi. I wasn't always certain what my father was doing when he was away from home. I knew he was in Rumeza frequently at his shop, but I also knew that often he was simply out with the other men in the community, including my uncles, and they weren't always occupied productively. Yet no matter where my father was, we always felt his presence. We would never eat our evening meal without him. Even if he was away from home hours beyond the customary dinnertime, we would not begin until he arrived. Invariably, he was the first person my mother or my sister served, and he always received the largest and the finest portion. Also, my mother was always certain to have enough food remaining so that if my father wanted another serving, she would be able to accommodate him. If he did not desire whatever was left, then we male children were allowed to have more. My sisters and mother somehow managed to survive on less. It was rare that my father didn't eat his full portion and beyond, but I never went hungry and simply accepted these arrangements and my father's dominant role in our family as a natural function of life.

That is not to say my father did not contribute greatly to our well-being. Some of my fondest memories are of days spent learning to hunt at his side. Each Saturday was devoted to hunting. The game we most frequently pursued was antelope. In Burundi, hunting was a communal activity. No one I knew owned a gun, so we hunted with spears and machetes. Consequently, we had to get very close to our prey before we would be able to kill it. The first time I participated in taking down an antelope was one of the most thrilling experiences of my childhood.

Antelope roamed freely through the countryside and mainly stayed fairly deep inside the bush. They ranged a fair distance each day, and with no roads and only a few scattered houses dotting the hills, finding and tracking them on your own was a difficult proposition. With so much other work to do, we couldn't afford to spend our time fruitlessly searching alone. So generations ago, we devised a cooperative system that allowed us all to benefit. When one person spotted an antelope, he would emit a loud trill to alert others that game had been identified. That person would take off on foot in pursuit of it, continuing to make those loud whistling noises so others could follow the animal's progress and predict its path to intercept it. In that way, we ran a kind of relay race against the animal. While it would be almost impossible for a lone man to run an antelope until it dropped from exhaustion and could be killed, working together and taking turns running after it gave us a far better chance.

Whether you were simply moving into position on the intercept or actually on the animal's trail, the hunt was always an adrenaline-fuelled pursuit. That first day I participated fully in the hunt was somewhat cool and misty. The treetops were shrouded in fog, and a heavy dew dripped from the tops of the banana trees to the vegetation below. My father and I were outside mending the compound's perimeter fence when we heard the shrill signal coming from what seemed very far off. Standing straight and turning his head in the direction from which the sound seemed to come, my father held his hand out palm up, signalling me to remain quiet. With the mountains and valleys, it took a practiced ear to know for certain where the sound was coming from. He set down his machete and signalled me to follow him. After he retrieved his spear, we set out on an easy jog to the north. We were travelling uphill and sticking to a slightly overgrown footpath. Ferns slapped at my legs, and a persistent gnat buzzed in my ear and my nostrils. My father remained intensely alert, his head swivelling from side to side. Our bodies were soon glistening with sweat, and my father shifted the spear from his right arm to his left. I could see the tight cords of his veins standing out in relief on his oil-black skin.

The calls grew fainter and then louder, and our course drifted from the north to the west, then back south. We seemed to be moving in circles, but at one point all we could hear was the sound of the rustling leaves, snapping twigs, our own thumping footsteps, our laboured breathing, and the panting of the local dogs we kept as pets who trotted alongside us. To my right I saw a flash of white, and I turned just in time to glimpse the antelope briefly coming toward us. As soon as it sensed us, it doubled back in its tracks, and without waiting for word from my father, I ran after it as swiftly as I could. I would like to say I spent the next few minutes running through the deep jungle underbrush, but I was lucky in that the antelope's route led me through a partial clearing, where I was able to move swiftly and not have to scrabble over rocks and leap roots or small streams. By the time I joined the chase, the antelope had been running steadily for nearly a half hour and was clearly tiring.

I chased it from the clearing, letting out my own child's version of the call to alert the others, and then we crashed through into some of the more dense foliage. For a moment my heart fell when I thought I had lost the trail. I came to a stop and, my blood pulsing at my temples, scanned the area. I was in a kind of domed clearing, and weak sunlight filtered through the overhead canopy, bathing everything in a pale green light. To my surprise and delight, not twenty metres from me, the antelope stood, its sides heaving, its nostrils flaring, its flanks glistening with blood, though no spear remained. Without a second's hesitation, I bolted towards it, yelling as loudly as I could. Almost reluctantly, the antelope dropped its head and ducked through some tangled vines of a banyan tree. Seeming dispirited, it circled back into the clearing, only to run into a group of about six men and boys, including my uncle Joseph Kiyogoma, who were joined shortly by my father. He didn't say anything to me, but I could read in his eyes how proud I had made him. I ducked my head and walked over to him, meekly accepting pats on the back from the other boys. My cousin Alphonse shook my hand formally, and then his look of grave seriousness was split by his smile and his wide-eyed shout of triumph. We would soon be eating meat.

The men made quick work of the killing, and soon my uncle stood smiling, holding the antelope's head while its blood flowed from its slashed throat. Within minutes the carcass was butchered and the meat divided. Everyone who had participated took home some of the meat, and I was especially pleased that my father was given the antelope's heart along with one other choice cut from its flank.

When we got back home, my father sent word to my grandmother that we had meat. As he stoked the fire in the outdoor pit, my uncles, aunts, and cousins drifted in from the fields as news spread that we would be having a feast. My father roasted the heart and the other meat on a metal rod, and everyone gathered around to advise him on his technique and the proper cooking time. He mocked them and we all laughed. We were in high spirits, since we were not able to have meat regularly – on most hunts, we had no catch. While we waited, we did what we usually do whenever the family got together – we sang songs. My uncle Buzosi led us in a hunting song, and his high lilting voice seemed to rise with the fire's smoke.

When it came time to eat, my father asked me to step forward. He took his machete and cut off a piece of the antelope heart. Though we were Catholic, we held on to some of our ancestral beliefs, and one of those was that an animal's spirit resided in the heart. Since I was instrumental in conquering that animal and its spirit, it was only right I should ingest some it. In doing so, I would take in some of the antelope's qualities, and I was eager to see if I would later be able to run faster and longer.

As a mere child of ten, I felt self-conscious with everyone's eyes on me, but I resisted the urge to turn my back on them. Instead, I took a bite of the still-smoking heart meat. Though I can't recall clearly the taste of the meat after all these years, I can still remember how wonderful I felt when I stood by my father's side in front of my collective family knowing that I had done something to please him and provide for my family.

Eating game was always a treat, since the only other time we had meat was when we lost a cow to illness or to old age – the cows were too valuable to slaughter regularly. Meat always tasted better when I played a part in bringing it home. My father seemed most pleased with me when I was able to kill a rabbit or other game for our cooking pot. My skills were a reflection of his abilities as a teacher, and had I remained on our farm, hunting would have put me in good stead for the remainder of my life. Though my mother was pleased I had developed some skill as a hunter, she never participated in the enjoyment of our bounty. She is a vegetarian – she'd forsaken her share of meat so that a man could eat it for so long that eating it held little appeal.

Besides teaching me to hunt, my father taught me how to build and maintain fences. For us as for ranchers in America's West, this was one of the most important tasks we engaged in, for the fences not only kept wildlife away, they also kept our cows out of our crops. For fencing material, we used branches from the thick undergrowth that ringed our property. Instead of stripping the leaves, we left them on, which gave the fence more heft. We did not sink posts into the ground and use cement or stones to solidify the structure. The fence was approximately a foot thick and was able to stand independently – until a strong wind blew it over or a particularly recalcitrant (or hungry) cow knocked it down. Once the leaves and branches dried, the fence weighed less and was more susceptible to the whims of wind and livestock. Consequently, we would have to replace sections at a time until the entire fence was renewed. It was a never-ending cycle of work that kept my father, and later me, very busy. To give you an idea of how labour-intensive fence building was, it took nearly a week to build the fence that surrounded our home, and that fence was but a fraction of the total length of fence we needed. While the weaving wasn't as intricate as basket weaving, there was still an element of artistry to its construction. A man could be judged based on the efficiency and, to a certain extent, the beauty of his fence.

My father taught me all I know about cows and how to care for them. With a total of about a hundred cows among our entire family's holdings, we had to be careful to not let them overgraze in one area, rotating them from one grazing area to the next. Getting the cows to move from one grazing area to another was probably the most difficult and dangerous task I had to learn. When I was a small boy, even the youngest calf outweighed me. And believe me, a grazing cow wants nothing more than to stand its ground and continue to feed. Encouraging it to move often meant putting my shoulder to a cow's hindquarters. This could earn you a swat in the face with the cow's tail or an encounter with fresh manure, or worse. When I was a little over eight years old, a particularly stubborn cow named Birenzi (we named all our animals) unleashed a powerful kick that caught me flush in the mouth. It happened so quickly that I don't remember the blow itself, but I do recall finding myself lying on my back stunned and staring at the sky, the salty taste of my blood in my mouth. My curious tongue grazed across my teeth and gums, finding the jagged stumps of two broken incisors. My lips swelled and I felt light-headed when I stood. Rather than going home to my mother, I decided it was best to complete my assigned task and get the cows to their appointed pasture. My father had warned me constantly to be careful around the cows and to avoid standing behind them. I knew that from my injury he'd be able to discern what had happened, and I wanted to demonstrate that I was a tough young man who would not go running home to his mother every chance he got.

Only after I'd successfully completed the job did I go home. My mother's sharp exhalation when she saw me let me know that what I'd feared was true. The cow's hoof had done some serious damage to my mouth and jaw. She sat me down, pressed a cold cloth to my face, and wiped away the blood. Peeling back my lips to look at my teeth, she winced, and her dark eyes narrowed. She spoke sharply to me, telling me that, despite my name, I needed to be smarter and more alert. Since she called me Tumagu, I knew she was more frightened by what happened to me than angry. She held me in her arms for a moment, then she pushed me back so that she could look at me again. She shook her head and I knew what she was thinking. How was my father going to react when he saw me?

She gave me a cup of water, and I rinsed out my mouth. A jolt of what felt like lightning ran through my head – the cold water hit the exposed nerves and my eyes welled with tears. I turned away so my mother would not see my pain, but it seared through me. She told me to go lie down for a while. For once, I was content to be still. I spent hours in an agony of dread waiting for my father to come home; fortunately he was sympathetic, and I imagine he felt a bit guilty as well. We did not have access to a dentist, but my adult teeth were still not yet fully in, so for the most part the damage was only temporary. My permanent top front teeth did not come in straight, however. To this day, even though I could choose to have them fixed, I have not. My pronounced overbite serves as a reminder to me of my homeland and my past life there, with all its pains and pleasures.

By seven o'clock on a school day, our teachers should have been in their classrooms busily preparing for the day's lessons, grading papers, setting up science labs. Given what I'd witnessed outside, I wanted some reassurance that whatever might be taking place elsewhere, order would rule our day at Lycée Kibimba. Classes were held in one of two low-slung brick buildings – one for the lower grades and one for the upper. I did a quick search in the classroom buildings and saw no teachers. I tried to tell myself they were simply running late that morning; whatever news had come out of the capital had delayed their arrival. Perhaps they were sitting at home listening to the radio trying to discern what had taken place and what it all meant.

I went outside and walked the short distance to the cafeteria, trying to keep my mind focused on my studies. In all my time at Lycée Kibimba, classes had never been cancelled. Since my prayers the night before had been more like asking for a miracle than a simple request, I began to wonder if perhaps I had been too full of pride in asking for God's intervention. I knew in the last two years I had drifted from Jesus's example and lacked humility.

The cafeteria was filled with students, and the clamorous din of conversation at first seemed typical of any morning. However, when I joined a group of grade-thirteen classmates, I quickly realised this was no ordinary gathering. In the run-up to the election, it seemed as though politics was on everyone's mind, but in the months since, those high-spirited discussions had slowed to a simmer. Now everyone was again discussing which of the two principal political factions, FRODEBU and UPRONA (with *its youth wing, JRR), were going to lead the country in the proper direction. I was only half listening when I spotted Mr. Muvyigo and Jeremy Ntirandekura, two faculty members, and heaved a sigh of relief. That they were both at school was a good sign; all would go on as planned. Mr. Ntirandekura was one of the adults who lived on the school grounds; in addition to his teaching duties, he supervised the students in the cafeteria. Mr. Ntirandekura was the equivalent of the dean of discipline in an American school.*

I managed to eat a few slices of papaya, but my earlier reconnoitering mission and conversations with my peers had taken up valuable time. My friend Marcel confirmed what had been to that point a rumour. There had been a putsch and President Ndadaye had been either injured or killed in the attack. Because Radio Burundi was shut down, they'd been listening to Radio Rwanda. We were 75 to 100 kilometres from Bujumbura, and that distance gave me some comfort. If Ndadaye had been assassinated, the violence would begin in the capital. I did not know what to make of what I'd seen, but at least for now, with mostly Tutsis gathered in the cafeteria, the day seemed to be settling in to some semblance of normality. Marcel noted my pained expression and said, "Do not worry so much, Gilbert. You are still too young to be president!" I managed to laugh along with the others.

As usual, at seven-twenty, we assembled in the school yard for the raising of the flag and the singing of the national anthem. Each level was responsible for this activity on a rotating basis, and today the tenth-graders led us. I stood at nervous attention, rocking from one foot to another like a player on the sidelines before a big football match. The one odd thing was the bell's failure to ring at the appointed time to signal us to gather; we gathered on our own through force of habit, perhaps, or more likely an unconscious desire to impose some order on this day. At the conclusion of the anthem, some students went back to the dorms to get their materials; those who already had them proceeded to our first-period classroom assignments.

When we got to the classrooms and saw that none of our teachers were there, we resorted to being teenagers. Though we had never had an opportunity to implement this rule before, everyone was familiar with the fifteen-minute waiting period. If our teacher didn't show up by then, we were free to go. While many of my classmates milled around in the classroom or in the hallway, I sat at a desk and pored over my notes one last time. I was convinced the tests would go on as scheduled, no matter how disorganised the first period seemed.

My first class of the day was to have been biology, and the teacher was Mr. Selemani Kaiko from Zaire. A slight, balding man with a gap-toothed grin, he self-consciously covered his mouth with a curled right fist even when speaking. Our speculations as to his whereabouts were added to the already volatile mix. As I looked around the classroom, I noticed again that there weren't many Hutus present. Where were they? Even at that moment, I'd already neatly cleaved what had once been a single unit into "them" and "us."

Increasingly, the students were growing restless. The tenth-graders, who only a few minutes before had led us in the flag-raising ceremony with great dignity and purpose, were now out in the yard running and playing like second-graders. Mr. Ntirandekura intervened and herded them back into the building. Having been around cows my entire life, I'd witnessed this phenomenon before. Like our cows, we students were better off when we were scattered about. Now that we were all penned up together, our individual anxiety fed off one another's. What had been a few minutes before a high-spirited, celebratory rambunctiousness turned into a riot of conflicting emotion.

Above the tumult of voices I heard Mr. Ntirandekura shouting that he wanted the members of the student government to gather in the boardroom. I did not have to shoulder my way through the mass of students gathered in the hallway – when they saw me coming, they stepped aside. A few of them clapped me on the shoulder or patted me on the back. I kept my eyes downcast and walked to the boardroom, where Mr. Ntirandekura and three other student board representatives sat at a long table. None of the Hutu students on the board, including my good friend Severin, were there. Mr. Ntirandekura made quick work of the meeting. He told us that rumours of the putsch were true. He didn't know if President Ndadaye had survived. He told us that we had experienced coups in the past that had not been accompanied by additional violence. It was important for us to return to our classrooms, to let the other students know what had happened, and, above all, to remain orderly. Our teachers would join us shortly, and the school day would commence.

I struggled with deciding whether or not to report what I had seen going on outside the school grounds. Mr. Ntirandekura had been so emphatic in encouraging us to keep calm, I saw no point in raising an alarm that was probably not necessary. He was right; we'd had instability in our government for years. I didn't want to say this, but I also knew that this situation was potentially very different. In the past, a Tutsi faction had deposed another Tutsi. Given the charged political atmosphere before the election, I wondered how this time might be different and what parties were involved. Cutting off that line of thinking, I rose to my feet and went outside to urge my fellow students to return to the classroom. I told them about the coup, but they shouted me down in disbelief.

I pointed to several students who had portable transistor radios with them and asked them to confirm what I was saying. "Look to them!" I shouted. "They can tell you what they know. There has been a putsch."

"Why don't you just go back to your studying, Gilbert. You don't know a thing. Study some more."

"You don't understand. Why aren't the state radio stations working?"

A few other students, both Hutu and Tutsi, lobbed more jibes at me. I was about to lose my temper when we heard adult voices shouting. Our physics teacher, Mr. Ntirandekura, came running through the school yard and tried to push his way through the throng of students. A moment later, a group of Hutu men, most likely from the neighbourhood near the school, came sprinting after him. After a brief struggle, they subdued him and two of the men started to lead him away. A moment later, we heard the voice of Mr. Ntirandekura bellowing over the crowd, "Let him go!" The power of his voice startled me, but even more so, his riveting gaze and flaring nostrils frightened me. The Hutu men turned to see where the voice was coming from, and when Mr. Nkuyujura, who was a head taller, stood in front of them, his face still a mask of barely restrained rage, they released Mr. Ntirandekura. The physics teacher stood sullenly rubbing his biceps, regarding the men with a mixture of loathing and fright. Like two street curs forced off a scrap by a larger dog, the Hutu men slunk off the school grounds.

The incident served as a catalyst. Suddenly, rather than milling around and waiting to see what developed, a host of students, Tutsi and Hutu, followed the two cowards off the school grounds. In all, maybe twenty students left. The rest of us, either trusting we'd been through a putsch before and had nothing to fear, or like me, with nowhere to go, remained. I returned to my assigned classroom and once again tried to study. A quick glance at my watch told me it was only 8 A.M. A few minutes later, Mr. Kaikoczairean came into the classroom. I was never so glad to see a teacher. Evidenced by his dour expression, he did not share my pleasure. His hesitant voice nearly failing him, his ever-present curled fist acting like a baffle, he told us he was postponing the test, due to what he termed "unforeseen circumstances." In part, his news was welcome, but I knew it did not bode well for us, especially considering what we had all just witnessed in the school yard. To give myself some time to think, I walked across the school yard to the latrine; at least there I could have a few moments to myself.

I could not get the image of Mr. Ntirandekura out of my mind. When he came running into the school yard, his eyes seemed as wide as billiard balls. Whenever he cast a glance behind him, his mouth contorted into a shark's jaws. It seemed to me he had witnessed something out there that frightened him even more than his pursuers. Why did the Hutu want to drag him away? Why were they blocking access to the town and to the school? What had happened to Mr. Kaikoczairean that had so devastated and dispirited him?

Walking back to join the rest of the students assembled near the school, I kicked up clouds of dust that spiralled skyward like smoke. I squinted into the rising sun in the east and stopped in my tracks. A much larger and darker cloud billowed and juddered in the breeze. Was this distant fire moving toward us or away from us? What I did know, based on what I'd seen early that morning, was that it would be almost impossible for us to flee or for anyone to rescue us. Somehow, we would have to resolve this matter ourselves.

CHAPTER TWO

EDUCATION IS OUR CHILDREN'S FUTURE

I grew up with one certainty in my life: education was the key to my future. My parents stressed this point to me at every opportunity, and they made sure I heard them and abided by their word. Because of the influence of European missionaries of various denominations and origins, Burundi did not develop its own system of education. Instead, our ministers of education followed the French system. My siblings and I first attended École primaire de Rumeza, the primary school in the village of Rumeza. Rumeza was a commercial crossroads, the place where we attended church, and the site of my father's shop. It was nearly a two-hour walk from my home, and for that reason, I did not start school until I was seven years old. I could have started at age six, but my mother feared the walk would be too much for one as young and as small as I was. We did have one other choice. We could have attended the public school much closer to home, but the education offered there was inferior to that of the private school at Rumeza, which was sponsored by an Italian missionary. This choice was, in many ways, the last real decision about my education the government allowed. In the West, I understand parents have a great many more choices

about their children's education. In Burundi, few parents have
that luxury.

Compulsory education, according to the government, was
supposed to begin at age six and last for six years, until the child
had completed primary school, or until age twelve. At that
point, parents might opt to discontinue their child's education.
This is what my sister did. Regardless of the law, not all children
between the ages of six and twelve were enrolled in school, as
the nation's 41 percent literacy rate testifies. Though I do not
have hard numbers to firmly establish this point as a fact, it is
true that the literacy rate among the Tutsis is far higher, perhaps
double, what it is for the Hutus. Part of the reason for this is
cultural, and inseparable from that fact are the economic
reasons. Because Hutus tend to farm exclusively and have larger
households, they normally are less well off financially. With
more mouths to feed, they need to plant more crops, which
requires a larger labour force to work the land. A lack of
education about birth control in combination with a cultural
imperative to have large families completes the cycle.

I know if it weren't for my parents (who each completed six
years of compulsory education) pushing my brother and me to
get an education, and without the example of my father's
brother Eliphaz, who completed a secondary technical education
and attained a *certificate technicien*, my life could have been far
different. Though I did not grow up in a house surrounded by
books, I was very eager to learn to read. This was primarily due
to my watching Dieudonné coming home from secondary
school with his books. In many ways, Dieudonné's success – and
his willingness to teach me a few things he was learning – helped
pave the way for mine. Add to that my inherent curiosity about
the natural world around me on the farm and in the hinterlands

surrounding our settlement, and you have a student perfectly suited for the strictures of the system imposed on us at the Rumeza school. I don't remember feeling that my one-year delay entering school was any kind of hardship, and in all the time I spent in school, no one ever mentioned the age difference to me.

In October 1983, when I donned my school uniform for the very first time, I was bursting with excitement. Stepping into the stiff khaki shorts and matching shirt, I felt like I was entering another phase of my life. Though it was one that offered less freedom of movement, fewer chances to slouch through the days as I had with my friends and cousins, those losses were offset by increased opportunities for socialising and a chance to become as prosperous as my uncle Eliphaz. I was familiar with the route to school, having walked with my grandmother or mother to the nearby church hundreds of times already in my life. But even that well-known walk felt different to me the first day of school.

Before I could set out, I had to be fortified for the five-mile walk. Days often began with a hearty helping of *ugari*. Made from a mixture of roughly mashed corn and water, *ugari* was one of my favourite foods. Not only did it taste good, but like any kind of porridge or oatmeal, it filled me up and stayed with me through most of the morning. My mother would ladle a large helping onto a hot metal plate, cooking it into a kind of corn bread. I'd dunk that bread in mashed spinach or other vegetables and down it very quickly. What surprises many people about my food stories is that my mother used very few spices in her cooking. Because everything we ate was so fresh, she didn't need to doctor it in order to make it flavourful. If I could have, I would have eaten *ugari* every day. Just like sorghum beer, it took a great deal of effort to make. The first step in the process was to grind the corn to make the meal. Many hours I spent sitting with my mother's *urusyo* – a stone grater we fashioned from rocks – scraping ears of freshly picked corn across its rough surface and tearing the kernels from the cob. Over time, the *urusyo*'s surface became too smooth from the corn wearing away at it and we'd simply start the search for a new stone. As we did with most activities, to make the time pass more quickly, we sang as we worked.

Kirundi is a beautiful language, filled with lilting consonant sounds and mellifluous vowels. It has no harsh sounds, and to my ear, makes the French we learned sound as guttural as German. That wasn't the reason my grandmother so objected to our being forced to learn French. Instead, she chafed against the idea that we were being forced to learn the language of our oppressors. She had no love for the Belgians who had ruled our country for many of her early years, or for any of the other groups who came into our country wanting to show us a new way of life. We were never allowed to speak French in front of my grandmother, even though, along with Kirundi, it was the official language of our country. Only once did I dare to ask her why she so disliked the French language, and her normally placid expression grew stern and her eyes narrowed: "Tumagu, there are some things you are better off not to know." I did not ask again.

I had spent much of my youth surrounded by and cared for by women, so I was pleased to learn that my first teacher was a woman. Miss Nyankobwa was stout, with a round face dotted with freckles and a complexion the colour of an avocado stone. She favoured brightly coloured mud-cloth dresses, *ikanzus*, that clung to her ample rolls of flesh. I had no idea how old she was;

she simply fitted into that indeterminate category known as "adult." She greeted us the first day of class and stood with arms folded as other teachers shuffled about herding us into the proper classrooms. There were two groups of first-year students, and all one hundred of us were massed in one large group initially. We stood nervously eyeing one another, smiling at those we recognised from church, eyes darting from contact with strangers. It took a few minutes after all the other students had been marched into their classroom before we first-years were divvied up into our sections.

Miss Nyankobwa introduced herself in a voice that rumbled like thunder. My mouth was dry from the exertion of the long walk and my nervousness, and when she asked each of us to tell her our name, I was barely able to muster something above a whisper. She narrowed her eyes at me and asked me to repeat myself. On my second attempt, I regained my voice and nearly shouted my name: "Tuhabonyimana." I was certain I'd startled and offended her, for she stood straight up and looked to the heavens. Instead of chastising me, she smiled and said, "Very good, Tuhabonyimana." My name had never sounded so dignified to me, and she won me over immediately.

We sat on low stools, two to an elongated desk, sorted by Christian name according to the alphabet. For the next six years I would share a desk with Jean-Claude. Miss Nyankobwa walked among us, explaining the rules of conduct, stooping to place her hand on the knee of any leg swingers. She left no doubt that she expected us to sit quietly and remain orderly throughout the day. And the school day would seem interminable for children used to being highly active. To sit quietly taking notes and listening to lectures like college students would not prove easy. Of course, in the first few years of school when the others were first learning to read and write (I had already learned this, thanks to my brother) we did a great deal of oral recitation and repetition. I have since become familiar with the American educational system, and I can assure you, the classroom environment is far less rigid than what I experienced.

The directors of education did make one concession to us youngest students. We attended school three days a week from seven in the morning until one in the afternoon. They made this change after realising we were incapable, no matter how severe the punishments, of remaining inside and as still as they wanted us to be. Because there was no such thing as a preschool or kindergarten in my village, many of us were not accustomed to being in a confined space and forced to sit for hours on end. It wasn't an easy adjustment for me, but my parents had been fairly strict with me, and I was so fearful of any bad reports on my conduct getting back to them that I was never really a discipline problem. I confess that my mind often wandered, and I fidgeted distractedly in my seat on occasion, but for the most part I was a top student. It helped that Miss Nyankobwa really liked me – mostly, I realise now, because I was not a discipline problem but also because she didn't have to teach as much as she did some students who could not yet read. For that reason, I became a kind of teacher's pet, asked to perform errands for her while she worked with the other students.

I loved to erase the board, and each time I stood with my face nearly pressed to the black slate watching close up as her perfectly executed letters were swept away, I was sorely tempted to pick up a piece of chalk and etch my name on its surface. To me, that chalk seemed as precious as any jewel, but its possession was the sole province of our teacher, a kind of forbidden pleasure we might only experience later. I also remember strutting up and down the aisles among my classmates, bearing the handheld pencil sharpener for them to use. The nearly intoxicating scent of the pencil shavings was enough to keep me on my best behaviour.

Over time, the walks to and from school took on their own rhythm. Many of us walked the same route, so as those farther from the school came into view, we would know it was time to leave. I was among the farthest away, so my walk began in relative calm. By the time I'd gone the first mile, the group would have enlarged and the chatter increased in volume and intensity. Unlike a mudslide, which increases in rate as it gathers momentum and material, our group got slower the larger it grew. Too often we would hear one of the teachers ringing the hand bell signalling the first warning. Depending upon how far we were from the school, we would break into either a jog or an all-out sprint in order to arrive in the next five minutes when the final bell tolled. If we weren't in our seats for the morning roll call, a beating awaited us. While the beating typically wasn't savage, it was painful physically and psychologically. Most of the beatings (imparted with a switch from a nearby tree) were handed out in front of the entire class, and it was difficult to remain stoic throughout the ordeal. But if you didn't, then you could be sure your friends would inflict a greater punishment on you later on – something I experienced on more than one occasion.

Similarly, contrition was expected of you by the teachers but frowned upon as unmanly by your inner circle. I confess that I did live in fear of the beatings and the accompanying humiliation, just as I feared the taunting of my classmates. Most of all, though, I respected my teachers and was eager to excel at school, while still fully enjoying my infrequent excursions into misbehaviour. In short, I suppose, I was a typical boy child.

The school year lasted from October until July, with a lengthy break at Christmas and time off for national holidays. I eagerly looked forward to each Christmas and our family celebration. Equally important on our calendar was the marking of the new year. While we did not exchange gifts or follow many other of the Christmas traditions you are most likely accustomed to (we did drape ribbons from trees), gathering the family together was a mainstay of the season. Any family get-together meant music and singing. My grandmother would sing some Catholic hymns, but primarily we sang our native songs, keeping time by clapping our hands or drumming our palms on our thighs or some household object. Later on in life, those singing, chanting, and drumming sessions would serve me well. At the time, I didn't realise how important my developing sense of rhythm was going to be.

These gatherings always included an appearance by my uncle Eliphaz. He would bring us each a small gift from the city and deliver an address to the whole family. While these addresses were not so formal as to be written out in advance or with an audience seated in neat rows, speech making played an important role in our culture. Before we ate our main meal, after everyone had enjoyed a drink of sorghum beer or the special treat of a Coca-Cola or Fanta Uncle Eliphaz brought from the capital with him, he would rise to speak. It would take a moment for all of us to settle, and then he would talk to us about the past year and how successful it had been. He would let us know how important it was for us to be grateful for what we had and to press forward to the future. I felt as though he was speaking to me directly, and oftentimes his eye would seek me out. He would tell all the children how important it was that we study hard. At times he seemed to me a sage or even a sorcerer, for he would produce the Bible and hold it up to us. He would tell us how so many things we might want in our lives could be found there. Hard work, he promised us, would lead us on the path to prosperity.

For me, the success Uncle Eliphaz spoke of was embodied in one thing – his automobile. The first time I saw a car, I was frightened by the noise but also completely captivated. The parish priest and the missionaries had automobiles, usually Volkswagen Beetles of uncertain age, with mismatched doors and fenders. Not Uncle Eliphaz. He often drove a French Peugeot coupe. In its own way as idiosyncratic-looking as the bulbous Beetle, the Peugeot was angularly Gallic, incongruously sleek with its divergent lines. If an education meant being able to harness the speed his Peugeot possessed, then an education was what I must get. For a boy who lived his first twelve years without benefit of shoes, a car was a prize nearly beyond comprehension.

As he usually did, during that first Christmas since I'd begun school, Uncle Eliphaz asked each of us how we had placed. In our education system, the teachers posted all our scores in each subject so that we knew exactly where we ranked in our class. That first year, I was in the top five, and I told my uncle so. He smiled broadly, patted my head, and gave me my gift. Later during the first break from the meal, he took me aside. He sat on his haunches so he could level his eyes with mine, and he spoke evenly, his breath redolent of my mother's yeasty brew. "Tumagu," he told me, "you must be serious, son. You must be. Focus. Focus will get you through the tough times. There will be many other fellows who will lead you astray, but you must resist. If you focus on your studies, the world can be yours." Even though I had only just turned eight, I nodded solemnly and vowed to take his words to heart. His statements echoed what my parents said to me anyway, but there was something about watching the jouncing taillights of his Peugeot recede into the dusty darkness that drove home the point. I didn't necessarily understand the symbolism of the rutted path he navigated on his way back to the smoother roads of the city, but I knew someday I wanted to be looked upon as he was, own the things that seemed to bring him so much satisfaction. As a consequence, later on when I was in school and my mind started to drift from geography or a civics lesson, all I had to do was think of those taillights, knowing I didn't want to always be the one left behind, that someday I wanted to be the one who was leaving.

Besides enlarging the sphere of my expectations for my life, school also enlarged my circle of acquaintances. After the first grade, I attended school every day five days a week from seven-thirty until four. In acknowledgment of the distances many of us travelled and the impossibility of going home for lunch, we had a two-hour break at noon for eating and recreation. That break, combined with our maturity and adjustment to the rigours and demands of school, seemed to settle the issue of disrupted afternoon lessons. I'm pleased to say school hadn't broken our spirit but merely channelled it in a more positive way.

As much as I enjoyed the challenges of the classroom, I also found great pleasure in our midday break. On rainy days we remained inside, and dominoes and *urubugu* took the place of running and football. Like millions of schoolchildren, I loved soccer – even though it would be several years before I would play with a regulation ball. Also like millions of other boys and girls around the world, we had to play an improvised game. Our ball was a tightly knotted and wrapped bundle of clothing scraps and rags. On weekends and after school, whenever we played, we used a similarly constructed ball and two stones or two pieces of wood to indicate the goal. I sometimes grew tired of the countless disputes over whether or not a kicked ball had actually gone into the goal or travelled over the marker. When I was the aggrieved party, I made my case strongly and added my shouts to the chorus of charges and rejoinders. At times our games resembled a debating tournament as much as a soccer match, but each, I suppose, helped to develop our lungs, win us allies and adversaries.

Who was on your side and who was your opposition never seemed to be a matter of tribal affiliation, and those friendships and hostilities – whether on the soccer pitch, in the classroom, or on our long meander to and from school – waxed and waned not as a function of our differing ethnicity but according to the timeless rhythms of shifting childhood allegiances and the pull of our changeable hearts and uncertain emotions. We were boys and we certainly said our share of unkind things to one another, but ethnic slurs were not a ready weapon of our vocabulary. In purely practical terms, this made sense, considering Hutus outnumbered us Tutsis by such a considerable margin. That we got along so well made what was to follow so difficult and so painful for so many.

I don't recall much of my lessons from those days, and my teachers have drifted from memory. It seemed that each year a few more boys became truant, and I have to admit there were times when I wanted to join them, when I was tempted to just peel off from the main group and dash into the bush for a day free from following orders and the constant demand to sit up straight and pay attention. My lessons were difficult and

unrelenting in their routine. Occasionally we read aloud from
our textbooks, but mostly we took notes from our teachers'
lectures and copied what they had written on the board. We
would do sums at our desks, answer questions from our
studies, and recite and recite until facts were embedded in our
brains. We had no filmstrips to watch, no overhead projectors,
no computers. While the methods and pedagogy were
rudimentary, the standards were high. The National Ministry
of Education established the minimum guidelines for progress,
and all teachers nationally used the same deciles to determine
our grades. A 90 percent score meant excellent, 80 to 89
earned you *la plus grande distinction,* 70 to 79 *grande
distinction,* 60 to 69 *distinction,* 50 to 59 *satisfaction,* and
anything below 50 percent meant failure and repetition of the
grade. Believe me, many students failed, and I know of no
exceptions being made to this invariable formula.

One of the reasons our teachers were so strict is that the
headmaster was held accountable for their performance. If the
teachers got their students to do well, then the headmaster
might be promoted to a position within the provincial or
national ministry or to a school with a higher ranking, and the
teacher whose students performed at the highest level might
be promoted to headmaster or similarly moved to a higher-
ranking school. To insure standardisation and eliminate the
possibility of cheating, the national exams administered at the
conclusion of the sixth grade were sent to the national office
in Bujumbura for grading. It was these exams that determined
the career paths of teachers and, of course, the educational
paths of students. From the time we entered first grade, the
threat of these exams hung over our heads. With so many
futures riding on that single exam, you can imagine why our

instructors took our education so seriously, drilled us so unstintingly, and demanded our unflagging attention so adamantly. The system may seem antiquated, and may not reflect the latest research on learning styles or grant teachers the opportunity to develop their own methods of instruction, but it demanded performance and accountability. While some children were left behind, those who could stand the rigours of the training received outstanding educations.

Outside of school, I was learning other lessons as well. As strict as my parents were, school had exposed me to the influence of others who were less constrained by their parents. I became aware of the many ways I could avoid my parents' wrath and also enjoy some freedom and fun. The walk home from school took on the qualities of a madcap adventure instead of being a burdensome task. With miles to cover and hours to do it before darkness descended, we enlivened the journey with footraces, impromptu soccer matches, and the occasional foraging expedition. The latter once got me into some real trouble. Given my fondness for sorghum beer, it probably won't surprise you to learn that I had a bit of a sweet tooth. While oranges grew nearby, they were not as sweet or succulent as the cultivated varieties available in the United States. What really enticed my friends and me was corn. I don't mean just the ears, though sweet corn was a favourite year-end holiday pleasure, but the juices that ran through the stalks. For the farmers and ranchers of our region, corn was a staple food for humans and for cows, so it was a doubly valuable commodity.

One afternoon when I was in the third grade, some friends and I decided to raid a cornfield owned by a man named Fidele. We picked the choicest ears, enjoyed the juices that ran down our hands and arms from the severed stalks, and laughed at our great fortune. Now, freshly picked corn is delicious even when eaten raw, but roasted over an open fire it is sublimely sweet, and on this day someone came up with the idea to roast it. We stomped down the stalks of the plants we'd plundered, pulled them out by the roots, and ran off into the bush. Someone produced a box of matches, and using the corn silk and tassels as fuel, we soon had a surging cornstalk fire going. I don't know what we were thinking. Something as green as stalks produced a lot of smoke, but we were too lost in anticipation of the pleasure we would have the moment our teeth sank into the tender kernels and our mouths were treated to a frenzy of caramelised goodness to think about that. The smoke brought Fidele running from his home, and we didn't spot him until it was too late. We stood meekly with our heads bowed while he chastised the four of us and solicited promises that we would never do such a thing again. As much as he lamented the loss of the corn, he was more concerned that we could have done serious damage with the fire. Sufficiently chastened, we trudged on home.

It took Fidele a few days to make the rounds to each of our homes, but rest assured our misdeeds went neither unreported nor unpunished. I came home from school two days after our corn feast to a mother whose fiery eyes and blazing anger made our little cooking fire look like a spark in comparison. It's funny how one's name can sometimes sound like an endearment and at other times like a deadly threat. When my mother called "TUHABONYEMANA!" and told me to get inside the house immediately, I knew none of my usual schemes would help me evade whatever peril I was now in. The switch was already at hand, so there was no use in denying my involvement. My whipping was as severe as any I'd ever received, and what was worse was that my mother remained silent throughout. I knew it was not a question of the value of what we had taken as much as it was the embarrassment I had brought to our family. Fidele was a member of our church, and in that closed society no secret was ever safe. My misbehaviour was sure to be a topic of discussion. While a certain boys-will-be-boys mentality existed in our society, my parents didn't subscribe to it. They held us all to high standards, and sometimes those standards and my parents' expectations confused me.

During the rainy season, our region experienced violent thunderstorms accompanied by torrential downpours. Most often those rains came in the late afternoon and coincided with our walk home from school. Since we were at high altitude, lightning strikes were frequent and we'd been repeatedly told stories of those who had been struck and killed or seriously injured by them. I had also been scolded frequently for not coming home straight from school. Looking back now, I can understand that because of the unrest and accompanying violence that rocked Burundi my parents were always concerned about my safety. They had repeatedly told me not to accept an offer to go to the home of anyone who wasn't family. On one occasion I was caught in one of those ferocious storms. The wind lashed the trees, the rain pelted us, and the air was so charged with electricity that the hairs on our bodies stood on end. I was frightened, but I knew my mother would be worried about me, so I refused a schoolmate's offer of temporary shelter and made a mad dash for home, leaping over puddles, falling on the rain-slick dirt, skinning my knees and elbows. About a half mile from home, a fusillade of hail came down. I ran stooped over, with one arm over my head to shield me from the blows. The temperature had plummeted, and a dense fog obscured the way. By the time I got into the house, I was shivering and bleeding.

My mother took one look at me and started yelling at me for not having the good sense to have sought out shelter. "Didn't you have someone you could have waited out the storm with? Someplace to go?" I sputtered some excuse, but I was too stunned to adequately defend myself. Hadn't she told me not to stop anywhere? Not to trust anyone other than family? When my father came home, he spanked me, telling me he wanted this to serve as a reminder of the importance of having good sense. All the spanking did was add to my confusion.

Most of the times I got into trouble were because of being late. I wanted to spend as much time with my friends as possible, and I never wanted to leave a game in the middle. Sometimes my mother seemed to grow weary of punishing me, and I learned it was often best to simply confess to my misdeeds. When she would confront me with "Where were you?" I wouldn't try to concoct some excuse, I'd simply say, "I'm sorry. I admit I was wrong." That would defuse her anger, and I'd get off without a spanking. I learned that the judicious application of the truth could be a wonderful salve.

I certainly learned something very different in my catechism classes. The Rumeza school was a Catholic institution, founded by missionaries. Our instructors were not a part of the clergy, so priests came to the school twice a week to teach religion. The entire student body attended church services each Friday. My earliest memories of religion are the treks I took with my paternal grandparents to church each Sunday. My father's side of the family was more religious than my mother's, and I was surrounded by my father's family, so they were far more of an influence in my life. In particular, my grandmother Pauline, a Protestant, led me to my faith. A truly devout woman, she attended church regularly and prayed with the fervour of a saint. The Belgians had instituted a government she abhorred; she loved the Catholic missionaries from all over the world. She couldn't read, but she had memorised the entire liturgy and many of the songs. Grandma Pauline loved the hymns. She would always sing them to us in Kirundi, since by the time we came along Vatican II had long been established and services were in the vernacular. She had a lovely, soothing singing voice that lulled us to sleep each night.

In her strong, sweet voice she sang:

Nzoririmba igitangaza Yesu Mwami Yakoze
Ndikumwe nabo Mwijuru Imbere ya yantebe
Ndacabona Ibimbabaza ariko yesu arnkiza
Aca Anshira mubitugu anjana iwe mwijuru
Nzoririmba igitangaza Yesu Mwami Yakoze

O victory in Jesus, my Saviour forever
He saved me and I love him
All my love is due to him
He suffered for me at Calvary
And shed his redeeming blood

The church we attended in Rumeza, Saint Anthony of Padua, was one of the largest and most beautiful in the province. It held nearly a thousand people. When I was very young and unable to pay close attention to the mass, I would sit and marvel at the building. Constructed like a Byzantine basilica, it had lovely stained-glass windows depicting the stations of the cross. What seemed to me to be enormous statues of the Virgin Mary, Saint Joseph, and of course Jesus loomed over me. Every bit of the church, with the exception of the mortar to hold the masonry work, had been imported. Supervised by members of the church, the local tradesmen and craftsmen spent nearly ten years completing the work, and several men lost their lives in construction accidents.

The pastor, Father Anthony, was a Xavierian priest from Italy. Father Anthony was reed slim and as pale as any *muzungu* (white person) I'd ever seen. Even after years in Africa, his alabaster skin remained a nearly blinding white. His wispy moustache and uneven thatch of beard contributed even more to his exotic look. The priests and missionaries were the only *muzungus* we'd ever seen and were natural objects of our youthful curiosity. My mother reprimanded me any time I asked questions about them – what they might eat, whether they slept in their vestments, and the like. The associate pastor, Father Desire, was African, and far more robust and jovial than Father Joseph. He liked to join in our soccer matches, and he'd run barefoot with us, after rolling up his pants to reveal ebony legs that positively glowed, even when coated with dust.

I was grateful to the priests for exposing me to the teachings of the Catholic Church, and I was extremely grateful that they exposed my friends and me to something else as well – the wonders of travel by automobile. My uncle sometimes let me sit in his Peugeot, but I never got to go for a ride with him. Father Joseph sometimes gave us a ride home from school. I would never tell my mother about it, given her stern warnings about strangers, but those warnings weren't enough to offset my curiosity about cars. The first time I rode with Father Joseph, I was with my cousin Emanuel Nkurunziza. He was a year younger than me, so he got to ride in the backseat of the VW, and I clambered into the front. The car's interior smelled of mold and something metallic, and rust had eaten away at much of the belly pan, so that when I looked down I could see the ground moving beneath us and the spinning driveshaft.

My attention was soon drawn to the scenery outside the windows. I knelt on the seat and watched the world recede as I moved faster than I ever had in my life. Each jolt from the car's suspension blurred my vision, and I was enchanted by the sensation of speed and visual disorientation. I got out with Emanuel and without a word ran from the car toward his house. Just short of the doorway, I turned and waved at Father Joseph, watching while he wrestled with the wheel as he tried to turn the car around. That accomplished, he gave the horn a brief tap and sped away. Neither Emanuel nor I had spoken the entire time, we were so entranced. It was almost as though someone had cast a spell on us and transported us from school to Emanuel's home in an instant. I experienced a brief sense of dislocation, but it didn't last long; there was a soccer match to get to and cows to take care of at home. Since it was my day to watch them, the game would be played in a clearing near our pasture. We had just gone through calving season, and I had to make sure the newborns had not migrated back to their mothers to nurse. After that, I had water to fetch and firewood to chop. Getting home sooner only meant I had more time to work, and one less excuse for not getting everything done before dark.

The clergy at Saint Anthony of Padua offered us another first-time pleasure: the wonders of cinema. I had heard stories about television, and though it has become a kind of clichéd joke, I truly was under the impression, based on how it had been explained to me, that actual, live, albeit tiny humans performed inside the box referred to as a television. Since we had no electricity, it is no wonder we had never seen a television programme. Rumeza did not have a movie theatre, so the first moving pictures I saw were the religious films shown to us as part of our catechism classes. The vast majority of these were in Italian, and they depicted the life of Christ. By today's standards, the movies would be crudely laughable, with their grainy, scratched black-and-white images, overblown acting, and ponderously melodramatic soundtracks. To me they were magisterial and majestic, transporting me into another reality as surely as any special-effects-dominated film of today could. It was as though I was a guest at the wedding feast of Cana, sipping the wine that had been transformed from water, or sitting on the hillside passing along the loaves and fishes that miraculously replenished themselves to feed thousands; I was there, though more wide-eyed and alert than any of the apostles, in the garden of Gethsemane on the fateful night Judas betrayed our Saviour. The film on the Passion of our Lord was the most terrifying and deeply affecting one we saw, not because of the graphic depictions of violence but because many of the scenes were shot at night – the inky darkness and shadows were as effective in creating atmosphere as any horror film. We'd read enough to know what torment Jesus was put through, and it was not uncommon for the classroom to fall silent throughout these scenes, save for the clicking of the shutter and the squeak of the take-up reel.

I suppose I was as mesmerised by the form as by the content. To that point, I had not read much that could be called literature or even fiction. The kinds of cultural touchstones that American children share with many of their peers around the world weren't available to me. Not only did we not know Barney the purple dinosaur or any of the *Sesame Street* characters, but we did not hear the fairy tales of the Brothers Grimm, Aesop's fables, or the tales of Hans Christian Andersen. My parents had no ready supply of bedtime stories to read to me, and much of what we had around the house was distributed to us at church. I do remember having a well-worn edition of a book that related the lives of several Catholic saints. It was a colouring book of sorts, with text on one page and a drawing on the other. The drawings had already been coloured in, and the paper was curling and aged to a dank orange-brown. Even though I could not read all the words in the text, I pored over those pages time and again, looking for the few familiar French words. I memorised some of the names and a few of the dates, vowing to one day learn more about Saint Catherine of Siena, whose palms bled an unearthly red from her stigmata, or the tenth-century bishop Saint Gilbert of Meaux, whose name I would eventually choose as my own.

Father Joseph was an extremely tolerant man. I wonder now if perhaps his patience with us had something to do with his sense that despite all his hard work, he had failed to teach us well the lessons of the Bible. If Burundi was truly paradisical, then the tree in our garden of Eden was not an apple tree but an avocado tree. I've already gone on about the deliciousness of all the fresh produce we consumed, but for some reason, the avocado tree growing on the grounds of the rectory in Rumeza was the most appealing of all. The priests kept a pair of dusty hounds, culled from the pack of street dogs that were ever-present but transient in number and composition. Despite their years in the streets, they possessed a keen territoriality and barked whenever someone approached the priests' house. Worse, if they were outside the house and anyone approached, they would charge you with their jaws snapping. For some reason, that only added to our temptation. A hard-earned avocado always tasted the best, I suppose. After school or on a weekend, my friends and I would sneak onto the property, sometimes creating a diversion to lead the dogs astray so we could feast on the tree's offerings. The hounds' alert would set Father Joseph in motion, and he would come tearing out of the house fast on the heels of the dogs, waving his arms and yelling at us. We'd retreat around the corner of the church or across the street to hide behind another building.

We'd peer around the corner, and Father Joseph would be standing in the middle of the clearing. He'd run his hand through his thick hair and then stare skyward and shout, "You don't have to steal, just *ask*!" We didn't ask because we were still very shy around the priests, mostly because they were priests but also because they were white men. It also felt a little like we would be begging, and none of us wanted to do that. Only when Father Joseph caught us in the act and threatened to tell the headmaster, which would have resulted in our being humiliated and having our parents summoned to school, did we relent and sheepishly knock on the door to ask permission. That wasn't nearly as fun, and it seems to me that the avocados we acquired that way never tasted as good as the ones we'd stolen.

We had many things to celebrate in 1981. Following successful completion of primary school, my brother took the national exams, which would determine his future. Even though I had just started primary school, I'd already learned the importance of these exams, and I paid particular attention to how events developed in Dieudonné's case, for in a few short years I would undergo the same stringent battery of tests. Based on his performance, he would either continue his education on the same track or be sent to a technical secondary school. If he scored well and went on to lower secondary school, he would attend what was called a *collège* for four years. Then, if he scored well on another national exam, he would go on to upper secondary school for an additional three years at a lycée. The *collège*-and-lycée track offered the only opportunity to get to the university level and the success and wealth completing a university education virtually guaranteed. If he went to technical school, his choices would be more limited, but we had seen in Uncle Eliphaz what a man could do with only seven years of education, so merely passing the exam and advancing to any form of additional schooling would be a boon.

Since the exam scores would come from the Education Ministry in Bujumbura, he had to wait until late August before learning the results. During that time, I noticed some changes in my older brother. He was even less likely to join me in playing games, less likely to shirk his assignments around the farm, and in general more distant. In retrospect, I understand he was preparing himself for the inevitable. Not only did the government agency score the tests, it also assigned my brother to a specific school. This was a matter of great importance and much concern, particularly because the decision of where you would go was completely out of your hands. The best you could hope for was to get assigned to a school close enough to home that you might be able to return on the weekends. Also, you hoped you would be assigned a school that at least some of your primary-school classmates would attend. Only a small percentage of students even passed the exams each year and advanced, so post – exam anxiety ran rampant.

When my brother heard that the scores were in, he and I made the trek to Rumeza together so he could meet with the headmaster and learn his fate. I was probably more excited than he was, and I kept running ahead of him. Each time Dieudonné caught up with me – or, more properly, every time I stopped and rested so he could join me – he told me he could not keep up, that I was too fast and if I wanted to, I could run ahead and wait an hour for him to get there. In truth, he was probably exaggerating a bit. I was a faster runner than he was, but not that fast, and he probably wanted to be alone with his thoughts. I did what he suggested and got to Rumeza ahead of him. My mother had given us each twenty-five cents, and I went to a nearby shop and bought myself an orange Fanta. I promised myself I would only drink half of it until I saw my brother come into view. In fact, once the sweet, cold liquid hit my mouth, I was done for and so was the drink. I held on to the bottle and sat leaning against the shop's wall hoping by some miracle the drink would replenish itself, but it did not. A few moments later, Dieudonné strode into view. I followed a few feet behind him and watched as he stepped inside the school.

When he returned, Dieudonné's face was solemn. I looked at him anxiously, and he merely nodded and kept walking. I trotted after him and tugged at his arm, but he swatted me away. My heart sank, and I feared the worst for him. When he broke into a run, I sprinted after him and easily overtook him. Still not smiling, he stopped, put his hand inside his pocket, and pulled out a paper. With great ceremony, he unfolded it and told me, "I go to Bujumbura. I have received my *certificat de fin,* and like Uncle, I will study technology." With that he exhaled loudly, and I could see the anxiety draining from his face to be replaced by a beaming smile of pride. I was glad I was able to share the moment with him. I would miss him, as I knew my mother and father would, but he would be back. Yet somehow I sensed that neither of our lives would ever be the same.

Three years later, in the late spring of 1984, I experienced much the same thing my brother did. As the day of the exams drew nearer, I felt the teachers hounding us even more than usual. As a young student, I had seldom taken books home from school, but in the upper primary grades I had become a beast of burden, my canvas book bag nearly bursting its seams under the groaning strain of my educational ambitions. I had continued to excel in maths and science, and geography and history caused me little trouble. I was a somewhat indifferent student of French, and French literature was my one great struggle, since I saw it of no practical value. From my early days as a top-five student, I had slipped each year, enough to concern my parents. In some ways, I was a victim of the expectations I'd created with my early excellent performance.

Many of my teachers felt the same way about me – I was somehow not realising my full potential as a student. I would rise to the occasion and score 75 to 80 on nearly any exam and higher in maths and science, but they sensed something I certainly felt. Perhaps it was frustration with my failing to reach my potential that led my sixth-grade teacher, Salvatore Nzumuremyi, to beat me for apparently no reason early in my last year in primary school. Several other boys in my class were far more disruptive and disrespectful than I had ever been, but for some reason Mr. Nzumuremyi focused his ire on me. We had all been whispering during a lesson; instead of punishing us all, he yanked me out of my seat and led me to the front of the class. There I had to bend over while he took a switch to my backside. My mother's whippings stung me, but my teacher seemed intent on flaying my skin. Generally a school whipping was more humiliating than painful, but Mr. Nzumuremyi's beating raised welts I couldn't hide from my mother. Her deep intake of breath when she saw me told me how bad it must have looked. I was shocked when instead of adding to my pain with a few more blows, she very calmly asked me what I had done. Her eyes grew steely as I related the story, and instead of admonishing me further, she got a cloth soaked in cool water and applied it to the backs of my thighs.

I don't know what else transpired in the next few days, but a week after the incident, I was no longer a student at École primaire de Rumeza. My parents sent me to the neighborhood public school – we often called it a pagan school because it offered no religious instruction at all. A good family friend was the headmaster at Kivumu, and it was within easy walking distance of home. Only the poorest families sent their children there, and the total enrollment for all grades was fifty students. At Rumeza, we had two classes of fifty students at each grade level. I'd loved that school and was sorry to leave so many friends behind, but I knew better than to protest too much. Fortunately, the sixth year in primary school is mainly a review for the national exams, and with the headmaster looking out for my interests, I settled in quickly.

While my yearly grades counted, it was the national exams that truly mattered. Just as I would later learn in my days running track, it made little sense to give your all in a preliminary round of a competition. The idea was to qualify for the next round and advance. Then, in the finals, give it everything you have in hopes you've conserved enough energy to win it all. I was confident of my abilities, but the collective anxieties of my teachers, my parents, and my classmates were nearly too much to bear. On the eve of the exams, I was eager to just be finished, to let the results speak for themselves.

The day of the exams dawned clear and hot. With my brother away in the military (he had failed a single class his first year at secondary school and joined the army at fifteen), I knew even on such an important day, I could not skip my early-morning chores. With no one else yet awake, I headed down to the spring for water. I'd slept fitfully the night before plagued by unpleasant dreams I couldn't clearly remember. The morning air was refreshing, and splashing cold water on my face revived me. Upon returning home, I stoked the fire, replenished the wood supply, and set the water to boil. I ate a bit of lentils and spinach left over from the night before. Just before I set out for school, my mother wished me well. She pressed her lips to my forehead and held me for a moment. I had no way of knowing then what she was really thinking, but now that I am a father myself and I see how quickly my own daughter has grown, I'm sure she was thinking of all the beatings she'd had to administer to my behind and how much I'd grown and matured.

Only a few weeks before the exams, my uncle Eliphaz's wife, Charlotte, had died suddenly. The family was grief-stricken, and I had been given the task of running to Bururi (the provincial centre located approximately 15 kilometres away) to relay the information to the shortwave radio operator there. He then relayed the news to the national radio service in Bujumbura so that it could be broadcast widely. Without phone lines in our area, this was the only way to alert her family in the north. My five paternal uncles' wives and my mother had similar stories to tell. Being married to the men in my family meant they had to come to Mount Fuku and live hours – in some cases hundreds of miles – from their own families. For that reason, the women were very closely knit, and my aunt Charlotte had been particularly fond of my mother. Charlotte had been ill off and on for a number of years, and my mother often cooked for her family when she was unable to, since she had no daughter of her own to help her. My mother performed many other duties on the farm as well, and frequently I would help her with planting, fertilising, or harvesting. For that reason, my mother and I had also grown close in the years since Dieudonné had gone away. My being selected to go to the radio operator was further sign that I was maturing, and the exams that were to follow this sad time were just another indication my time on Mount Fuku was growing short.

My mother must have felt a painful mix of emotions that morning, but once I kissed her goodbye, my mind was on other matters. The passage of time has blurred my recollection of the exams, but some images persist: my face resting on my flattened hand and my pencil dancing before my eyes as I breezed through the algebra problems. Even today I can run my thumb up and down and feel the bump along the side of my middle finger from squeezing my pencil so tightly. And I can recall the initial buzz in the hollow of my stomach when I came across a question for which an answer escaped me, and the swelling of my chest when I was the first to put my pencil down after completing one phase of the exam and was able to watch my classmates continue to struggle. By the end of the day, I was pleased with my performance, but I had no idea whether I had done as well as I hoped to do. When I stood outside the school during breaks talking with my classmates, I experienced some of the mixed emotions my mother must have had that morning. Later, after the final answer had been marked and we'd been dismissed, we all gathered outside to talk. Some of the students grew emotional, crying over what they sensed were missed opportunities.

From the fifty students who had started in my first year of primary school, we had added and lost a few, but the core group of my friends remained. There was Gabriel, the tallest of us, a superb soccer goalie and a budding basketball star. Antoine, the most boisterous and mischievous of us all, the ringleader of the corn feast, always seemed to be on the verge of being expelled for his poor performance. He had a knack for just slipping by. Gordien and Bruno were cousins who seemed opposite sides of a coin. If Gordien was enthusiastic one day, Bruno was disconsolate. If Bruno scored well on an exam, Gordien was certain to have failed. They were both the first in their family to attend school at all, and the fact that they had survived to the sixth grade was a testament to their strong will. They were Tutsis, and their parents didn't necessarily want them to go to school. Without the kind of support and encouragement I received from a family who valued education as much as mine did, I don't know how the two of them found the motivation to continue when the odds seemed stacked against them. We had all tried to help them the best we could. In the beginning they had struggled with reading but had rebounded from that early setback. I was glad to have them in my grade and my section. They reminded me of how blessed I was and that being in school was a privilege I should not squander. We didn't talk about those things that early evening; we simply enjoyed the feeling of shared hardship our education forced upon us. We were as world-weary as sixth-graders from the hinterlands of Burundi could be, but we were still boys, and the taunting and laughing would begin as soon as we set one foot in the direction of home.

Using Dieudonné as my role model, I continued to accept more responsibility that summer. The more I worked, the faster time would pass, and I wanted nothing more than for August to arrive so that I would know my fate. Dieudonné had not shared with me one dilemma seventh-graders faced at secondary school. Along with all the other adjustments they had to make, it seemed as though everyone who came back for the summer from their various schools told tales of the torturous initiation rites they had faced. The main gathering place for returning students was church, and I attended regularly as much for social as for religious reasons. It gave us a chance to exchange information about schools scattered around the province and to catch up with the best and the brightest students the Rumeza school had produced. All that receded into the background once I got word some of the school's upperclassmen engaged in initiation rites. I realise now that my friends and former classmates remained purposely vague about the nature of their torment. They wanted our overactive imaginations to fill in the blanks.

I had been used to the playful teasing of my friends, which could sometimes cross the line and become abusive, but one additional element came into play at these schools. With so many students living away from home, they had no place to retreat from their tormentors. I doubt the older students who returned to Mount Fuku had conspired to create these stories merely to frighten us. Besides, the stories varied from school to school, and I don't think my former schoolmates had time to concoct such elaborate and authentic-sounding reports.

Along with the initiation rites, I also wanted to know about each school's academic reputation. I wanted the best education possible so I could go on to university. The government published reports of each school's performance – the graduation rate, the number of students they sent on to university, and the like. Besides these official documents, we relied on word of mouth – often a more accurate gauge of what our experience would be like than the numbers the government released. I was still in a bit of a quandary about where I wanted to go. I wanted the best of all possible worlds, of course. I wanted to go to a secondary school close to home, one that had an outstanding academic program and older students who would not torture the incoming seventh-graders. For a while, I had considered entering a seminary school. While I was not as devout as that kind of commitment might suggest, a seminary school met most of my criteria. Besides, I enjoyed the interactions I had with the priests, and they often mentioned the important role that priests played in the community and the kind of valuable contribution we would be making to the greater good if we became the next generation of religious leaders in Burundi. The priests and missionaries made a fairly persuasive case, and the fact that the nearest seminary school was within a few hours of my home was a further inducement. I could also avoid the government telling me where I had to go if I chose the seminary option.

My parents, however, were strongly opposed to the idea of me becoming a priest. They were still possessed of the mind-set that agriculture was our family's future. They wanted one of their sons to take over the farm. While my older sister was as capable as any man of doing much of the farmwork, our society didn't allow her to. It would not have been proper for Beatrice or Francine to be left to operate the farm. As soon as they married, they would go off to live with their husbands on his land. So, even their husbands would not be as desirable an option for my family as Dieudonné or me.

To say I felt as though I was being pulled by conflicting forces would be an understatement. In truth, at that point in my life, I lacked the deep spiritual devotion it would have taken to become a priest. I suppose I was simply trying the idea on for size, and it took little effort on my parents' part to convince me it was an ill-fitting solution to my personal dilemma and potentially dangerous to our family's long-term future.

As I waited for my scores, the days passed quickly and life returned to its normal rhythm. I remembered my second year in primary school when Dieudonné had reported back on what life was like in the capital, and it seemed as though he was talking about life on another planet. I could understand his words, but none of them translated into images that fit my frame of reference. Dieudonné was as smart as I was, but he fell victim to the distractions and temptations of the big city. Living with Uncle Eliphaz during his first year of secondary school had been a good thing in some ways, but not even my ever-vigilant uncle could keep Dieudonné from wandering. I don't mean to imply that he got involved in drugs or drinking or anything of that kind. But he did see that there were other options for him besides school. Failing one class and passing all the others isn't a horrible performance, but in our school system it meant having to repeat all his classes. Dieudonné wanted more chances to experience the world outside of the classroom. He told me that once he had been in the city, life back home seemed very different.

After his first summer break, Dieudonné told my parents he was going back to the city to work with Uncle Eliphaz and attend school. Even though he was a year shy of the age-sixteen minimum, he joined the military and added to the deception by telling my uncle he was back in school. Eventually my parents would learn the truth, and his deception and academic failure put even more pressure on me to do well. I wanted to be the first in my family to attend university. Of course, I would have to focus on my classes, and according to Dieudonné, that was easier said than done.

We both knew I was in for a shock no matter where I went to school. When word came to us that the scores had come in, I set out for Rumeza. I went alone; I could have joined some of my friends, but something told me this was a journey I was better off making on my own.

The primary school's headmaster, Mr. Jean Nibigira, was the one who would deliver the news about my scores. For some reason, the year Dieudonné took the tests, there had been a delay in the scoring so he was told both his scores and where he would go to school at one time. I knew I would not be told what school I would be attending for a few weeks. Mr. Nibigira had always been kind to me. Since I was one of the better students at the school, he knew that his future depended upon my success. He sat me down in his office and shuffled a few papers before he rubbed his eyes and peered at the score sheet.

"Tuhabonyemana," he said, the beginning of a smile lurking at the corner of his mouth, "I have some good news. Seventeen of my students have passed and will be attending secondary school in October. Congratulations. You are among them."

He continued to talk, but my mind and heart were a jumble of conflicting emotions and thoughts. I was relieved I had passed, frightened at the prospect of being sent far away, glad I would most likely be leaving home, but sad I would be leaving some of my friends and family behind. I had heard one of the most repeated and therefore reliable certainties of secondary-school life: The food was terrible. I would miss my mother's cooking. There was no chance I would remain in Rumeza, since the secondary school was not suitable for me, but I hoped to attend Lycée Bururi. A two-hour walk from home, it was the school that produced our president back then, Jean-Baptiste Bagaza, and so had a fine academic reputation. I would be able to come home on weekends, and I would be able to bring back my mother's food to get me through the week. My heart was set on Bururi.

Mr. Nibigira sent me home with a firm handshake and an even firmer command that I do him proud wherever I was sent. He didn't need to say anything about pride. I was fairly bursting with it. I had scored high enough to remain on the track for a university education. Though I had gone through some rough patches, I had managed to rise to the occasion when it mattered most. Each of my scores was equal to or higher than my averages had been at Rumeza. I hadn't simply squeezed through the gate that sorted us, I had made it with relative ease. I don't think my feet touched the ground the entire way home. I'd done what I had set out to do. I thought of Uncle Eliphaz and wondered what he would say to me when he learned that I'd been the first in the family to achieve this goal.

My mother took the news extremely well. I knew she was concerned about my leaving home, but she was thrilled I had scored so well. She and Beatrice and I danced a bit in the house in as spontaneous and joyful a celebration as we had ever had. I knew my departure, regardless of where I went to school, would be a hardship for the two of them. I suppose for some African women this was to be expected and therefore not mourned but rejoiced at. My mother and sister had already worked very hard and sacrificed much for the men in their lives. I was grateful to them, and after we'd quieted for a few moments, I told them both how thankful I was to have been given this opportunity. My mother told me to run along and tell all my aunties and my grandmother the good news. We would have one more thing to celebrate in the coming weeks, and she wanted everyone to share in our joy.

In October 1993, I was just shy of my nineteenth birthday. For thirteen of those years, I had been in school. My excellence on the running track had afforded me opportunities few of my classmates would ever enjoy. I had been places and seen things few of them could imagine.

I'd come to think of my brain as a highly developed problem-solving machine. My education had reinforced this notion: what I needed to do whenever I was confronted by an unfamiliar situation was to gather as much data as I could, process it, and arrive at a satisfactory conclusion. In many ways, the scientific method was as familiar to me as my own name. I applied many of its principles to my running. If I wanted to decrease my time in the four hundred metres, I had to refine my technique and do my speed work at increasingly faster rates and with less rest in between, and the logical result would be a new personal record.

Though it would take me many hours to realise this, the events of the morning of 21 October defied logic. Even if I had been able to devise a brilliant schema of irrefutable reasoning, I probably could not have stopped what was already unfolding. Of course, it's easy to see this in retrospect, but at the time all I could do was rely on one of the two things that I did best – run or reason.

I chose the latter.

A glance at my watch told me it was now getting close to ten o'clock. I'd been up and around for nearly three and a half hours, and still the vast majority of the Tutsi teachers had not shown up on campus. Just as I was taking a mental inventory of which of them were present, Mr. Damas, the technology teacher, tugged at my sleeve. Mr. Damas was an almost preternaturally imposing physical specimen, his appearance marred only by the thick lenses of his horn-rimmed glasses and a scar on his thick forearm from an industrial-acid spill. He ushered me out of earshot of the collection of twelfth- and thirteenth-graders I had been talking to. He leaned in close to my right ear and said, "Gilbert, we must do something. The president is dead. The Hutus are rising up against us."

I stepped back from him, shaking my head. "How do you know this?"

"The radio, son. The radio. I fear that the Hutus are going to attack the school. I've seen some of their preparations on the road. They are going to do everything they can to keep the military out."

For decades the Tutsis had dominated the ranks of the military leaders and the troops as well. Mr. Damas must have observed what I had on the roads.

He saw me thinking and took this for hesitation. "You must be able to see what is going on," he said. "So few Hutus are here this morning. This cannot be a coincidence. They must be planning a coordinated response in retaliation. We either have to stop this attack on us, or we must get away from here."

"But there are still reports that Ndadaye is alive."

"You cannot believe that, can you?" He pointed over the school building where more smoke smudged the sky.

I didn't know what to say to him. Worse, I did not want to tell him what I was really thinking. If the Hutus found out that I was a part of some organised resistance effort, they would certainly arrest me or worse. At that point, I wasn't sure I wanted to be involved in any scheme.

Apparently, Mr. Damas wasn't the only one who didn't want to wait around to find out what was going to happen. Our dean, Mr. Ntirandekura, assembled the rest of the Tutsi faculty members who'd made it to the school. Together, they went into

Headmaster Niyonkenguruka's office. I had not seen the headmaster arrive on campus, but at that point many other people besides the students were milling about. I stood with a small group of Tutsi classmates, watching from a distance. We could not see because the headmaster's office had no windows that faced the school yard. The faculty members were inside for only a few minutes. When they came out, I could tell their meeting had not gone well. They went off to speak among themselves, and from time to time I saw Mr. Damas looking over at me. Each time, I dropped my eyes to the ground.

By ten o'clock, none of us could deny that this was to be an extraordinary day. For the most part, the students now stood in segregated groups – Hutu and Tutsi. It seemed that we were all still wondering what we should do about the school day. We had been so well trained; I suspect that many of us feared that if we left the classroom area, we would be punished. I thought of going to the dormitory, but at this point, so many other people from Kibimba had gathered in the school yard that it felt safer to stay where we were.

Finally, I got so frustrated by standing and waiting to be told what to do next that I decided to take charge. Some Tutsis were talking about escaping, but I knew that would be a futile effort. We were far outnumbered, and with each passing minute, more Hutus joined the ranks of those already surrounding the school. At that point, I saw no weapons, but I could read the malice in their collective eyes and expressions. Even if we could get beyond the school's boundaries, all the major escape routes were blocked. We would need some guarantee of safe passage.

Though it seemed that the teachers had failed to get Mr. Niyonkenguruka to commit to holding classes or releasing us, I thought that if the students approached him, he might advise us as to the best course of action. I gathered a small group of Tutsi students and told them of my plan.

I was very careful to keep my eyes focused straight ahead of me as I walked, careful not to exchange glances with anyone in the crowd. The dull pain of a headache was building up behind my eyes. I also realized I was terribly thirsty. I'd yet to drink anything at all that morning, and I was constantly licking my lips to keep them moist.

Mr. Niyonkenguruka was seated at his desk when we arrived. He stood when we crowded into the doorway. A small ceiling fan in his office clicked with each revolution as it strained to push the moist heavy air. The boy we'd appointed to speak stepped into the office. Sahabo Bonaventure was a skilled orator; he had excelled at reading aloud in the lower grades and aspired to be a lawyer. He clasped his hands behind his back, and I could tell that he was nervous; he repeatedly worked his thumb into the spaces between his fingers as he spoke. He made a personal appeal to Mr. Niyonkenguruka, claiming that it was the Hutu headmaster's duty to ensure the safety of the students in his school.

The headmaster leaned back in his chair and held our gaze individually for a moment before he spoke in a measured tone: "I need not be reminded of what my duties are. Your duty is to do as you are instructed. You are to return to your classrooms to await the arrival of your teachers."

Something inside me told me that I had to speak. "But Mr.—"

He swiftly cut me off. "I will speak no more of this. I have told you what to do. The president has been assassinated. There has been a coup. I am working on getting the teachers here. That is all you need to know."

As soon as we were back out in daylight, our fellow Tutsi students surrounded us. We had nothing to tell them. We decided *to join the Tutsi teachers who were standing by the cafeteria. As we walked toward them, I saw the philosophy teacher, Mr. Hikintuka, and his expression told me something was wrong. I turned around and saw a group of Hutu students approaching us, each of them brandishing a machete. From the back row, my track teammate Severin shouldered his way to the front and stood before me, his face a menacing mask of hate.*

"You killed our president." His voice was thick with anger. "And now I am going to cut you, Gilbert." He ran his finger across his throat. "Ndagukera izosi."

His gestures and attitude seemed straight out of Rambo or one of the other Saturday-evening Hollywood videos we watched.

The young men then started shouting for Mr. Jeremy, alias Mwihevyi. I don't know what grievance they had against him, but I suspected that since he was the largest and strongest among us, they thought it important to eliminate him first. We Tutsi students closed ranks around Mr. Mwihevyi and began shouting back at the small cadre in front of us. I'm not sure if we were being stupid or brave, but the whole scene had taken on an unreality that was difficult to grasp. I didn't know if it was laughable or horrific, but in either case, I could feel adrenaline surging through me. After our brief shouting match, they backed away. Severin locked his eyes on mine, and I could see the rage in them.

We tried once again to reason with the headmaster. This time a smaller group of us went to talk to him. I acted as our spokesperson and began by telling him that some of the Hutu students were armed and threatening us. He let me go on for a while, and when I was casting my eyes about thinking of what to say next, I saw a green-and-white FRODEBU ribbon draped over the back of an empty chair beside his desk. On the wall above it, a portrait of President Ndadaye smiled down on us.

Mr. Niyonkenguruka was not smiling. "You do not seem to understand. I cannot be more plain. You killed our president. Now you must die."

Collectively, we took a step back from his desk. If he was joking, his face did not give it away. At that moment I realized this man was crazy. When I heard a rumble of shouts from outside the building, I sensed he was telling the truth. The Hutus meant to kill us. I chased the thought away.

When we reported back to the dean and other Tutsi teachers, we swiftly came up with a plan. One of my classmates and a member of the JRR Party, a young man named Diomede Cishahayo, said, "We have to do something. They say they are going to kill us tonight. We can't wait around for that. Go pack your things and meet here at two o'clock. We're going to march out of here then. It is dangerous here, and we are in trouble."

After further discussion, we decided that we would march to Mwaro Camp, a military installation a few kilometres away. The dean told us we shouldn't try to take all of our things with us. "Take your clothes and a few items you can carry, and we are going to have a peaceful march." He paused for a moment. "And, boys, do not take with you anything that you can use as a weapon. We march in peace."

We had a little over an hour to pack our things and assemble for the march. At this point, not just Tutsis were going to leave the school grounds – Hutus were going to join us. Including day students and boarders, about eight hundred to a thousand students attended the school. Six hundred were Tutsis. At that stage, it seemed that the group planning to march out represented only about a third of the student body; the vast majority were Tutsis.

We assembled in front of the main upper-school building. We formed about thirty lines of approximately ten across and linked arms. Staying tightly packed, we must have presented a formidable front to the hundreds of Hutus who had gathered on the school grounds. Even though they were armed with sticks and machetes, they let us pass by them, but we were still clearly and decisively outnumbered. As we marched, some of the older students rode herd on the younger students, keeping them tightly bunched up in our pack. Everyone agreed that since I was the most recognisable person in our group, I should stay in the centre. I did not object.

When we marched along, I heard people shouting my name. Their voices encouraged me. I thought they were going to help me in case anything went wrong. Somehow just moving forward gave us all hope; anything was better than the countless and fruitless hours we had spent talking. I almost felt like breaking into song, as I had done so many times when leading our track team on a long-distance run.

Just as I was about to open my mouth, I saw a spear arcing over the Hutus gathered to our side, and then I heard a piercing scream.

Chaos broke out. Suddenly what had been a peaceful march was transformed into a riot. My first concern was for whoever had been hit by the spear. I tried to make my way toward him, but my panicked schoolmates blocked me. I saw a bloodied body being dragged away, and I could only hope that someone was taking my classmate to the hospital. Though we were now a less tightly packed group, we had sped up, but the Hutus, now clearly pursuing us, speeded up as well. To our left and to our right, groups of them were running ahead, to try to outflank us and pinch off our exit. I started to run, and that was a mistake. Everyone knew my speed. If I were to escape, I could get to Mwaro Camp before any of them and summon the military.

I ran until a wall of Hutus stopped me. I can only estimate, but the throng that now confronted us had to be at least five hundred people, not counting those on our flanks and those we'd left behind. My mind raced. I could not believe this was happening. What had we done?

Severin and a few other Hutu men stepped forward and told me to go back to the school. At first I could not understand why. They could have just as easily killed me where I stood. They thrust their spears at me and kept shouting. "Go back. You are not going anywhere!"

I looked around. Men. Women. Children. I spotted a few of my classmates by their uniforms. Even some of the younger children from the lower school were among them. I noticed something unusual: as much as the Hutus were looking toward us, their heads were constantly pivoting, as though they were awaiting something or someone. It became clear to me that they were, at that point, leaderless. Occasionally, some ruckus would break out – raised voices, drawn machetes, spears thrust skyward – then spread to another nearby group and then around the circle.

I wanted to shout at them to leave me alone, to give me space, but I had read the fear in the eyes of my youngest classmates, here at the school for only a few short weeks, and I remembered how frightened and nervous I was during my first days away from the familiarity of home. I could not agitate these students further. So while they clamoured and shouted around me, I went where I usually did during a race. I found the quiet place inside me where the distractions of the other runners and the shouting crowds disappeared. I turned back toward the school and started walking. A whorl of images passed before me, and I thought of Severin and his joke. Somehow, it seemed more threatening than it had before.

A clamour of shouts pierced my reverie. I looked to my left and saw one of my classmates staggering, clutching his arm, which spewed blood. Then dozens of Hutus were slashing indiscriminately with their machetes. We reeled from the blows, and hands held up in defence were nearly severed. The smell of blood and the horrific shrieks of agony filled the air.

I felt someone grab my arm, and I turned to see a machete raised above my head. He was about to cut off my ear, but another Hutu grabbed his arm. "No! Don't hurt him. Bring him safe back to the headmaster."

As they led me back toward the headmaster's office, they taunted me, asking me where I thought I was going. I refused to answer.

They shoved me through the door of the school and down the hallway to Headmaster Niyonkenguruka's office. As before, he was seated in his chair, but now a smug grin split his face. I shut my eyes to try to block out the anguished wails of my classmates outside.

"Look at me!" The headmaster's smile was gone, replaced by a pinched scowl. A bead of foam crusted his bottom lip. "Where were you going!"

I did not respond.

The silence lingered. Mr. Niyonkenguruka leaned forward and, his voice full of malevolence, shouted at me, "Why are you here now!"

"They brought me back."

Startled, he jumped back at my answer, but then he narrowed his eyes at me and said, "You are now going to see what Jesus saw on the cross."

CHAPTER THREE

ACTS OF CONTRITION

Faith in God has always played a major part in my life. Though I had got off to a slow start in the Catholic Church, I was about to catch up with the rest of my classmates. The summer of 1987, when I graduated from sixth grade, I was to receive the first sacraments. I was to be baptised, receive First Holy Communion, confess my sins, and be confirmed. Unlike most Catholics, whose baptism is performed shortly after birth, I remember mine. Mostly, I remember that it meant the end of one source of my friends' teasing.

Because for reasons not known to me my parents hadn't had me baptised as a baby, I didn't have a Christian name as did my brother and sister. As a joke, my friends would call me whatever suited them on a particular day – sometimes it was Jean-Baptiste, sometimes Jean-Claude, sometimes Peter. Friends who had gone off to other schools wrote me letters addressed to Tuhabonyimana Jean or whatever other name they felt like calling me. I took the joking in my stride and kept everyone guessing about what my chosen Christian name would be. In some ways, I was sad to lose the attention. On the

Saturday night prior to the Communion and confirmation mass, I was baptised along with a few others, and only then did I reveal my choice of name. Of course, I took a bit of abuse from my friends about my somewhat unusual selection, but it was worth it – I was glad to be baptised and to have a name that was as uncommon as Gilbert.

The lengthy instruction we received before we could take the first conscious step in our path to follow Christ was a matter of great seriousness to the priests. For weeks we learned about the rites of Communion and confession, memorised our Act of Contrition, and practiced folding our hands as reverently as possible and presenting our tongues in as dignified a manner as we could so we could properly receive the Body of Christ into our own bodies. The boys were required to purchase a new white shirt and tie for the occasion, while the girls had to get a white neckerchief or other white lace to wear on their heads. Some of the wealthier families were able to provide the traditional white dress for their daughters. On the first Saturday in August 1987, we walked in a procession into the church in front of the entire congregation. Though we were instructed to keep our eyes focused on the main altar, I stole a glance to my left and saw my family beaming at me, especially my grandmother, who stood stooped by age, rosary beads dripping from her hands and her head bowed in prayer. Later, at a family gathering following a brief reception in the church's social hall, she presented me with her rosary. She clasped her hands around mine and told me it would protect me always, just so long as I put my faith in the Lord.

The confirmation process that followed wasn't as momentous as First Communion, but it was an important rite in its own way. In most traditional African cultures, adolescents experience some initiation rite, earning their way into adulthood. Confirmation was the Catholic version of that rite of passage. The bishop of Buruli Diocese, Bernard Bududira, came to Rumeza to officiate. We had taken an exam on church teachings and the life of Christ in order to be eligible for confirmation, and I had earned one of the highest scores in our group. As a result, Bishop Bududira presented me with a card. I have kept it ever since, and it has inspired me on many occasions. Its simple wording, "Always love people and God," has an eloquence beyond language, and I've tried to live my life by that precept. It hasn't always been easy, but in those wonderful days just after receiving the sacraments and learning of my success, my heart was as light and filled with joy as it had ever been.

The other sacrament I received for the first time that year was the confession or, as it is known today, reconciliation. Telling a priest your sins and being forgiven for them is one of the fundamental precepts of the Catholic religion. At first I was frightened at the prospect of going into a darkened booth to confess my sins and receive a penance. I was well aware of what happened to me at home when my misdeeds were discovered or confessed. I was old enough to understand that God wasn't going to whip me, but in some ways that would have been preferable to the gnawing of my guilty conscience. The first stage of the sacrament was to examine my conscience and list my sins. Somehow, speaking them aloud in the confessional made them seem far less serious than they had in my imagination. My faults and failures always loomed large in my mind, but being able to say a simple Act of Contrition and having the priest give his blessing was a wonderfully restorative process.

O my God,
I am heartily sorry for
having offended thee,
and I detest all my sins,
because I dread the loss of heaven,
and the pains of hell;
but most of all because
they offend thee, my God,
Who is all good and
deserving of all my love.
I firmly resolve,
with the help of thy grace,
to confess my sins,
to do penance,
and to amend my life.

Amen.

To celebrate my graduation, passing the exam, and my First Holy Communion and confirmation, my mother hosted a major family get-together. I helped her prepare with a fervour that surprised me. Suddenly, carrying water seemed more like a blessing than a burden – even if we hadn't been making sorghum beer. We kept a few sheep along with our cows, and we slaughtered one to serve. I welcomed the opportunity to be the centre of attention, and I was lavished with it from family and friends. I was disappointed that Uncle Eliphaz didn't show up until the party had been going on for a while, and he spent most of the time talking with my mother and father. I didn't know what they talked about or if any of it pertained to me, but I hoped it did. I received a few small gifts: a pen and pencil set, a poster of my favourite soccer team, and a necklace and cross.

Over the next few weeks, I thought about little else besides to what school I would be assigned. Reluctantly, I came to the conclusion that Lycée Bururi really wasn't the best choice for me. In reality, if I were to remain in our province, another school was better academically – Lycée Kibimba. A seven-hour bus journey from our home and to the northwest of Fuku, it was a short drive from Bujumbura. Like most of our schools, it was coeducational, though the boys and girls boarded in separate buildings. I had heard horror stories about the hazing of incoming students there, including forcing them to walk naked in front of the girls' dorm. Nudity is a major taboo in our country.

When the time finally came for me to learn which school I was going to attend, I received the good/bad news. It was Lycée Kibimba. I would have only ten days to prepare. The school sent me admission forms as well as a list of items I needed to bring with me. It seemed as though each day I added something new to the growing pile of supplies I was going to take with me – a bath towel, a sheet, a pillow and case. Each time my mother set something on my bed for me to pack up, I could see her eyes getting sadder. I knew the prospect of my leaving was painful, but she did her best not to show it. Every now and then, especially in the last few days before my departure, she would cry. As soon as she started, she would cover her face with her hands. If I rushed to her side, she would pull me close and run her hand over my head and down my back and assure me it was going to be okay, I would be fine, and I had nothing to worry about.

For days before I left, I had an upset stomach and little appetite, though I still managed to eat, knowing my days of enjoying my mother's cooking were slipping away. My mother must not have slept much the night before I took the bus to Bujumbura to stay with Uncle Eliphaz before going on to school. She had packed a sack of food for me, including an avocado, some *ugari,* and a pot of pinto beans and spinach. My father was far less emotional, but he spent more time around the house than usual. We worked on the fence together, and though he wasn't as eloquent as Uncle Eliphaz, he reminded me of many of the same things his brother had told me over the years. I think my father understood me in ways no one else did. He knew that like him, I had a frivolous streak that if left to run riot could cause me great trouble. He knew I needed discipline imposed from without as well as within. I had a natural curiosity and intellect that served me well, just as he did, but I would always prefer the company of others to the solitude of my studies. I'd demonstrated that in my somewhat spastic attention to the cows, but I was determined to change all that. Now that my future was within my grasp, I was even more determined not to slip up.

With the exception of Dieudonné and my father, my whole family, including a number of cousins, made the trip to Rumeza to see me off. My chest felt tight and my stomach unsettled, but I was eager for this next phase of my life to begin. I had said goodbye to my uncles, aunts, and cousins, and with each subsequent farewell, I felt more and more like a visiting dignitary who now was returning to his people and his home. Everyone was very pleased for me and very proud that I would be doing such a good thing for our family and our reputation. We truly believed that as a family our prospects were heightened by the success of any one of us and diminished by any of our setbacks.

The hardest person to say goodbye to was my mother. I tried

to assure her I would be home again in a few months, and each time I did, she would grow serious and tell me I had to remain resolute. Then I found myself reassuring her that I would come home only during school breaks. It seemed the ever-shifting sands of our emotional states would strand us, but knowing Uncle Eliphaz would be there to help ease my transition gave us both the traction we needed to move forward.

The crowd at the Rumeza station was ebullient. Any trip to the capital was cause for excitement, and it seemed to me I was the only child travelling unaccompanied. The other passengers had boxes, bags, and baskets knotted up with string and yarn; a few chickens clucked from their makeshift stick cages, adding to the colour and noise. When the bus pulled into the station, I made one last trip to the latrine before receiving final instructions and hugs and kisses from my family.

Bus travel in Burundi was a full-contact sport. No one waited in a formal line. Instead, as each bus – actually a Toyota van or a pickup truck – pulled onto the street, a stampede of humanity went to greet it. At first I wasn't as aggressive as I needed to be, and I lagged behind. My mother chastised me and told me that I had to be quick. Finally, after a few hours of missing one opportunity after another, I clambered aboard the last bus of the day. The crowds had thinned at that late hour, so the seat next to mine remained empty for several minutes, and then much to my surprise, another young man came and sat alongside me. He was one of the few children besides myself I'd seen travelling alone that day. He introduced himself as René Ndacayisaba, and he too was heading to Lycée Kibimba, where he was returning for his second year. I liked and trusted him immediately and on the seven-hour ride to Bujumbura, we grew to be fast friends. I was grateful for the company, and because he was beside me I didn't linger at the window for too long after the bus had pulled out and my family's figures diminished.

René filled me in on the most important information, such as who the prettiest girls were. Fortunately, he wasn't too far removed from his own first year to feel too superior, so he answered my questions honestly. We shared our food, and he told me stories of his initiation during the first few weeks at school. Essentially, he confirmed that the psychological pressures were very real, and though he had heard rumours of physical abuse, he'd not seen any evidence of it. Of course, he said, there were sometimes fights on the playing fields, but they were ordinary dustups and not fuelled by any attempt to intimidate the younger students. Mostly, the upperclassmen wanted to test the younger students' knowledge, to be sure they belonged at a school with such a prestigious reputation for academic rigour and achievement. While that may seem hard to believe, in many ways the educational system in Burundi is far less egalitarian than that here. With less than half of my section advancing to secondary school, those with any chance of attending university were an even smaller and more select group. René was a serious student, destined eventually to rise through the ranks of the military to become a lieutenant colonel. He assured me that if I kept my head and didn't panic, I would do fine.

He produced a deck of cards from his bag, and we played cards to help pass the time. Eventually, the heat of the day, the rhythmic rocking of the van, and the aftereffects of the previous days' adrenaline rush caught up with me, and I fell asleep. I didn't sleep for long, but when I next opened my eyes, the landscape had altered radically. We had descended from the highlands onto a broad high plateau. Instead of the lush trees and vibrant greens that were so familiar to me, I saw the dull yellow-brown of the savannah, dotted occasionally by stunted trees and, rarely, an enormous baobab. The paved highway was nearly spear straight, and the farther we travelled, the flatter it became. In the hours I was on the road, I saw more cars than I had in the entire time I went to school in Rumeza. I soon grew accustomed to the sight of Toyota pickup trucks, their rear springs straining under the weight of a bed full of passengers, hay, or grain. There seemed to be only one rule of the road – the larger the vehicle, the more of the roadway it insisted upon occupying, and it was up to all other drivers to dodge it at their own peril.

As the sun set, the colours of the fields turned to a burnished bronze, and the horizon seemed to go on forever. When you live your life in hilly terrain, the horizon is always foreshortened, and now gradually the world seemed to be opening up, as if the roadway cleaved it in half. As night fell, I could see a halo of lights in the distance, and gradually that indistinct glow took on form and substance. I had never seen anything like Bujumbura from a distance, and I was overcome by awe and uneasiness. Soon, I could see the shafts of light were in fact individual lights glowing in the windows of the tall buildings. The traffic increased, approaching from multiple directions. Illuminated streets signs spelled out words in Kirundi and French. As we slowed and wound our way along the streets of the capital, vehicles and pedestrians seemed to merge into a seamless flow of traffic: bodies, bicycles, scooters, automobiles, and trucks. Horns blared; shouts and laughter floated past the opened window. My shirt now clung to me, and I could feel the heat and the fetid air of the markets. The smell of rotting vegetables and diesel exhaust hung heavy in the cramped bus. A glittering concoction of varicoloured broken glass lay in the street. The scene reminded me of a kaleidoscope that I'd once received from Uncle Eliphaz for Christmas.

Beside me, René seemed unfazed, but I felt as though an electric current was coursing through my veins. The pulse of the city matched my own racing heartbeat. I was just a boy from the mountains, and this city of some 300,000 could easily swallow me or shunt me aside and discard me like so many shards of glass. It was thrilling and repellent simultaneously. I didn't know if I should get off the bus and join the revelry or cower beneath my seat and hope that no one saw me so I could take the van back home. A few moments later, we rolled to a stop.

The sight of Uncle Eliphaz standing just inside the doorway of the bus station was a tremendous relief. I slung my bag over my shoulder and, resisting the urge to sprint to his side, walked across the pavement with the others. The hot blacktop surprised me. It was nine o'clock at night and still warm enough that if I stood in one place for too long, I could feel my skin burning. Uncle Eliphaz greeted me with a handshake and then took my canvas bag off my shoulder and embraced me.

"Tumagu, it is wonderful to see you. Congratulations on your accomplishment. I hope that your trip was a good one."

I began to share with him all of my impressions from the journey, and I must have been talking very quickly, for he held up his hand and, smiling broadly, told me I should slow down, that we had a brief ride to his house and we could talk on the way and afterward. Driving in his Citroën only reinforced what I had experienced in the van. The streets were choked with people and vehicles, even at that hour. Being at the same level instead of sitting up high was nerve-wracking. I could see only a few feet ahead of me, and Uncle Eliphaz drove quickly, weaving between slower cars and cyclists, changing lanes with a casual tug at the wheel. I was riveted by the sights and sounds assaulting me. The few trips I'd taken with Father Joseph were never like this – in Rumeza we seldom saw another vehicle, let alone a traffic light. Uncle Eliphaz and I chatted, but my attention was drawn to the music coming from his radio. He saw me staring as I tried to figure out how music could be playing, since the national radio station usually broadcast news at that hour.

"Cassette tapes." He pressed a button to show me. I'd seen and heard them before, but never in an automobile. "Most convenient."

Uncle Eliphaz lived in an apartment building, one that he owned, on a side street about a quarter mile from the city's main thoroughfare. His apartment occupied the entire top floor of the four-story building, and the rest was used to hold meetings and store merchandise. We walked up an internal staircase, and the fluorescent lighting gave the cinder-block walls a garish pallor. When he opened the door to his apartment and switched on a light, my impression of the building changed completely. The apartment was really two units he had combined into one by removing a few walls. A bank of windows ran along the far side, and I could see the downtown buildings easily. The walls were decorated with posters and prints by artists whose names were unknown to me. What I could not comprehend was how bright the space was. Even with just a few table lamps and one overhead light in the kitchen, his place was brighter than my family's house was in the daytime. He showed me the kitchen, and I marvelled at the refrigerator stocked with brightly packaged foodstuffs. He turned on the faucet in the kitchen sink and a stream of water gushed out. I thought of all the trips down the mountain I had taken and how easily he could get a drink or bathe. Truly this was a marvel.

He showed me to the room I would sleep in. I had never slept on a bed with a mattress and box spring before, and when I sat on it and I bounced back up after sinking momentarily, I shook my head in wonder. I tried to imagine what it would feel like to sleep so far above the ground. I ran my hand across the bedcovers.

"You must be tired, Tumagu. Why don't you shower and then get to sleep. We have much to do tomorrow."

In truth, I wasn't tired at all. I had been weary on the ride, but now with my senses awakened on nearly every level – from my feet, which trod on soft carpet for the first time, to my backside, which sat on something more cushioned than it had ever experienced – my nerves felt raw and exposed. Uncle Eliphaz led me to the bathroom and explained how to use the shower. You must understand that my standards of hygiene were probably much different from yours. Growing up in a home without indoor plumbing, and having to haul water up a mountainside as opposed to twisting a handle, we bathed maybe twice or sometimes three times a week. You can probably guess that my first experience in a shower required lengthy consideration to determine whether or not I enjoyed it. Only when Uncle Eliphaz knocked on the door to tell me I had better get out did I conclude my investigation of the relative merits of a sponge bath versus a shower. The evidence proved inconclusive, so the next morning when I awoke from a restless sleep, I repeated the experiment. I loved the feeling of the water pelting my skin, and I especially liked the sound

I heard when I plugged my ears and let the water beat on my skull. It was as though the water could wash away nearly all of my anxieties, and the comforting embrace of Uncle Eliphaz's absorbent towels soaked up the rest.

Nothing Dieudonné had told me about Uncle Eliphaz's apartment had fully prepared me for the actual experience. For the most part, Dieudonné hadn't even tried to describe these things to me – he simply told me to wait and to see for myself.

After a quick breakfast, Uncle Eliphaz and I went into the city centre. Though it was only eight in the morning, the streets were already crowded and the air thick with a foul humidity. What struck me was that although there were thousands of people out and about, they seemed to have no real destination. Nearly everywhere I looked, people were clustered about in groups large and small. When we slowed, and especially when we came to a stop, men surged toward the car, waving their arms and shouting.

"Beggars," Uncle Eliphaz said, his expression clouded. "They've nothing better to do than hang out in the streets and ask for handouts. Without education, they can't find work."

"How do they feed themselves?"

"Oh, they manage to find something to do to get by. They're enterprising enough."

I expected Uncle Eliphaz to continue, but he changed the subject by asking me if I had my list. I took it from my pocket and we reviewed it. When we parked the car, I watched as he negotiated with a man before slipping a bill into his hand. Though street parking was free, Uncle Eliphaz had paid the man to watch over the car for him to be sure that no one vandalised it. I understood then at least one form of enterprise these men engaged in. It seemed as though nearly everyone else we walked

past on our way to the first shop tried to sell us something –
watches, videos, fruit, sandals, mats, chipped cups and plates.
And they didn't just stand idly by waiting for a customer, they
tried to outshout one another, and my sleeves were constantly
being tugged.

Uncle Eliphaz's first mission was to buy me my first pair of
shoes. The shop we went to was really more of an outdoor stall
that had corrugated steel sides subdividing a much larger space.
Within those walls we found bins filled with shoes. To keep the
pairs together, either the laces were tied together or spring
clothespins were used. Uncle Eliphaz told me to take my time
and that I could have any pair I liked. Several weeks before this
in Rumeza, I had stood with a group of men and boys outside
a bar watching an American movie with Eddie Murphy. He
wore a pair of shoes that had toes made of one colour leather, a
centre section of white leather, and the rear section like the
front. I didn't know then that they were called saddle shoes, but
I decided I had to have a pair just like them. I didn't want to tell
Uncle Eliphaz I wanted a pair of movie-star shoes, so we spent
quite a bit of time looking. He showed me various styles, some
with buckles, some with laces, some with higher heels, some
boots, some sandals. I must have tried on ten different pairs, and
each time I had to force myself not to laugh – the sensation was
so strange, the idea that I was now going to own a pair of shoes
so exciting.

I finally spotted some saddle shoes. They were a creamy dark
mustard colour with white bands, and I was overjoyed to have
found something so cool. I showed them to Uncle Eliphaz, and
he scrunched his face up and looked at me with knitted brows.
"You want those? But what about all these others?" I could have
any pair, he said, and the ones I'd chosen were of questionable

quality, but I couldn't be dissuaded. Reluctantly, Uncle Eliphaz agreed to purchase them for me.

That day we also bought my school uniform – a pair of khaki trousers and a white shirt. Uncle Eliphaz insisted on buying me two of each, and I was extremely grateful. In one day I had been transformed. When we got back to his apartment, I went into the bedroom and tried on my clothes. I had never worn a pair of long trousers before, and at first it felt very strange to have my legs covered. Uncle Eliphaz showed me how to tie the shoes, and at first I struggled. I feared he would have to tie them for me and I would have to just slip them on and off, but eventually my fingers grew more nimble.

The next morning Uncle Eliphaz was going to drive me to school, and on my last night in the capital, he took me to a restaurant to eat. I wore my new clothes, and though they felt stiff and foreign to me, he assured me soon they would be as well worn and familiar as my others had been. He ordered for both of us, and I had to make a conscious effort not to stare at the waiter and the other patrons. It was as though every pore in my body was wide open, aching to absorb and assimilate as much of these experiences as possible. Even the condensation beading on a steel pitcher of water was new to me. I had come hundreds of miles, and I still had farther to go. I did not know much about the city of Kibimba, only that it would be smaller than Bujumbura. For that I was grateful. While I enjoyed some of the aspects of the city, and another lingering shower on the morning we left confirmed my earlier findings, the noise, the dirt, and the crowds were too much for my senses to handle. Though I was only there for a little more than a day, I had had my fill. Besides, I was eager to get settled in at Lyceè Kibimba.

Kibimba is located in Gitega and Muramuya Province in the

central part of the country. It lies at the intersection of three provinces and halfway between the country's two largest cities – Gitega and Bujumbura. Unlike Bujumbura and like my home region, it sits on a relatively high plateau at four thousand feet and is hilly if not mountainous. It is still two thousand feet closer to sea level than Rumeza, and this would prove advantageous for me later on when track came to dominate my school life. We had a two-hour drive from Bujumbura to Kibimba, and as soon as we left the shores of Lake Tanganyika, we began to climb. Classes were scheduled to begin two days hence, but I had to report for check-in. The teachers would be there to greet us and to make certain we had brought the proper supplies. Kibimba was in many ways similar to the much smaller Rumeza. At twenty thousand, Kibimba's population was significantly larger, but I was glad some elements seemed immediately familiar.

The school sat near one of several small central districts of low commercial brick buildings dotted by a few homes. This district, encompassing several blocks, was surrounded by an outer ring of many more homes closely clustered and made of various materials. The sprawling city contained many such neighbourhoods, unlike Rumeza, which had only one central district. Construction was ongoing, and new homes and commercial buildings sat cheek by jowl with half-completed and apparently abandoned projects. Like most cities in Africa, it evidenced little planning, had a more spontaneous catch-as-catch-can sensibility. Dirt roads and paths meandered through the town haphazardly, with the main road to Bujumbura a heavily trafficked paved highway.

Lycée Kibimba sat on the city's high ground. Founded by Quaker missionaries, who built a hospital as well, it was very Western in its architecture, blocky redbrick structures with lots of divided-light windows in white-painted frames. Though the Quakers had built it, the school was administered by and under the jurisdiction of Burundi's Ministry of Education.

Check-in at the dormitory proceeded smoothly. I was one of the first new students to arrive, and Marie Niyonzima, one of the mathematics teachers, showed me to my place. The dormitory was about what I'd expected from former classmates' descriptions. The bunk beds were not nearly as plush or as comfortable as my uncle's bed, but they would suffice. I quickly unpacked my sheets and blanket and made up the bed, asserting my rights as the first of my bunk mates to arrive by choosing the top bed – I'd heard that this was the prime spot. I stowed the rest of my belongings, a few clothes, and toiletries in the wooden cabinet I was assigned. I had been instructed to purchase a padlock to keep my belongings safe. My mother and father didn't think I could be trusted with a combination lock, but I assured them that unlike a key, which could be lost, the numbers would never leave my head. 12-22-4 – to this day I still remember that combination.

I owned very little that was of any value and seemed worth the risk of expulsion to steal. We all wore the same uniform, and I seldom, if ever, removed my prized possession. For my graduation and confirmation, my parents had asked Uncle Eliphaz to purchase a watch for me. I had seen other men with fancier analog watches, but the Casio digital I received was invaluable. Later on, I would use it as a stopwatch to time my workouts, and it had an alarm that I used to wake myself up each morning. I no longer have that watch, and I still miss it, but I have to laugh at myself for thinking its green body and band were the definition of cool.

Uncle Eliphaz took me into Kibimba for my last dinner

before school food became my only choice. I was disappointed by Kibimba's atmosphere. While I had expected the noise and the crowds of Bujumbura, I hadn't expected to be assaulted by people with the same desperate commercial sensibility as those in the capital. I saw all manner of wildlife for sale, skinned monkeys, ibex, and other mammals hanging in the market stalls. I also saw many young boys chasing after the banana trucks hoping for some cargo to fall off so they could scoop up the large bunches for selling. Failing an act of fate, they would try to jump up and grab them as the trucks slowed or came to a stop. On many of the fruit trucks, the driver enlisted a man to ride along on the running board hanging on to the sideview mirrors to keep an eye out for thieves. It seemed that everywhere I went in Kibimba, people were engaged in some form of commerce. Sadly, since the mostly Hutu people did not have property of their own on which to raise food, they had to resort to what was little better than scavenging to live. I did not think I could survive that way – I needed farm fields and cows. Much of the time I was in Kibimba or in Bujumbura, I experienced claustrophobia. Too many bodies pressed too tightly together seemed to choke the community spirit from them. My first impression of city living would never alter.

Saying goodbye to Uncle Eliphaz wasn't easy. I thanked him profusely for everything he had done for me. He told me I could best show my gratitude by excelling at school, and I assured him I would. I knew he would be the last family member I would see for a while, and that saddened me. After he drove away, I experienced a moment of panic when the realisation hit me that I would be living someplace where I knew absolutely no one other than René. That thought struck me with fear but also freed me. Whatever people from my past thought of me didn't matter. While I felt that I'd always been well liked before, this was a chance to start fresh. No matter what else might happen, I knew my future was in my control now.

The first student I met when I got back to the dormitory after seeing my uncle off was Eddie. Eddie was a loose-limbed and gangly Hutu with a seventh-grader's indiscriminate sense of humour. Anything and everything seemed to make Eddie laugh. And when he laughed, he expected everyone else to join in with him. Eddie had grown up with two brothers very close to him in age, and he was used to being affectionately physical with them. Even though we'd known each other only a few minutes, Eddie felt comfortable putting his arm around my shoulder when he went weak-kneed from laughing so hard. At first I thought his stumbling was genuine, but then his grip around my neck tightened and he tumbled me to the floor. We would soon learn such nonsense was not tolerated in the dorms, but our brief wrestling match bonded us immediately.

We shared stories of home and school and family, and long after the lights had gone out, we continued to talk quietly, our whispered words echoing in the silent, nearly empty room. When I told him my friends and family called me Tumagu, he immediately picked up on the other meaning of that name – "smoke" or "dust."

"So you must be fast," he said, and laughed.

"I am." I surprised myself by making that admission. I wasn't prone to bragging, but based on my experiences with my friends back home, I knew my legs were as lively as anyone's. To back up my claim, I explained to Eddie how back home we played a game called Kick the Lion. Because of my speed and leaping ability, I was always one of the first chosen. The game involved two teams, each of whom had to jump over the stream that flowed down from the mountains and joined the Muhorera River. The game also had elements of tag: One person would be selected as "it," and as soon as that player tagged another player, that player joined "its" team. Eventually it would be everyone against the one person still left untagged.

As the person selected to be "it," I had the responsibility of yelling, "Are you ready?"

When I heard, "Yes!" I'd shout back, "Are you afraid of the lion?"

"No!"

With my last call – "Kick the lion!" – the other players would scramble to avoid being tagged. Being fleet and fearless – depending upon whether we played during the rainy or the dry season, the stream was either a torrent or a trickle – was necessary to succeed. I possessed both qualities, and knew that I could outrun nearly everyone. At first I'd pick on some of the slower players so they would be on my side. We'd work together to capture the rest. To give you some idea of how fast I was, among my schoolmates and friends back then was Aloise Nizigama, who would one day finish fourth in the '96 Olympics in the ten thousand metres. During our informal runs as children, Aloise and I were always stride for stride. What happened when I got on a running track was yet to be determined, but I knew that secondary-school athletics would play a big part in my life in Kibimba. Before then, though, I would have to adjust to a new academic routine.

At Lycée Kibimba, classes began at seven-thirty and went straight through to our noon lunch hour. After an hour-and-a-half lunch break, we returned to classes until 3 P.M. At that point we were expected to be involved in some school-sponsored activity until dinner at six. We studied until lights-out at nine o'clock. Needless to say, it was a very full day, and it took me some time to adjust. The strict regimen was good in one way: I was seldom left with time to think too long and too hard about my family and friends back in Fuku.

Other aspects of the school were all too familiar. Once again, I sat at a two-person desk; the roll was called in every class, and soon I knew the names of my classmates nearly as well as my own. I got to know who my rivals were in the classroom. As before, our teachers read out all our scores on tests and homework assignments. Once each month, on what was designated proclamation day, the headmaster announced our aggregate percentages to the entire student body, and the number one student from each level was identified and presented to the student body. The system promoted competition, and unless you developed a close and trusting friendship with someone, you could count on little help from your fellow students if you were struggling to understand a concept and the teacher's efforts to explain it had fallen short. Peer pressure and fear of failure were powerfully motivating to a group of students who were already considered overachievers. There was far less ruckus making in the classroom, though we weren't always completely serious.

That I was well behaved did not matter to my fellow students. They cared about how well I performed in the classroom. And, as René had warned me, the upperclassmen did test me on my knowledge of Burundi history, among other topics, when they cornered me in our dorm section. I kept a level head and stalled for time by repeating their questions, and I apparently satisfied them with my answers. Every now and then in the first few months I'd face another challenge, but the ordeal was not as bad as I'd envisioned. The same was true of the food. Though I can't say I liked it, I did grow accustomed to it, but I still greatly missed my mother's cooking. I didn't like having to clean up the cafeteria after meals, but it did provide a chance to socialise. Working alongside my classmates made mopping a less tedious chore.

The other thing I missed was my uncle Eliphaz's private shower. We had to shower every night, but this meant waiting in line in order to use the single shower in the dormitory's lavatory, and it took me a few months to get over my fear that somehow the older students were going to seize this time to force us to march about naked. I also tried to sneak in some study time while waiting for the shower, but I soon gave up on that idea in the face of enormous pressure from the others to relax and socialise for a while. Only now do I realise the contradictory nature of my classmates' attitude toward school. Simultaneously, I was under pressure from the upperclassmen to demonstrate that I had the knowledge to uphold the school's strong academic reputation while also being encouraged to take it easy and not think about my classes so much. It strikes me now that it is these contradictions that make us human. This was just one of a few contradictions I would encounter in my time at Kibimba, and learning to recognise and negotiate them was a fundamental part of my education.

That first year, I had little difficulty adjusting to the rigours of my classwork. My teachers at Rumeza had prepared me well for secondary school. In fact, I was doing so well in my algebra class that my teacher asked me to help some of the struggling students. I also distinguished myself in physical science, history, civics, economics, and agriculture. As I had in primary school, I struggled a bit in French and in English. I still saw them as of little utility at that point in my life. Twice a week we took physical education classes that included a written curriculum; we learned the history and rules of various games and took written tests as well as engaging in activities.

I had enjoyed soccer, but my parents had not encouraged me to play it. There was too much physical contact in the game, and they felt my slim build put me at a disadvantage and could make me prone to injury. Many of my Hutu counterparts were wild about soccer, but as much as I liked to listen to the games on the radio, I didn't aspire to play professionally as several of my classmates did. My uncle Leonard was disappointed I didn't pursue that dream, in part because he himself never got to despite his passion for the game and also because he thought I was wasting a talent – my speed and endurance. Perhaps there was something else at work besides a reluctance to bang bodies with my fellow soccer players: I discovered a game that I absolutely loved – team handball. Most Americans are not aware of the game – if they've heard of it at all, it's from the Olympics. Team handball combines elements of basketball, soccer, water polo, and rugby. The object of the game is for each team to succeed in throwing an inflatable leather ball, about half the size of a soccer ball, and segmented like a volleyball, into a goal. Each team has seven players, and the team that possesses the ball advances it toward the opponent's goal by dribbling, running without dribbling (a maximum of three steps before and after dribbling), and passing. It is a fast-paced game played indoors on a court slightly larger than a basketball court. The goal is two metres high by three metres wide and is defended by a goalkeeper.

I fell in love with the game the first time I played it. Blessed with speed and agility, I was a capable attacker who could dart in and around the opposition's defence with little trouble. There is no tackling but the same degree of contact that exists in a basketball game. Something about being able to run up and down a court nearly nonstop for thirty minutes at a time appealed to me on the most fundamental level. I didn't care so much for the running of set plays or strategising; what I enjoyed was the mayhem I could create by being the quickest person on the court and remaining almost perpetually in motion. While soccer, with its high-level offensive and defensive strategies and low scoring, has proved a difficult challenge for American tastes, team handball's frenzy, its high scoring, and the athleticism required to play seem ideally suited to U.S. sensibilities. I don't understand why it does not have a stronger following here. If I could not run and coach for a living as I do now, I'd undoubtedly choose to play team handball. Nothing else I've done, with the exception of running track, has so successfully brought back the sheer pleasures of being a child.

Weekends at Kibimba were not entirely our own. We had to clean the dormitories, and some of the clubs and sports teams met or practiced on the weekend. Attending church services was not mandatory as it had been in Rumeza, but I still went each Sunday to a neighbouring Catholic church for mass. The school also provided us with some social activities, but as a somewhat shy and bookish seventh-grader I didn't participate in them much those first few months. We were required to attend the dances and other functions, but we first-years mostly stood in segregated groups, talking and whispering among ourselves. I enjoyed the fact that the school was coeducational, though the girls' dormitory remained for all of us a deep but desirable mystery to unfold.

Sexual matters were always a ripe subject of discussion and an easy target for anyone looking to inflict wounds on another's psyche. Like most agrarian-based cultures, our culture places a high premium on fertility – for both humans and animals. Farming is labour-intensive, and the larger the family, the larger the workforce. I remembered how my friends had teased me when they learned I was considering the priesthood – perhaps I had only one testicle and was consequently infertile. The English language tends to be more brutish and blunt when it comes to profanities, so few of the more colorful expressions and put-downs we levelled against one another would make much sense to you, but we employed them with the same frequency and intent as our youthful American counterparts, except they were more metaphorical and most (at least the ones I used) did not violate any commandments.

The teachers and the headmaster actively discouraged boyfriend-girlfriend relationships, but they were more lax with the twelfth- and thirteenth-graders than with the younger students. In such a small and closed community – fewer than four hundred students attended the secondary school, with eight hundred to one thousand total between the primary and upper levels – it would have been nearly impossible for couples not to form and for those couples not to become known. Teen pregnancy was not a problem among our secondary-school students, nor were sexually transmitted diseases, drinking, or drugs. I don't mean to imply we were more virtuous than anyone else – we simply lacked funds, access, and time to engage in immoral or illegal behaviour.

Outside the school, those issues were another matter. Teen pregnancy was rampant in some schools, and the AIDS epidemic ravaging many African nations plagued Burundi as well. If my religious beliefs did one thing for me, they kept me from engaging in sexual activity of any kind. My secular education made clear the link between sexual activity and AIDS. I was fortunate to have had both those concepts instilled in me. That's not to say I had no interest in sexual matters or that I was expert in my knowledge. In Bujumbura when I was with my uncle, I saw many women dressed in outlandish and revealing outfits. He caught me gaping at them once and told me I had better wise up. "Those women have no respect for themselves or for you, Gilbert. They sell men sex. All they care about is money. If you don't stay focused, you will never find a girl from a nice family, and those other women will have nothing to do with you anyway if you don't have a good job."

With so few distractions, I found it relatively easy to focus in my first semester at Lycée Kibimba. We had a few transistor radios in the dorms just as we had at home, but with only one station broadcasting, we were, for the most part, at the mercy of the government for our news and electronic entertainment. That first year, I joined several clubs to meet the requirements: the French Club, the Agriculture Club, and the Chemistry Club. It seemed as though only an instant passed and I was headed home for the Christmas break.

No bus went straight from Kibimba to Rumeza, so even though Bujumbura was in the opposite direction to my home, I rode the bus there and transferred to another bus to Rumeza. It was a two-day journey, but I got to stay with my uncle again for a night before going home. I was excited to be going back, especially since I could report to my parents that my progress was excellent. At the midterm I was in the top fifteen in my class. My teachers were pleased with me, and I'd even managed to get an 80 percent in both French and English. The rest of my grades were in the nineties. Not too bad for a small-town boy faced with the challenges of what was to him big-city life.

When my bus arrived in Rumeza, my mother was there to greet me, along with my sisters. I was amazed by how much Francine had grown. She was now twelve years old and nearly a head taller than the last time I'd seen her. She was a year away from taking her exams, and she'd already distinguished herself as a scholar. My mother and Beatrice both looked tired, and as much as it pained me, I knew that meant good things for my stomach. I wasn't to be disappointed.

In some ways, the farm looked like I had never been away, except the corn we had planted just before I departed was now ready for harvest. Some of the calves had grown quite large. If there was one constant in my life, it was the presence of the cows. I resumed my milking chores immediately, and though it had been months since I'd done it, I fell easily into the rhythm of the work. A few days after my return, we went to church. I was eager to see my old schoolmates and exchange stories with them, but the pleasure of our reunion was short-lived. With only seventeen of the fifty going on to secondary school, a small percentage of them could really understand what I had experienced. Some of my peers had repeated the sixth grade, while others had opted out of the education system entirely. We could reminisce about the past years at school and mock our teachers' peculiarities, but I sensed a distance growing between us. Each time I came home, that distance seemed to grow. I suppose it was natural that we would drift apart, but it made me sad to see some of the choices they were making. It also made me even more grateful for the opportunities presented to me. I'd been places and done things someone from a rural area like me might never have got to do. I also got a chance to see what awaited me if I didn't continue to bear down and concentrate.

The Christmas holiday passed all too quickly. It seemed as though Dieudonné and I had only a moment to share stories before he had to report back to his military camp. Uncle Eliphaz continued the annual traditions that had meant so much to us all over the years. Besides my father, no man had ever taken so strong an interest in my welfare. I was pleased to see Father Joseph, whom my grandmother had invited to our home for a meal. I wondered if perhaps he had done something to displease his superiors, for instead of taking his car, he had pedalled a bicycle – an odd contraption, with narrow tyres and a hard leather saddle shaped like a bellows. As it turned out, Father Anthony had had aspirations of being a cyclist where he grew up in cycling-mad Italy. We talked about the spectacle of the Giro d'Italia, a multistage race that wound through his mountain village of Dimario. He thrilled me with his story of the pack of racers speeding recklessly down out of the Dolomites and kicking up a torrent of dust on their way through his village. He sat wistfully gazing into his empty cup before someone filled it with beer. He'd let my cousins have a try at riding the bike, but when my turn came, a quick glance at my father let me know I'd be sitting this one out. I knew why my father wouldn't let me have a turn: I already had a spotty driving record.

Though it seemed now like a memory of what someone else had done, I recalled how several years earlier I had built a two-wheeled cart out of some lumber scraps and the wheels from a discarded barrow. I'd fashioned a T-handle steering mechanism out of eucalyptus branches. I rode with one foot on the cart and the other treading the ground as a skateboarder would, pushing off a few times and then letting gravity take over. As fun as the banana-leaf sled was, my cart was capable of even greater speeds. Then on one trip, I hit a large stone and was tossed off my cart. I scraped a good-sized chunk of skin off my right forearm and elbow. It didn't bleed so much as ooze a clear fluid, and the bare spot reminded me of the skinned flesh of an antelope.

I had kept my toy a secret from my mother and father, so I had to come up with a plausible explanation of what happened to my arm. I knew that my "I was wrong and I'm sorry" tactic wouldn't be of much use this time. Instead, I told my mother I had seen one of our calves mixed in with the adults, and I'd jumped over the fence to get to it as quickly as possible. I'd not made it over and had tumbled to the ground, scraping my arm. I knew I would get in a little trouble for not being more careful, but since my accident was in the service of a good deed, I wasn't likely to be punished. And I wasn't. Not until several days later when my father whipped me for lying to them about my arm. My mother had been diligent about keeping the wound clean and wrapping it in a cloth, and I had lied to her. My father wanted to know where my scooter was, and I took him into the bush beyond our house. He brought it back into the yard near the woodpile and used his hatchet to chop it into pieces. He made me add what was left of my fun into the cooking fire. I never did learn how he found out about it.

While we watched my cousins master the art of the skinny-tyre bike, my father came up to me and said, "It wasn't so long ago that you would have been the first to engage in foolishness. I see you changing. You have better things to do with your time now." He rested his hand on my shoulder, and I could see how gnarled and abraded his knuckles were. My father worked hard, and I could now sense his appreciation for my efforts.

I didn't have too much longer to think about how wonderful I felt, for Uncle Eliphaz whistled to get our attention. It was time for him to give his speech and deliver gifts. But I knew I had already received what I'd really wanted and needed from my father.

If my seventh-grade year was notable for one reason only, it would have to be my emergence as an athlete to be reckoned with. In gym classes and in informal races I'd proven that I had speed, but I'd never competed against the upperclassmen or the members of the track team. I set that as a goal for myself. Toward the end of my first school year in Kibimba, I heard about a race that was sponsored by the JRR – the Tutsi president at the time was a member of this political party. Like all political parties in Burundi, the Rwagasore Revolutionary Youth Party recruited students. I had already joined it as one of my school activities. Politics was always an important part of student life, and with a government that had such an unstable history, there was often much to talk about. I don't want to lead you to believe that we debated the great issues of the day and were conversant in the nuances of every government programme and policy. The parties served a social function as much as a political one for students, but we also learned some valuable information that shaped our opinions and, ultimately, our fates.

In early July 1988, the JRR was sponsoring its annual five-mile race, with prizes offered to the winner from Lycée Kibimba. The race was a way to draw attention to the party, get its name in the news, and build goodwill. They were also interested in finding athletes who could compete on their club team. I desperately wanted to run in the race, but it was generally understood that it was for upperclassmen. This year the first prize was a portable stereo system with built-in speakers – what Americans would call a boom box. I loved music, and my tiny transistor radio was not of the highest fidelity.

At the first mention of the race – the headmaster, Mr. Ntibazonkiza, the Tutsi I so admired, made the announcement during an all-school assembly – I'd planted the seed with all my teachers that I wanted to run. They scoffed at me and told me I was too young. I couldn't compete with seventeen-, eighteen-, and even nineteen-year-old boys. I had only just turned fourteen. Only a few young boys were competing, including a Hutu named Zepherin Ruzoviyo who was in ninth grade and sixteen years old. My teachers asked me if I was as fast as Busigi, a thirteenth-grader whose nickname meant "fast." When I nodded, they laughed at me and shook their heads.

On the day of the race, a Saturday, the whole school was buzzing. The race was one more sign that the year was coming to the end, and a semester's worth of pent-up energy was nearly at a boiling point. The race would be run through the streets of Kibimba, and the surrounding community was abuzz as well. The school's drumming team was performing in the streets, lending a carnival atmosphere to the race and the other festivities associated with it.

An hour before the race was scheduled to start, I was in the field with the rest of my agriculture class, cultivating and weeding, upset that I wasn't going to be allowed to run. In my frustration, I fantasised about tearing up all the plants; instead, I worked as slowly as I could in silent protest at what I considered unfair treatment. Though I had never run in a formal race before, I was certain that I could compete with these older boys. I was stooped over and dissolutely pulling at a weed when I saw a shadow come toward me and then merge with my own. I looked up, and Mrs. Mia Nzedekaza, the agronomy teacher, stood looking at me. A grin split her wide, round face. "So, what are you doing here? Don't you have a race to run?"

I jumped out of the furrow and took off toward the race's start, turning and yelling my thanks over my shoulder. Mrs. Mia Nzedekaza waved in response. I was glad that they had relented and equally glad that they'd come to get me while I was working in the field. In any other class, I would have been wearing my uniform, but now I had on a pair of shorts and an Adidas T-shirt. When I got to the starting area, I saw that many of my competitors were wearing running shorts and singlets – either their Kibimba team shirts or ones from another club team. More important, a few of them wore running shoes. I wasn't too worried, though. I'd been running without shoes for my entire life. I'd also studied the route in the week leading up to the race, and I knew that although there were some rocky and rutted sections, I could handle it. I didn't have a choice anyway, and when we were told to take our marks, I edged my way toward the front of the pack.

When the gun went off, a shot of adrenaline coursed through me. I was clearly the youngest in the field and also the smallest. Taking the lead immediately, I was greeted with a burst of encouragement and warning from the crowd. They wanted me to be careful and not use up all my energy too quickly. I heard them, but I didn't listen. I kept going as fast as I could. The day was pleasantly warm, with just a little breeze to cool us, and where possible, I ran in the shade to take advantage of the slightly cooler temperature there. After a quarter mile, I could barely hear the crowd at the start/finish line. I was running along the main road that paralleled the school grounds, and when I looked to my right, I could see that the students in the field were no longer working but had dropped their tools and stood in a group alongside the road. A few of my friends shouted my nickname and laughed. They began a chant about my name and how the only thing anyone would see of me was the dust that I kicked up. I slowed slightly, trying to get my arm swing and my legs to work together. I ran with my hands up high and my shoulders tucked up close to my ears, as though I could muscle my way around the course.

When I got to one of the rocky sections, I picked my line and stuck with it no matter what stones I stepped on. The road took us uphill and away from the school, but I kept my pace. My breathing wasn't laboured, and each gulp of air I took in was sweet. A quick glance to my rear let me know that I was still well out in front – in fact, I couldn't see any other runners.

As the hill steepened, I leaned forward slightly and chased my shadow over the crest. The downhill section was almost more difficult for me than going up had been. Ultimately, I gave up trying to control my legs and just relaxed them completely. I lost all sense of time and effort. I looked straight ahead of me, and before I knew what was going on, I saw the first members of the crowd gathered at the finish. When they saw me, they emitted a full-throated roar, and I wanted nothing more than to be swallowed up by that sound. The last quarter mile was as easy as the first had been, and I kept looking around trying to see if anyone was closing on me. I crossed the finish line, stunned by what I'd accomplished. I kept thinking that someone must have been ahead of me, but in my heart I knew that wasn't the case.

When the leader of the JRR delegation came toward me with his hand out in front of him, he confirmed what I already knew but was reluctant to admit – I had won. He shook my hand vigorously and raised my arm above my head like I was a boxing champion. My sweat was stinging my eyes, and I needed a drink badly, but he stood there with my arm in the air and spun me around so I could acknowledge the people on each side of the course. I heard a few people from the community shouting my name, but I wasn't sure who was talking to me or how they knew my name. I felt a bit light-headed and out of sorts. One minute I was sulking in the pea patch, and the next I was outrunning some of the best runners in the province. I'd even beaten some national youth champions, and only after about a minute did the second-place runner finally come into view. By the time he crossed the line, my margin of victory had grown to a full two minutes. Not only had I won, but I'd ground them into the dust.

Only when more of the field crossed the line did I start to think about what any of this meant, including what prizes I was going to receive. More than the material rewards, I received the gift of confidence. I'd been running almost since the time I could walk, and I knew I enjoyed it and that it came easily to me, but now I had confirmation of an important fact – I was fast. I might have taken the others by surprise, and I readily admitted that might have been a factor, but my victory planted a seed in my head. I hadn't really trained for this race, and I had had no coaching, so if I was somehow able to win without those two things, regardless of the reason, the future seemed wide open. If I applied myself the way I did with my studies, if I focused the way Uncle Eliphaz and others had exhorted me to, then I could improve and perhaps excel at the sport. I'd taken on getting into secondary school as a challenge, and I set a goal to excel in my schoolwork that first year, and I'd made both those things happen, so why not with running? In that moment I decided I was going to dedicate myself to becoming a champion runner.

After the race was over and the prizes (the radio, bars of soap, and a few other items) were presented, Lycée Kibimba's track coach approached me. He shook my hand and leaned close to my ear to be heard over the shouts of the crowd. "Son," he told me, his voice conspiratorial and certain, "you can be the best. Not just the best around here, but around the world."

A few days later the school held its final proclamation day. The top students in each class were introduced, and various awards were handed out based on academic and athletic achievement. When my name was called as the student with the third-highest average in my class, I was thrilled. I had to stand up, but I kept my head down and made little or no eye contact with my fellow students. I was still very concerned about what everyone thought of me, and I did not want them to think me too proud or vain. Inside, I was bursting with pride, but I had to be careful not to show it too openly. I need not have worried; later that evening in the dormitory, several of my classmates congratulated me. More important, several of the older boys on the track team spoke to me as well. Third in my class and a racing victory were as fine an end to the school year as I could have hoped for.

Later, just after we were dismissed from the proclamation-day assembly, the headmaster, Mr. Ntibazonkiza, took me aside. He told me that because of everything I had achieved during the year, I was to receive one semester's tuition payment. I knew this would please my parents a great deal. They had sacrificed a lot to send me to private school, and now, in this way, I was going to be able to pay them back.

I suppose that one of the benefits of an education is that it enlarges our field of vision, opens up possibilities we might otherwise not have encountered. It is easy in hindsight to say this, and I wonder sometimes if it is just human nature to believe these things, to place more importance on events than they deserve, but I truly believe that if it weren't for my victory in that race, my life would have taken a very different turn. In the years since the attack, I've thought often about the lessons that athletics taught me, and I've no doubt they played a large role in my survival and overcoming the many challenges I've faced.

At the time, though, I had no time for such thoughts. I had to begin packing for the long ride home to Mount Fuku. There would be cows to tend to, and they cared little that I had won a stereo and a few bars of soap, that I'd made my mark and earned respect. All they knew is they needed to be fed, watered, and milked. No matter how much I changed, the cows would always be the same.

By the time that I had been dragged into the headmaster's office and told I was going to see what Jesus Christ had seen, I had an immediate and visceral context in which to place those words. Mr. Niyonkenguruka left me sitting alone in his office. The mob outside had grown into the hundreds, and I could hear them screaming, "Bring him! Bring him out here to us!"

I sat in the chair with my head in my hands, and my mind was flooded with images from those grainy movies I had seen as a young boy during my catechism classes at Saint Anthony of Padua. Christ's Crucifixion figured prominently in many of those movies. The image of Jesus's beatific smile as the crown of thorns was placed on his head, as he staggered beneath the weight of the cross, as he was scorned and mocked by the jeering crowds, provided me with a safe place in my mind, however briefly, to retreat from the horrific reality of our situation, knowing what my Saviour had done for me.

I could not deny this truth: I was Gilbert Tuhabonyemana – christened "child of God." I make no claim that I suffered as Christ did or that I can offer the world the lessons of my Saviour. I claim only this: What I relate to you is the truth as I remember it. That I am here today to relate this truth is not of my doing.

From outside, I heard the repeated screams of my fellow Tutsis and the angry shouts of the Hutu mob. I could only imagine what was being done to my classmates and others. I'd already witnessed much cruelty. The Hutus were bent on torturing us, and the slashing blows of their machetes had already taken their toll on many of us. I sat slumped in my seat, my head resting on my thighs. I realised for the first time how much my jaw ached. I'd *been grinding my teeth all day. My belly was empty and gnawed at me. I'd had little to drink and my head throbbed. What frightened me the most was that these pains were nothing compared with what others had suffered.*

I remembered my grandmother Pauline and the song she had sung to me as a child:

Nzoririmba igitangaza Yesu Mwami Yakoze
Ndikumwe nabo Mwijuru Imbere ya yantebe
Ndacabona Ibimbabaza ariko yesu arnkiza
Aca Anshira mubitugu anjana iwe mwijuru
Nzoririmba igitangaza Yesu Mwami Yakoze

O victory in Jesus, my Saviour forever
He saved me and I love him
All my love is due to him
He suffered for me at Calvary
And shed his redeeming blood

At this point, I still held out hope that we would survive this ordeal. I could not imagine the violence escalating beyond this point. I'd never seen anyone die in real life. The concept could not fit inside my head, nor did I want it to.

I must have sat in the office for more than an hour. No thoughts of fleeing ran through my mind. I knew the school yard was thick with heavily armed Hutus. Eventually, two Hutu men came into the office, their coffee-coloured skin flecked with blood and viscera. My stomach turned and I felt faint. They each took an arm and led me out the door. It was now three o'clock, and a light rain began to fall. I turned my face to the sky and let some of the drops fall into my mouth. The rain tasted of metal.

The Hutus had gathered the Tutsi students and other residents of Kibimba into groups of fifty or so. When I was led to one of the groups, I could see they were bound by rope. Everyone had their hands tied either in front of them or behind them, and they were all roped together into a kind of organism or cell. I was the last one to be added to my group. For the most part, the Hutus had gathered up the men and boys. I would later learn why the women were not there.

While I was being bound, I listened to the Hutus as they chanted and drummed. The Hutus have a strong tradition of drumming, and I'd always loved its pulsing rhythm, so I'd never imagined it could sound so sinister, so freighted with ill intent.

A few in our group were already wounded. Several had their ears cut off. I recalled the passage in the New Testament where Saint Peter slices off the ear of a Roman centurion and Jesus heals him. I'd never considered before the violence of Saint Peter's act, the jagged gaping wound he inflicted and the horrible scent of blood fouling the victim's skin and clothes.

Nearly everyone's eyes were glazed, and we alternately stared at the ground or rolled our heads to the heavens. The air smelled of blood and urine and fresh excrement. I fought back the bile rising in my throat.

When at last my hands were secured, the Hutus used the points of their spears to prod us along. Ours was the last group to move out. I craned my neck to see how many groups were ahead of us, but I could see only a few directly in front of me. I don't understand why, but knowing our number was important to me. I also remembered that I had nearly a hundred dollars in my pocket that I'd retrieved from my locker earlier. Though it seems strange to say, I hoped it would be safe and not fall out of my trousers. With my hands tied, I'd have no way to retrieve it.

As we walked along, I scanned the crowd of our tormentors. Their singing and chanting had grown louder, more heated. As they marched along in step with us, they thrust their weapons – machetes, spears, clubs, tree branches, scraps of lumber – into the air. They were celebratory, their eyes dancing with malevolence. A few people pointed at me and shouted my name and laughed or drew a finger across their neck.

To this point, I'd been more numb than anything else. Walking the same streets where I had once raced and won or walked and enjoyed the acclaim of Tutsi and Hutu alike saddened me. These people who were now calling for my blood had once been my friends. I had loved Kibimba, the school and the city. It was my adopted home, the place where I'd become a man, found a purpose and a direction. The people there admired me and honoured me, made me welcome in their shops and their homes. I'd once run these streets singing gleefully, with young children running at my side, joining me in song, mothers shouting my name and encouragement. Now they taunted me. Now this was the place where I was to die.

It made no sense. None of this made any sense at all.

As we continued our forced march, it became clear to me that Mr. Niyonkenguruka had played a major role in organising this attack. He had also been smart enough to remove us from the school grounds. This way, no one could accuse him of being directly responsible. I remembered our debater, Sahabo Bonaventure, reminding him of his duty to protect us. "I need not be reminded of my duty," he had said. His duty was to his fellow Hutus, his students be damned. And we were.

For a moment the rain intensified, the raindrops pounding the eucalyptus leaves beating a counterpoint to the insistent drumming and chanting. Those of us bound together did little talking. Perhaps we had all retreated to some place in our minds where we could consider strategy, pray, or remember. My mind was a jumble of all three. I thought, not for the first time that day, of my mother and my father. I prayed they were safe, that Comina Songa remained as peaceful as it had during past periods of ethnic violence.

We lurched to a halt. I stood in the silt-slick mud and looked to the sky again. A few more drops of rain down my throat revived me a bit, but I was so very tired. We had gone only a kilometre or two, but hunger, thirst, and sleeplessness conspired against me. A strong wind lashed the trees, and a bolt of lightning fractured the whorl of clouds above us. The air was charged with electricity, and I felt the hair on my arms and legs stand on end. A powerful sulphurous odour nearly gagged me.

We were stopped within a few metres of a familiar off-campus building. It was to be a gas station but was not yet occupied. Fluted plaster and stone columns supported a wood roof. I could see Hutu men going in and out of the building carrying wood inside. My body began shivering and I couldn't stop it. I wasn't cold, but something had overtaken me. At first I hadn't known why we were stopping, but now I feared the worst. I understood what they meant to do with us.

Somehow stopping had reanimated the Tutsis around me. For the first time since we'd been on our forced march, we began talking to one another again, speculating about what was to happen next. I could not speak the words.

In a minute we had an answer. A line of Hutu men came toward us; they began taking off our clothes. I thought of the money in the pocket of my shorts, but I didn't say anything. I could smell alcohol on the breath of the man who stripped me. His broad nose was divided by a diagonal scar, and his yellow, bloodshot eyes tried to blink clear the rainwater. Next to me, a Tutsi man I did not know shouted and spat at his tormentor, but a blow to his head with the handle of a machete quieted him. The blood ran down his face and he spat again. A moment later he stood uncomprehending for a few moments, blood bubbling from his slit throat, before he collapsed twitching and gyrating in the mud. A minute later he lay still, his blood mixing with the rain and mud. I turned away when another Hutu approached the inert body, his machete about to hack at the dead man's groin. A few sawing motions and then he held his prize up for all to see.

After we'd been stripped, the Hutu man who seemed to be in charge walked among our ranks. He stopped in front of one man. I'd noticed him before because he was clad in military garb and because he was the tallest and most powerfully built among us. Now he was naked, the thick cords of his muscles even more clearly visible. He stood completely straight, keeping his military bearing even under these circumstances. The Hutu leader had to tilt his head up to see his face. He gestured to two of his associates, and the soldier was untied from the rest of the human chain, but his hands were still bound.

"You guys have been eating our blood!" the Hutu leader shouted. We'd heard this all before, how the Tutsis had taken advantage of the Hutu people. They claimed we were like a vampire feeding on a live victim sucking out its life.

The soldier remained ramrod straight and staring forward, even when the Hutu leader stepped around behind him. I didn't see the first blow, but I heard it. The sound of the Hutu's machete slicing into the soldier's body reminded me of the time when I had helped track down the antelope and then watched it being butchered.

The sound of the soldier's flesh being penetrated was both solid and wet. He only cried out briefly before falling to his knees. I wanted to look away, but I could not. In a moment, a group of Hutu men joined the leader in hacking and slashing at the body, their snarls and cries a guttural and inhuman expression of their exertion. When they were through, they raised their bloody weapons, chanted, and stomped their feet in the blood and the mud. What was left of the man was in the centre of their circle, barely recognisable as a human form, just bits of flesh and stark white bone against the oozing soil.

The soldier's killing, instead of horrifying the others watching, incited them to action. Suddenly, a swarm of Hutus attacked us, swinging clubs and machetes. They pulled some of us out of our group, slashed the lines that bound us together, then butchered men and boys like they had the soldier. I felt some of the tension in my ropes ease. Trying to ignore the horror going on around me, I worked myself free. Self-preservation allowed no time for thought or panic; I simply had to flee.

Completely surrounded, I had little chance of escaping. A Hutu man charged me and swung his club at my head, but I managed to duck out of the way. He recovered, swinging wildly, and I deflected his arm enough that he struck me full on in the chest. I staggered, the air rushing from my lungs in a wheezing hack. I fell to one knee, and the coppery taste of blood filled my mouth. I was gasping for air, but each breath ravaged my chest. Something felt broken – my sternum or my ribs – and I was in agony. My eyes welled with tears, and vertigo overtook me. Hands grabbed at me, trying to drag me back into the killing zone, where those with machetes and spears could finish me.

The shouting, the chanting, the drumming, and the rain pelting the leaves and the metal roof of the building all beat at a fevered pitch, and I wanted to scream in anger and anguish and disgust. How could humans do this to one another? What had we done to these people to make them so angry?

The smell of blood and urine and vomit clutched my throat. For an instant I thought of surrendering, of just letting myself be dragged away to the butchers. I was tired, I was wounded. What was the use?

From somewhere, I found a deeper well of energy, and I managed to pull myself away and make a mad dash toward the gas-station building. I didn't have time to think of the consequences. I was too busy avoiding the blows from clubs raining down on me to know that large numbers of Tutsis were being herded into another killing zone. Once inside, I believed for a moment I was safe.

If only we'd known how safe and how short those moments were going to be, we might have all made a different choice.

The site of the attack, my escape window, and the monument, which reads "Never Happen Again."

Above: Recovering from my burns, one week after leaving the hospital.

Left: Carrying the 1996 Olympic Torch for the Burundi Federation through Birmingham, Alabama.

En route in the 2006
Freescale Marathon on a
very cold day in Austin,
Texas. *Photograph by
Holly Reed*

Above: Meeting
President Clinton in
the Oval Office.
*Photograph courtesy
of the White House*

Left: With Muhammad
Ali, who presented
me with the Most
Courageous Student
Athlete of the Year
Award in 1999.

CHAPTER FOUR

RISE TO GLORY

Winning the JRR race taught me to accept victory gracefully. I had been well liked before that, and I was determined to keep my status unchanged. I treated everyone just as I had before, and I hoped they would do the same for me. When I returned home that summer of 1988 and told my parents about my victory and showed them the portable stereo I had won, they were very proud of me, but I could see something about the news troubled my mother.

She told me she worried about me carrying something as valuable as my new radio on the bus. She had heard stories about the city and the kind of thievery that went on there. She didn't want anything to make me a target for violence. I thought of her brothers who'd been killed in 1972 and suspected her worry was related to their fate. She never talked about what happened, and to this day the subject is still taboo. I don't know if my mother was any more or less of a worrier than other mothers – she's the only one I've lived with. Who could blame her for worrying? She had lived through violent times, and an undercurrent of unrest was ever present.

I wasn't always aware of the looming threat, but in the summer between seventh and eighth grade, one experience revealed to me the potential for harm awaiting me if I wasn't completely vigilant. Two friends and I wanted to go to Bururi, the provincial capital, to see the national championship track-and-field meet being held on July 1, our Independence Day. We had heard about it on the radio, and with my new goal of becoming a track champion myself, I thought it important to go. Bruno, Antoine, and I set out on foot for Bururi just after breakfast. It was a ten-mile trip, and we wanted to be sure to arrive by the time the first events started. We alternated walking and running, but we underestimated how long it would take, and we got there after the meet had begun. I didn't really care that much because what I really came to see was the fifteen hundred metres and some of the other middle-distance events. The stadium was one of the few places nearby where I could see men's and women's open competitions live. I had listened to the national finals on the radio, and I envisioned something as vast as the Colosseum in Rome. It was like that in one respect: the running oval was dirt, not synthetic. Bleachers ran the length of each straightaway, and the crowd could mill around each curved end, separated from the track by soldiers and a braided rope from which pendants hung. I wanted to get as close to the action as possible, so I opted for the standing-room seats at the top of the back straight. From there we'd be able to see the start/finish line and the all-important final turn for home.

This was the first full track meet I'd seen, and I was amazed by all the different events. I saw for the first time the steeplechase, and I appreciated the endurance and athleticism of the runners as they circled the track time and again, leaping over hurdles and water barriers. It reminded me of our days spent playing Kick the Lion, but the agonized expressions of the runners made it clear this was no game. One of my favourite field events was the high jump, and we were fortunate it was held in the infield at our end of the stadium. The crowd clapped and chanted rhythmically as each jumper prepared for the attempt and then grew silent as the spindly figures flung themselves into the air. We were so close to the action we could hear the bar if it was rattled in its stand and the grunt of the athletes when they landed on the mat. I loved how the crowd's attention was focused on just the one athlete competing in the event, and I wondered how I would do if I was in this situation, with thousands of eyes focused on me and me alone.

I was somewhat distressed to learn that the fifteen hundred metres wouldn't be run until five o'clock. Even if we left immediately after that, we would have trouble getting home before dark – when I would be expected. But I got all wrapped up in the meet, the colour and the spectacle of it all. I was most impressed by the runners' speed, especially in the four-hundred- and eight-hundred-metre races. They ran so fast around the final curve that they became just a blur of pumping arms and legs and seemed to float effortlessly above the track. Before I knew it, the fifteen-hundred had come and gone, but still I didn't want to leave. Bruno was bored, since he favoured soccer over track and field, but Antoine and I convinced him to stay for one more race – the five thousand metres. As the race wound down, the stadium grew dim, and in the one patch of sunlight directly in front of us, the runners cast elongated shadows that spread twenty yards in front of them. By the time we got out of the stadium, only a half hour of daylight remained. We set out at a jog, and before long we'd cleared the streets of Bururi and were into the unpopulated area, and darkness had fallen. At this point I was less worried about what my parents would do to me and more concerned about our safety. We'd grown up hearing warnings all the time about the dangers that lurked in the jungle and the wildlife we could fall victim to.

After an hour, the moon rose high enough to give us some light and we could see the dark footpath as it wended its way through the nearly reflective leaves of the undergrowth. We kept a constant flow of conversation going, recalling highlights from the meet, singing songs, and discussing anything we could think of to keep our minds occupied. I had to constantly slow my pace to allow Bruno to keep up, and we took frequent walking breaks. With about two miles to go before I was home, Bruno and Antoine said goodbye to me and split off the path toward their homes. I was both relieved and even more frightened at the prospect of being alone – even though I was now fifteen years old. I could set my own pace, and knew that if I pushed it, I could be home in twelve to fifteen minutes, but I would be totally alone. Add the fact that the first mile would be beneath the canopy of banana, banyan, and eucalyptus trees, all of which combined to block out any light, and my heart was racing. Since it was summer and a holiday, I knew many people had been travelling that day. Generally only a few people were still out at such a late hour, and those who were likely had mischief on their minds.

As I got to within a mile of home and the canopy thinned, I could see more clearly. Unfortunately what I saw was a man standing in the path about twenty-five feet ahead of me brandishing a machete. I came to a complete stop, and in an instant I thought of all my options. I could see well enough to know this man was not one of my uncles or a neighbour. I thought maybe I had startled him and that was why he had raised the machete, but even after a few seconds when he could easily see I was just a boy, he did not lower it. I took off through the bush. I knew I shouldn't scream because that might alert any accomplice he might have. The tangled brush slowed me, and with leaves and vines slapping at my face and arms and nettles stinging my flesh, I was nearly in a panic. I fought my way around a loop, hoping to reconnect with the path. I felt that if my way was clear, I could outrun him.

As I neared the path, I saw him standing on it, blocking my access. I turned and ran back the way I had come, zigging and zagging, hoping that he wouldn't follow me. I had been in this forest enough to be able to keep some sense of my location, and eventually I made my way to a neighbour's house. I told my neighbours someone was trying to kill me, but they dismissed my fears as youthful exaggeration. They told me I was only a few metres from my home and I should continue on. They would go outside to see me off, and if anything should happen to me, I should shout and they'd come to my aid. I couldn't believe that they were so indifferent to my plight, but after a few moments their attitude helped to calm me. I thanked them and took off running. I couldn't escape the feeling that someone was behind me, but I blamed my overactive imagination and continued on. A few hundred yards from the edge of our cleared land, the man with the machete jumped out of the bush. I was moving pretty fast, and I ducked as he swung at me. He missed me, and I sprinted into the clearing and jumped the fence as I'd seen the steeplechasers doing hours before.

I wanted to grab one of the spears my father kept leaning against the side of the house, but I decided against acting on my own. I also decided not to say anything to my parents. I would be in enough trouble just for being late. If I told them I was nearly attacked by some strange man within sight of our home, they might not ever let me go anywhere again. As it was, my parents were very angry with me, and they told me that was the last time I was going to Bururi on my own. I couldn't be trusted. After my frightening experience, I offered only a token protest. Sticking close to home was all right with me.

In retrospect, I wonder if the man was a Hutu. Though it was a dark night and I never saw him clearly, he was short and stout, and I'd imagined he had the Hutu broad nose. I knew he wasn't anyone I'd seen before, and I knew most of the Hutus in our surrounding area. At that time of year, after crops were planted and before harvest, we saw a lot of travellers moving through our area. We had to be especially vigilant with our cows to prevent thievery.

For my family, the violence of Burundi and Rwanda was more something we heard about on the radio than something that directly impacted our daily lives or influenced our attitudes. I can only compare my experience to what some in the United States might have felt during the 1960s when race riots occurred in cities such as Chicago, Detroit, and Los Angeles. I read about these events in school, and I can imagine that many Americans sat at home shaking their heads sadly, untouched by the violence. The destruction may have sickened and disturbed them, but it did not affect them directly, nor did it change their attitudes toward the blacks in their immediate community.

For the rest of the summer I was on my best behaviour. School had disciplined me in such a way that I no longer needed to be reminded of all the things I was responsible for. Even though my mother told me that Francine was now assigned the water-bearing duties, I did the chore myself. No one had to ask me to do anything – I simply got the work done. As before, I saw less and less of my old schoolmates who had failed the exam. After church I sought out a different group of students with whom I had more in common. I tried to tread a fine line between remaining humble and acting with my new maturity. I was surprised to find that I was looking forward to school resuming in October. At least when I was at school, I could fully be myself, and people only knew me based on that first year's experiences. It would be difficult to top my first year, but I was determined to give it my best effort.

If my eighth-grade year was notable in any way, it was because I was finally able to fully incorporate my two passions – running and music – into my school activities. I had experienced only one down period my first year – after not being selected to participate in the school's drumming program. If you know anything about African music, or Africa, for that matter, then you know how central drumming is. In many of our cultures drums are sacred instruments, and we use them in healing ceremonies, rites of passage, naming ceremonies, and on social occasions like parties and weddings. Among certain peoples they are still used as a means of communication. Drumming, both doing it and listening to it, is also a popular form of entertainment. Dance and drumming are intrinsically linked, and the kind of drumming we did at our schools incorporated dance. I wanted nothing more than to be a part of the showmanship and musicianship I'd seen on display my entire life. What really spurred my passion was a performance by the Burundi University drum team my first year. I was deeply affected by how much they energised the crowd, how soul-stirring their movements and music were. From then on I had to drum. Failing to be selected for our team was probably a good thing in retrospect.

First, drumming was such a popular activity and so important culturally that the team spent a lot of time in practices, competitions, and performances. I don't think I could have handled my class work and the responsibility and commitments of drumming my first year. Second, I lacked the confidence needed to compete at the highest levels. I would be starting at a disadvantage my first year anyway. Most primary schools had drum teams, but I had not participated in one at Rumeza. I was fascinated by it but not yet disciplined enough to participate.

Winning that JRR race at the end of my first year gave me confidence in all areas of my life. I am sure this had something to do with my being selected to participate in the drum programme my second year. When I saw that I'd been chosen, I literally jumped up and down in celebration – an appropriate response, since jumping was part of the team's performances.

I don't know if my words can capture the beauty and athleticism of the drumming and dancing, but I can explain how difficult and demanding the performances are. Imagine you have placed upon your head a tall, broad, twenty-five-pound drum. In Africa we grow up learning to carry things on our head, so for us this task isn't so difficult. But a drum isn't really a drum until you are beating it. So, imagine beating this drum with drumsticks while it's balanced on your head. And you can't just beat it, you have to play music on it and keep a steady tempo. Now, if you know anything about African music and drumming, you know the tempo is not going to be like a funeral dirge – it's going to be a rapid and complex rhythm. So far so good? You've got the drum balanced on your head, you've got the drumsticks in your hands, you've got the rhythms in your heart and your soul. The next step is to dance while playing this complex rhythm on the drum balanced on your head. And I don't mean a slow waltz, I mean a type of dancing that involves leaping and spinning and running and turning.

This would be difficult enough if you were going it solo, but this is a group performance. Not only do you have to play your drum, but you have to keep in rhythm with the other seven to ten drummers and keep your dance steps in synch with theirs. If you have never seen such a performance, you have not yet lived, in my opinion. It is awesome in every sense of the word. From the colourful costumes – always red, green, and white for our national colours – to the pulsating rhythms and chants, to the incredible endurance exhibited during the ten to twenty minutes of each dance, I know of nothing that comes close to displaying the amazing capabilities of humans. I have run a marathon, but I think performing a flawless drum-and-dance routine is a far more difficult and fulfilling task.

In Burundi and other East African countries, the lead player uses a drum called the *ngoma*. Unlike the goblet-shaped drum of West Africans, the *ngoma* is more like the typical Western drum – a simple cylinder. It is made of a soft wood and covered with cow skin. To accompany the lead drummer, who has to be the strongest member of the group because of the size of the drum and his central role in the dancing, we play the *ibishikizu,* a single-headed peg drum, similar to what many people refer to generically as a bongo drum. The third piece of the ensemble is the *amashako,* slightly larger than the *ibishikizu,* with which we play the basic rhythm line. In a sense, our drumming is three-part harmony, with a rhythm line, a melody, and an accompaniment.

For a while in the early eighties, Burundi drumming enjoyed popular attention in the world music scene, thanks to Western groups such as Adam and the Ants and Bow Wow Wow, who incorporated authentic Burundi beats and drum lines into their songs. Because a group called the Burundi Drummers recorded an album in the United Kingdom, every now and then a group will sample some of that album into its records. Even today, the Burundi Drummers (sometimes referred to as the Drummers of Burundi) perform around the world and their CDs are available in the United States.

At school, the drum squad practised three days a week, but once I was given a drum, I practised on my own for an hour each day. The first thing I was taught was simply how to play the drum. I had presumed that I could carry a drum on my head with no difficulty, but the first time I tried it, I realised my error. Because I was slightly built, I struggled. I undertook a training regimen of push-ups, pull-ups, and other exercises to strengthen my upper body. If you ever see a Burundian drum group perform, you will see some of the fittest men in the world. It would take me some time, but I would develop drumming muscles, of which I would be proud. It got to the point where all I could think about was drumming. I had a lot of catching up to do, and I was determined to do it.

Once I got the basic technique down, I learned the songs. Most of the music dated back hundreds of years and was passed on from generation to generation of drummers. I was unusual in that no one in my family had ever been a drummer; nearly every other drummer in our group (and in the other school teams) had a family tradition to fall back on. Anatole, Senda and Jean-Paul Kirimutumye were the leaders of our drum squad, and each had such a family tradition. Like most of the school activities, the drum squad had a faculty sponsor, in this case the physical education teacher, Mr. Kimwenjegeri, but the real leadership roles were undertaken by the students. In this way, the administration hoped to foster good leadership skills in its students. Eventually, I would take my place on the drum squad's advisory board, but it would take me two years to do so. First, I had to be good enough to actually perform. Since I had been so physically active my entire life, I was fit enough to last through an entire performance, but it took more than stamina to get good enough to perform with the group. I believe I was born with a natural sense of rhythm that – along with my inability to sit still – made me perfectly suited for drumming. My sense of rhythm also suited me well for my other passion – running.

When I returned to school, the track coach presented me with my first pair of running shoes – red Adidas track spikes. They were beautiful, and I took care of them as if they were my first car. After I ran in them, I would carefully clean them, paying special attention to the three white stripes. My teammates teased me about my perfectionism, but I believed paying attention to the small details would pay off in good results. I always made sure the spikes were tightly secured, and the other guys ribbed me for sleeping with a spike wrench tucked beneath my pillow. I didn't – I kept my drumsticks there.

One of the proudest days of my life was when I got to carve my name into the drumsticks the school presented to me when I earned a spot on the drum team. By May, I was chosen to accompany the squad and perform in a Labour Day celebration. My skills as a dancer and a drummer had improved greatly over the course of the year, and I'd also demonstrated my value to the group with my singing. Just as important as having a good voice was the ability to create lyrics. I've told you how in Burundi people sing all the time, and the words to the songs are seldom the same – we improvise and tell stories. Instead of listening to the radio on our trips, we sang songs – about what we saw along the way, about traditional themes, but mostly about the events of our daily lives. Though our lyrics don't incorporate rhyming in the same way that American hip-hop does, there are similarities in the spontaneity and the playfulness of the composition.

My first trip to perform, in Gitega, was a wonderful bonding experience. Though I'd been welcomed into the group, until I had the shared experience of actually performing with these boys, I felt like I was kept on the outside to a degree. Unlike schoolchildren in the United States who travel by bus to sporting events, all twelve of us on the drum squad had to fit into a compact Toyota pickup truck. We put four in the cab, and the rest of us, along with our drums, squeezed into the back. I enjoyed the trip almost as much as the performance. One of the traditional songs we sang is one that is sung in preparation for a wedding. It starts out with "When a woman wants to go and get married, they will have a lot of trouble." The rest of the song details these troubles – mostly caused by the fact that in our culture, especially in the old days, the two people getting married don't know each other well or sometimes at all. The song jokes about this, intermittently offering advice about relationships.

We performed before a large crowd in the city's central plaza. The mayor of Gitega was there, along with the provincial governor. They both made speeches before we were introduced, but I could barely listen to what they were saying. I kept shifting my weight from one foot to the other, running the music and the movements through my head. I was well prepared and nearly bursting with pent-up energy. When the speeches ended I was so grateful that we could begin.

As soon as we started dancing and drumming, my nervousness

disappeared and I lost myself in the explosive percussion and the meditative chanting and movement. For those twenty minutes, it was as if the rest of the world disappeared, and we were alone with our instruments and our ancestors. Even now, when I listen to Burundian drumming songs, I travel to a very quiet and serene place in my soul. Although to an outsider the music must seem anything but quiet, when I hear all that frenetic moving and pounding, I am slowly circling what is for me the center of my universe. It's what I imagine being hypnotised would feel like. Only when the song is over do I come out of the trancelike state. At the end of a performance I am energised and refreshed. For a few moments my muscles cramp or I'm aware that I'm thirsty and sweating, but those sensations quickly pass. I've read a lot about these altered states of consciousness, and of course, I know about the elusive phenomenon known as a runner's high. To me, though, what I experience both when running (although not every time) and in those drum performances is a state of grace and innocence.

The irony that I have been able to find such peace in activities that are very much the opposite of the stillness that Buddhism and other Eastern traditions strive for is not lost on me. I don't mean to make too much of this, but I hope you can understand why it is that despite all its faults and its legacy of violence, I so very much love my country and my culture. It is an amazingly rich, vibrant, and active way of life. So, it is possible that in one country you can find such extremes as genocide and grace. In the tamping of my footsteps, the beating of my heart, and the thundering of my drumsticks, I was constantly declaring I was alive, I was strong, and I was proud to be Gilbert Tuhabonyemana, a son of the mountains and a child of God. In large and small ways, I have sung my country's praises over the years, and even though in a few short years I was to experience Burundi at its painful worst, it was very easy for me to forgive my country and its people. I will not, however, ever be able to forget the lessons all my experiences have taught me.

During my second year at Lycée Kibimba, I was fortunate to earn the chance to learn other extremely valuable lessons and benefit from the advice of another very important man in my life. Adolphe Rukenkanya is a legendary athlete, coach, and educator from Burundi. He was a versatile athlete in his day, excelling in track and field, cycling, and other sports. His greatest claim to fame, however, was as a coach of young athletes. Adolphe was a physical education teacher but not in the usual sense. He taught physiology at the University of Burundi and took a very scientific approach to his coaching of runners. Long before others used slow-motion filmography and computer analysis of stride, Adolphe had unravelled the mysteries of efficient running form and was passing along his knowledge to national, world, and Olympic champions from a host of countries. When I was in secondary school, the Burundi Athletic Federation signed him up to train its national track team. Adolphe also supported himself by taking on private clients from among the professional ranks.

I got the opportunity to work with him and be a part of his Olympic development squad because of my performances on the track during eighth grade. At the age of fourteen I became the national scholastic champion in the four hundred metres and the eight hundred metres. I was competing in what was referred to as the middle-school events, against runners from the seventh through the ninth grades. Tenth- through thirteenth-graders were the upper-school or high school division. In eighth grade I also ran the anchor on our 4-by-400-metre relay team in the upper-school competition.

Our track season had relatively few meets compared with American high school programmes, which have weekly dual meets and weekend invitationals, culminating in conference, district, regional, and state meets. We had only a few dual meets and then some regional, provincial, and national meets. That meant we spent a lot of time training and relatively little time racing. Training is hard and tedious; racing is fun and exciting. Since we trained all year and had no real off-season, it took even more discipline to maintain a high level of fitness and then peak at just the right time. To be honest, my school coaches were earnest men who had studied track and field from textbooks and lectures, but they didn't have the practical know-how and technical expertise that Adolphe did. I didn't realise any of this until I actually worked with Adolphe, of course, but just from seeing the approach that many of my teammates took to the workouts, I knew we were mostly getting by on natural ability. With the right training and motivation, we could have been even faster and stronger.

Just after getting back home, I heard on the national radio station that I had been selected for the national team's developmental programme. I was to report straight to Bujumbura, where I and a few other young runners would begin two months of training with the rest of the national team. Being selected was a great honour, but it was going to be another adjustment challenge for me, for I had been eager to spend time home with my family on Fuku Mountain, but I'd still have a few months with them after my training.

I might have been even more eager to go home after that second school year if I had had better academic news to report.

By concentrating so much on drumming and running and a bit more socialising, I had slipped far out of the top five in my class. My average was still quite good, in the low eighties, but not nearly as strong as the year before. I was learning that life was a series of trade-offs. I couldn't have everything I wanted handed to me, either. My earlier high grades had been the product of hard work, not a natural gift. I was satisfied with my grades, because I had made a conscious choice, but I wasn't so sure that my parents would see it that way.

I also had to face Uncle Eliphaz, since I'd be staying with him during my training. And I assumed we would have to have another of those discussions – the kind when he noticed me eyeing the cars and the girls of Bujumbura and reminded me that instead of having my nose up a tailpipe or sniffing a young girl's perfume, I should keep my head firmly planted in reality. For me, he said, reality was books and education. Running could be an interesting diversion, but it could never replace education. Running could teach me to be disciplined, to set goals, but that should always be in service of achieving academic excellence and not the pursuit of fame. I understood what my uncle was telling me, and the truth is, I had already been thinking most of those same thoughts. But there was also this voice in my head that was asking me, "What if?" Like any adolescent, I had my dreams of glory and riches. I had had my first taste of success and minor fame. I liked it.

I believed in being outwardly humble, and at the time I probably wasn't consciously aware of the impulses that I can now put into words. At nearly sixteen, I must have sensed there was more to life than just an education and a job. I wasn't foolish enough to throw everything away and turn professional as a runner. I knew I had talent, I knew I was disciplined, and I knew I owed it to myself and to my parents, who had sacrificed for me, to do my best to achieve some kind of major breakthrough. I knew I had to somehow send that message to my uncle and to my family that I wanted to focus on running.

Maybe that's why I stole my uncle's car. Well, I didn't steal it exactly. I took it for a short ride. I had been so tempted to take it over those two months I spent with him. That summer I was left with a lot of unsupervised time. So one Saturday morning after my uncle had gone out, I took the keys to one of his cars, a Mercedes, eased it out of the driveway without starting it, and then drove it around the block a couple of times. I could have been driving Father Joseph's lowly VW Beetle, and I would still have felt that surge of power in my heart. I was asserting my independence, proving to myself what I was capable of.

Maybe my taking the Mercedes for a ride was a product of being exposed to Adolphe and the other runners. At first, I was absolutely frightened to show up at Adolphe's training centre. Located in one of Bujumbura's poorest waterfront neighbourhoods, the running track and brick office building, which looked like a cement bunker, were hardly what you would expect of a training facility for world-class athletes, but back then, I was impressed. The running track had a composite surface, and I had never run on anything so soft and springy in my life. However, the infield, where we did our stretching and calisthenics, was a hardscrabble patch of dirt with a few weedy clumps of grass stubbornly clinging to life. Adidas had partly funded Adolphe's developmental program and donated money for the track and other facilities. Somehow, all the money appropriated to us did not go into the construction of the office or weight-training or locker-room facilities. Over the years, I would hear Adolphe raging against the corruption and bureaucracy that plagued sports in Burundi specifically and the government generally. While the officials in the sports ministry and the governing bodies of the various sports grew wealthy and enjoyed the largesse of the International Olympic Committee, shoe and apparel manufacturers, and the like, the athletes suffered. Adolphe hated the system, and unlike most of the other coaches and lower officials, he refused to keep quiet about it. As a former athlete, he was on our side, and that's why we respected him so much and would do nearly anything he asked of us.

As one of the new invitees, I was a bit of a mystery to everyone, even to Adolphe. The first time we met, he didn't say much to me except "Let's see what you can do." I was dressed in a pair of shorts and a singlet; at five feet eight inches and only ninety-five pounds, I must have looked as thin as a rail. Even though it was 9 A.M. and the sun was barely high enough to climb over the low-slung industrial buildings and warehouses in the district, I was already sweating. "A thousand metres, Gilbert," Adolphe told me, and he held up his watch.

I'd been stretching with the others, struggling to follow their lead as they contorted themselves in ways I had never seen before. I was wondering how stretching my arms and fingers was going to help me, but I would soon learn. I knew enough to jog through a couple of laps before I toed the starting line under Adolphe's seemingly indifferent, yet alert gaze. When he shouted go, I took off.

The sensation of the track was different – I felt like I had springs on the bottom of my shoes. It took a few hundred metres, but I adjusted, and I no longer felt like my limbs would scatter in four directions. Once I was comfortable, I really kicked it into gear, and near the end of the thousand, I felt like

I was running as fast as I ever had. After a quick warm-down, I walked over to Adolphe. He pointed to a group of runners who were lining up along the back straight. They were a mix of schoolboys and older runners. "Your training group. They'll help you. They've all been here before. Show them the respect they deserve." He turned and walked away.

I wanted to know what my time was, but I saw that Adolphe had clicked the button on his stopwatch to clear it. I would find out in due course. For now, Adolphe was the master of my running universe, and he would let me know everything I needed to know. I suppose a part of maturing is knowing when to surrender some of your willfulness in the face of an authority figure who can do much to help you. Adolphe was just such a man, and I was fortunate he came along at exactly the right time. I have been truly blessed in many ways, and I was only then beginning to see that God had a purpose in mind for me, one that was just coming into sight, like the finish line from the top of the home stretch. It didn't matter where I was at that point, it was how I was going to draw on my reserves that would determine what kind of a man-child I was going to be.

When you are facing certain death, you find comfort any place you are able. I'd avoided being hacked to pieces. The blow intended for my head had struck me in the chest. Though it stunned me and the taste of blood polluted my mouth, I was still conscious. The gas station that we'd all been herded into was filled with Tutsis, but at least our enemy was outside. There were so many of us, all we could do was stand shoulder to shoulder.

I leaned against a wall for a few moments trying to catch my breath and clear my mind. I pictured my home on Mount Fuku, saw myself running downhill toward the well, the tug of gravity momentarily forgotten, my feet expressing my joy. Around me at that moment in Kibimba, I saw no joy. I saw my fellow students and other Tutsis numbly staring at me, their expressions devoid of understanding but their eyes alert with a combination of fear, recognition, and desire. In a way, I was envious of some of them. Some had been rendered senseless, clubbed on the back of the neck with tree limbs as thick as a man's thigh; some had been temporarily paralysed, dragged into the building. I cannot be certain, but I believed that many of them felt no pain. They did not cry out then, nor did they respond at all when the situation grew far worse.

At one point, a couple of Hutu men came into the building and poked their heads around; they seemed to be counting. I suspected that they were trying to determine if everyone inside was a Tutsi. They ducked out a minute or two later.

I was not envious of those who had been attacked with machetes. The concrete floor was slick with their blood. They clutched their arms, their heads, wherever they'd been cut. But for the most part they stood dripping blood, immobile, their expression vacant. Their

151

moans and mutterings tore at my heart. Each time I looked in another direction and saw another gaping wound, my stomach dropped – as though I'd crested a hill at high speed in an automobile. I sucked in my breath past teeth I'd clenched for hours. I stretched my aching jaw and felt my pulse pounding in my temples. Trying to massage the pain away, I shut my eyes and let my fingers work on various pressure points in my head and neck. For some reason, when I closed my eyes, the volume rose. Not only could I now hear the shouts and cries of my fellow captives, I could hear the Hutus clapping their hands, banging drums, chanting and singing, "We did it!" over and over again. Rain pelted the corrugated-steel roof, adding tympani to the chorus. The increase in volume surprised me – it was as if I'd been swimming and had water in my ears and now it had drained.

The pungent odour of seared flesh and hair attacked my senses. Opening my eyes confirmed what I suspected. The crowd inside was like an amoeba, and each person's movement sent a ripple effect among us. Across the way, a flaming eucalyptus branch fell from a hole in the roof. The odor of gasoline was now strong in the room, and in a flash of recognition, I saw that the Hutus had planned this all along.

A strange calm descended on me. Despite how horrific the situation was, I felt tranquil. I heard this voice in my heart say, "Do not worry. You will survive. Gilbert, you will be fine." That reassuring and measured voice penetrated the din of shouts and pleading.

In a panic, people began clawing at one another to escape the heat and the flames. Smoke started to sting my eyes and choke me. My already labored inhalations now seared my lungs. A few people tried to climb out a window, but the assembled Hutus pelted them with rocks and sticks, and they stopped trying. One man, his face a mask of fear, his forehead gashed, his back in flames, charged out the door, his shrieks drowned out by the sound of his body being clubbed.

Along with a few others, I managed to crowd into a small alcove off the main room. I had seen on television the atrocities committed in Bosnia, but I'd never imagined that I could have been a part of something so inhumane. It disturbs me to think this, but I wonder now if it wouldn't have been better to have been gunned down by automatic weapons than to suffer the crude and torturous methods of the Hutus.

From my vantage point, I could see most of the main room, and the sight sickened me. People were on fire, and they thrashed about before sinking to the floor. As each person fell, the fires joined together. More branches and gasoline rained down on the pile of flesh and bone. Anything made of wood in the building was now being consumed, and the heat was intense. The smell of burning flesh was nauseating, but what I saw was even more horrible. I watched as the skin on my Tutsi classmates and friends bubbled and blistered and then disappeared. If you have ever held a sheet of burning paper in your hands and watched it closely, then you have some idea of what I witnessed. Their skin rolled back on itself and flared a bright orange when exposed to oxygen. What none of you are likely to have ever seen is this: people whose skin has been burned completely away, exposing bloody sinew and bone. And they were not yet dead. Their brains were alive, and they spoke: "I'm not scared, man. I'm not scared."

Through it all, the voice in my heart kept telling me to be calm. I would be safe. I would not die.

The smoke was fiercely choking, and my eyes stung, but I felt it my duty to watch everything going on. I had to bear witness to this murder. I had to remember the names and the faces of the victims *so I could tell their families that they had died. I took an awful kind of roll call in my head. Anatole. Desirée. Martin. Delphine. Robert. Monique. Leonard. Solanga Beatrice. Hubert. Brigitte Patience. All dead. All my classmates.*

We had been put inside the building at about six o'clock in the evening. In the first hour or so, most of us had died. All that remained of the building was the steel roof, the cinder-block exterior walls, and one cinder-block partition. The rest had been incinerated. Where the main pile of bodies had been was now an unrecognisable mass of flesh and bone.

Those few of us who had survived could move fairly freely around the room. The main fires had extinguished themselves, and but for the occasional sound of a water drop hissing as it hit the embers, the night was still. I could still hear the voices of the Hutus outside, but I could tell fewer remained. Though more may have been alive, I recall that two other men and I were the only ones who were able to stand and move. Hours passed. I knelt on the concrete floor. Puddles of what had once been liquid congealed; fatty remains floated like prisms atop the pooled rainwater. Though a fierce thirst possessed me, I could not bring my lips to it.

At one point, hours after the fires had first started, two Hutu men came into the building, probably to see if anyone was alive. We quickly scrambled and picked up any rocks or sticks that had been hurled at us earlier and threw them at the two men. They retreated, but a moment later more stones pelted the building. We sought refuge away from the windows and gathered as much ammunition as we could. Even when the Hutus threw a few more lit branches inside the windows, we remained safely out of harm's way.

One of the other survivors was a soldier named Jean-Paul, and together with a local named Frederick, we plotted a strategy. Frederick had been cut by a machete and was very weak, but he could gather things for us to throw. When we looked out the window, we could see that more Hutus had returned. A group of nearly fifty stood just outside the firelight. We were certain that another major attack was imminent. They could not afford to let anyone survive.

The crowd dispersed, and we could hear some of them moving outside the far wall behind us. Soon they shoved more gasoline-soaked branches into the building. The heat was again intense. I would have tried to throw the branches back out the window, but they were blazing so fiercely that I couldn't even get close to them. I kept pressing myself as far from the fire as possible. I noticed that Frederick was lying on the floor. I watched to see if his chest rose and fell, but it did not. Now there were only two of us left.

I sat on the floor with my head in my hands. I wanted to cry but I didn't. My tongue felt as swollen and rough as a tennis ball. Still the voice in my heart soothed and reassured me. I was going to survive. Jean-Paul and I had talked about how important it was for one of us to make it out alive. We wanted to be certain that those who did this to us would be held accountable.

Now, with the hour well past midnight, I was struggling to stay awake. I may have dozed for a while. I was startled awake by the sound of a section of the roof being torn away. I yelled Jean-Paul's name but got no response. A moment later, gas was being sloshed all over the inside of the building. They must have hauled up a large container because even in the dim light of the embers, I could see a dark pool spreading before it burst into flames. I looked up and saw more fire raining down on us. With nowhere to run, I burrowed my way underneath a smoking mound of bodies. They were still so hot that contact with their flesh burned mine.

Gritting my teeth against the horror and the excruciating pain, I continued to claw my way under the bodies of my dead classmates. I recoiled as I felt chunks of seared flesh coming off in my hands, but I pressed on. I knew that in a moment, the Hutus would come into the building to see if anyone was alive. I hoped if they found no one, they would leave for the night and I would be able to escape. If they found me, they would certainly kill me. I tried to lie as still as I could, fighting the urge to cry out as I felt the flesh of my back and hip bubbling and blistering. I had heard that burns are among the most painful injuries you can sustain, and I can believe that. In agony, lying spread-eagle beneath the bodies, I thought I was going to die.

After a while, I crawled out from my hiding place and crept to the window, each movement feeling like a razor blade dragging across my raw and exposed nerves. A small group of Hutus, now fewer than fifty, stood clustered around a burning tyre from an eighteen-wheeler. The acrid smoke snaked skyward, and the nauseating smell of burned rubber added to the already putrid mix of odours.

Even though the voice in my heart kept telling me I would survive, I lost faith when I realised I was the last one alive. I tried to find Jean-Paul or at least his body, but I could not. I wondered then if Jean-Paul and Frederick had been apparitions, products of my fevered and tortured imagination. Being alone disturbed me in such a visceral, soul-shattering way, I immediately climbed onto the concrete partition dividing a service bay from the office. It was waist-high, and I stood up on it unsteadily, intending to dive off onto my head to break my neck.

Instinct took over, and just as I was about to hit the ground, my reflexes had me duck my head and twist my body so I landed on my shoulder. I tried again, with the same result. I stood on the partition and sobbed. Sooty tears and mucus ran down my face. Again, I heard the voice in my heart – louder and more insistent this time

– telling me to stop. I thought again of what Jean-Paul had said. We had to make certain the Hutus were punished for their crimes. He had told me he had seen me race. He knew who I was. His acknowledging me had given me some strength. I could not end my life this way.

I needed to know what the Hutus would do if they found someone still alive inside the building. The body of a young girl lay close to the door farthest away from the most intense fires. I picked her up and carried her to the window. I laid her across the sill. Her legs scissored and twitched, and she tumbled over the edge. To my horror, she got to her feet and staggered away from the building. She didn't get far. The Hutu men pounced on her, and I had to turn away as they pounded and hacked at her with machetes, clubs, and spears.

I collapsed to the floor. The sounds of the fire snapping and popping unnerved me. I could not believe I'd contributed to that young woman's death. My mind started to race. Guilt, anger, remorse, and revulsion were a volatile mix, and I wanted to end my life again. I had little time to think about it. From above, another shower of gas came down. It ignited, and as the fires burned, I smelled something. The smoke, which previously was black and grey, was yellow, and the strong smell of sulphur pierced and burned the tender flesh of my nostrils. The fire was burning in a kaleidoscope of colours.

Mr. Firmat Niyonkenguruka was back at work. Only a chemistry teacher could have possessed the chemicals that had been added to the fire. If they couldn't burn me alive, they were hoping to poison me with the fumes. I knew I had to get out of there. Even if I escaped the building and they captured me and chopped me to pieces, at least my parents would have something to bury. I did not want to die in the fire.

I picked up a femur, the largest one that I could find, and hefted it in my hand. The bone was still hot and it burned me, but I had little choice. I went to the far window, the only one still intact, and the one that faced away from the tyre fire where most of the Hutus still stood. I swung the bone like a hammer, and the heat-softened glass shattered easily. Fresh air swept in through the window, and the fire behind me roared and flickered. I kicked one leg onto the sill and through the broken frame. Jagged bits of glass tore at my calf, but I didn't hesitate. Using my arms, I pulled myself through the breach and out into the damp night air. Without pausing to consider what my best escape route might be, I sprinted into the night, flames still licking at my body.

The Hutu men shouted and pursued me. I fully expected that just as Severin had promised me, someone was going to slit my throat. But they were going to have to outrun me to do it.

CHAPTER FIVE

INITIATION AND ADVANCEMENT

The secret to running fast is unity. Adolphe preached and taught a unity of mind, a unity of purpose, a unity of the various parts of the body, and a unity of the soul. Only when we had all of those disparate elements in place could we expect to achieve our potential. I had a natural gift for running. In technical terms, my VO^2 max, the maximum amount of fuel (oxygen) my cells could carry from heart and lungs to my muscles, was greater than most people's. Even if I didn't train, I would have a natural advantage.

What makes sport so intriguing is that we can seldom reduce performances to the differences between us on the cellular level. In most regards, we are far more alike physiologically than we are different. In terms of our mental and spiritual attributes, we are all quite different. What Adolphe tried to do in training us to become world-class runners was to eliminate some of the differences in our physical and mental makeup. He firmly believed that form and function needed to be united. Though he allowed for some individual differences in our running style, he had conceived an archetypal stride length, hand position, and other biomechanical factors; if we adapted our natural style to these, we would maximize our effort and become faster.

It sounds easy on paper, but of course, you know that it is very difficult to adhere to a model of perfection in practice. I'm not certain what separates the winners from the losers in a race. If we presume, for the sake of argument, that everyone in a particular heat runs in perfect form and each has trained with equal rigor, why does one person come out ahead of the others? Is it sheer human will or the will of God that makes the difference?

I don't know the answer, but what I do know is that as I got older and matured as a runner and as a man, I saw the possible answers in a very different light than I did as a young man. As a young disciple of Adolphe, I believed deep down, at the very cellular level of my being, that I could learn to command my body to perform as I wanted it to. I could control my fate in a race by maintaining my focus, holding my form, and believing in my training methods and my race preparation. The only one who could prevent me from winning was me. Or so I believed then.

The truth is, I trusted Adolphe because I saw immediate results from his teachings. For the two summer months I was with him, life was reduced to the essentials. Each day we woke up and had a light breakfast. We were at the track by nine o'clock, and after a slow jog once around, we gathered in the infield for polymetrics (a specialized form of movement and stretching) and form drills while Adolphe circulated among us offering insights and instruction. Some mornings we simply stood in place and worked on our stride and body position for hours. This work never felt tedious to me. I loved every second of my training – though I loved some parts of it better than others.

I was among the younger runners at the training camp, but some of my peers were already enjoying great success. My childhood friend Aloise Nizigama would turn professional in tenth grade, as would Vénuste Niyongabo. They were both two years ahead of me, and along with the older runners, they did participate in my initiation into the group. The first time we went on a long run through the streets of the capital, I learned that a definite hierarchy existed among the runners, and the veterans of the camp did not always listen to what Adolphe told them. The first day I spent at the camp, Adolphe told us that we were to go on a forty-five-minute run. I didn't know the route, so I had to rely on the others for guidance. Adolphe wanted us to run at a steady pace of five-and-a-half-minute miles.

We took off through the streets, and I kept to the back of the cluster of about twenty runners. I had just come down from high altitude at school and at home on Fuku Mountain, so I was very fit and breathing the thick air of the capital was like getting two intakes of oxygen with each breath. The pace was easy, and I easily settled into a rhythm. Suddenly, as though in a spontaneous response to a surge in adrenaline, the pack shot out ahead of me. I took off in pursuit, confused by their apparent disregard for Adolphe's admonition to keep a steady pace. It took me nearly a quarter mile to overtake them, but as soon as I did, the pace slowed to its previous tempo. The veterans repeated this sprint-and-slow pattern a couple more times,and with their sidelong glances they let me know they were testing me.

We must have made quite a spectacle running through the traffic-clogged streets of Bujumbura. The collective attitude we projected was that we owned the roads, and the vehicles and pedestrians needed to get out of our way. As we ran along, we sang, and I came to really enjoy watching the expression on the faces of those we passed. The smiles of the children delighted me, and I imagined that they looked at us with pride and envy. We represented the best that Burundi had to offer the world of sport, and our exploits were broadcast nationwide.

I understood the necessity of demonstrating that I belonged and could do my part to maintain the tradition of excellence that Adolphe's group had established. In order to solidify my place among them, as we neared the training facility and the streets became more familiar to me, I picked up the pace and took the lead, eventually being the first to run through the gate and back onto the track. Barely winded, I came to a stop near Adolphe, and I could read the pleasure in his eyes. Some of the other runners came in and stood stooped over, tugging at their running shorts or clasping their hands atop their heads, their chests heaving.

Adolphe looked at his watch and shook his head in a long slow arc. He held it up so that we could all see the digital readout. His expression was now fierce. "Forty-two forty-eight." He sounded like he was announcing someone's passing and not our time. "When I say forty-five minutes, I mean forty-five minutes and not forty-two forty-eight. You must learn control and tempo management. If you don't do this in practice, how can you expect to manage your race?"

He let the question hang in the air. I saw some of the older runners looking away from him, barely suppressed smirks undulating across their lips. Adolphe was not one to tolerate any form of disrespect. "Five hundred by fifteen at one-twenty. Get to the line!"

For the next half hour or more, we ran five-hundred-metre repeats. Adolphe had called out the distance we were to run, the number of times we were to do it, and the exact time we were to take to complete each repeat. He allowed us one-minute rests in between. We did these workouts regularly, but this one was his attempt to reassert his authority over the group and to drive home his point about the importance of learning your pace. We had to run each sprint at exactly one minute and twenty seconds. No faster, no slower. Each failure to do so added another repetition. Fifteen good ones and we could stop. Adolphe believed it was essential to train your body to become its own stopwatch. We were not allowed to wear a timing device when we trained. Our bodies would be all the metre we would ever need. Just as Uncle Eliphaz had preached to me for years – discipline and focus were the keys to success in any endeavor.

Adolphe also was a master motivator. In many ways, his methods reminded me of farming. He had a good eye for raw talent, and he took those seeds and planted them. His rigorous training methods ensured that only the strongest plants survived. He then weeded out those that would not be productive and watered and fertilised the ones remaining. I think he took great pleasure in nurturing young talent. He'd travelled all over Europe and had had many opportunities to coach athletes from other nations, but his heart was with Burundian runners. He was always looking out for the athletes, at his own expense. When he saw funds going into the pockets of the administrators and his athletes thus being denied travel opportunities, equipment, and facility upgrades, he would protest. He was frequently censured by the governing bodies, but as a university professor, he enjoyed some protection and respect in the community. I think those in power also understood that the athletes would rebel if he was dismissed, and no one wanted a stain like that to mar their record.

I don't know how I can ever repay Adolphe for what he did for me. Like any great teacher, he enlarged my vision and showed me possibilities I would never have seen on my own. As a way to motivate me, just before I returned to Kibimba at the start of ninth grade, he gave me a USA singlet and equipment bag. He'd gotten them at some meet from a USA Track & Field representative. He gave them to me because he wanted me to be ever mindful of the very real possibility that I could one day go to school in the United States. U.S. schools needed good athletes. I could receive a scholarship and a wonderful education, but he couldn't send me there unless I was going to succeed. After all, his reputation was on the line and he needed to be certain I would represent him well. If one of us failed there, it would be as if we all failed. I would have to work very hard if I was going to get this opportunity.

To increase my chances of winning a college scholarship to a school in the United States, Adolphe wanted me to attend school closer to Bujumbura so I could train with him year-round. Uncle Eliphaz thought I should attend a medical training school, where I could train to become a nurse and be nearly guaranteed a secure job when I graduated. I was torn by conflicting allegiances and desires. I did not want to disappoint either man, but I knew that Kibimba was the best place for me. I'd enjoyed both academic and athletic success there, and I was getting comfortable as well and making many friends. I often wonder how my life might have turned out differently if I hadn't made that choice.

At our last meeting, Adolphe handed me a sheet of paper. On it, he had laid out a training schedule for the upcoming school year. For every day from September to the beginning of July he had penciled in a specific workout tailored to my needs. I didn't really know what to say to him, other than to take his offered hand and thank him. Looking back on it now, I realize that although I was only fifteen years old, this man was treating me like a man. He was entrusting me with a responsibility to control my own destiny. If not quite his equal, I stood the chance of becoming someone like him. I did not want to ever let Adolphe down, and I vowed to validate his trust and belief in me.

In most ways, I accomplished that mission – especially on the track. I also became a de facto coach of the Kibimba track team and was a devout acolyte of Adolphe's philosophy and training methods. In the church of Adolphe, self-control was the highest aspiration. I was determined to let nothing stand in the way of my succeeding. My track coach at Kibimba understood that what I'd learned in a few months at the national camp far exceeded what he knew. He allowed me the freedom to structure the team's workouts and to instruct the other runners. I do not know if it was my new Adidas running shoes and my USA singlet and bag or if those were merely the outer trappings of a less visible transformation, but I do know that when I arrived back at school, other people sensed a change in me.

I'm ashamed to admit that I let my discipline slip. I no longer attended church regularly. When the other students assembled for services, I was granted permission to go out for a run. I must confess that instead of making me feel blessed, these privileges made me feel superior – as though I deserved special treatment and was only being accorded my due. In short, I lacked humility. I hope this change in character wasn't so obvious that others viewed me as conceited, but my increasing confidence must have been apparent.

Unfortunately, I didn't have many opportunities to put my athletic prowess to the test. Each year, Lycée Kibimba participated in only two dual meets. We did not have a strong winning tradition, but as we followed Adolphe's workout program, our times dropped and we won more frequently, eventually becoming regional and district champions at the scholastic level. Outside of the school meets, I ran in the open junior events – where runners under the age of eighteen were eligible to compete. To give you some idea of how much I'd improved in only one short season with Adolphe, my personal record in the eight-hundred-metre dash, at the age of fifteen, dropped from 1:54 to 1:50. In ninth grade, from September to May I cut three seconds off my best time. To put that in context, in 2005 the top high school athlete in the United States ran a 1:46 at the age of eighteen. Those additional three years, and the advances in training methods, nutrition, and hydration, mean a lot. Americans excel at sprints but are less adept at the middle and longer distances. When I was fifteen, my personal best in the metric mile (fifteen hundred metres) was 3:53. At the 2005 USA Track and Field Junior Olympics, the winning time in the fifteen hundred was 3:58.

Despite my prowess in what is loosely called the mile, I much preferred the four-hundred-metre and eight-hundred-metre races. In order to challenge myself in our four-hundred-metre runs during practice, I would take on a team of two runners each running a two-hundred-metre relay leg – and I would still win by a considerable margin. In the words of a Texan I met after coming to America, "It ain't braggin' if it's so."

I knew I was fast enough that if I trained hard, I could place highly in any event from the one hundred metres to the five thousand. At times, picking what races to specialise in seemed harder than running in them. I won a number of national championships at the junior level in the four-hundred-metre and eight-hundred-metre distances, competing against boys older than me. After I won those two championships the first year I entered, the organisers changed the race order to make it more difficult for me to win both; they scheduled the final of the eight hundred so that it went off only ten minutes after the four-hundred final ended. Their strategy didn't deter me, and though I had only barely caught my breath when I toed the line to begin the next race, I still managed to win.

I loved running at Prince Rwagasore Stadium in Bujumbura. The president had a special box there, and in addition to attending soccer matches, track championships, and the national drum finals there, he also delivered key speeches from that box. The vociferous crowd was a great motivator, and running in front of thousands of chanting and screaming spectators was an incredible thrill. Hearing my name announced over the public-address system the first time sent a chill up my spine. As time went on, the radio announcers and TV commentators grew tired of having to say my entire name and shortened it to Gilbert Tuhabonye. I didn't really mind – all that mattered was they were letting the rest of my countrymen know who that figure streaking around the track was. Having a few syllables cut off my name was a small price to pay.

My experiences at the nationals and with Adolphe brought me into contact with the best runners in the country – juniors and the older runners who ran in the open division rather than the schoolboy division. Among them was Dieudonné Kwizera. Kwizera would be a true trailblazer, being among the first runners from Burundi to go to the United States on a track scholarship. He ran at the University of Nebraska and later turned professional and stayed in the United States. Track and field in Burundi was its own community, and we followed news of Dieudonné's exploits with great interest. We were pleased to learn he was doing as well as many of the Kenyan runners. They were the first African athletes to gain fame in the international community, and they never let the rest of us Africans forget it. Even today, when I'm out in the city wearing my running shorts, people will strike up a conversation with me and invariably ask if I'm from Kenya. I tell them no and try to get them to guess my country of origin, but no one ever says Burundi.

When I first started to compete outside of Burundi, the misperception that all dark-skinned runners from Africa must be Kenyan bothered me – only because I love my country so much and want our contributions to be recognised. Back then, I was simply grateful that guys like Kwizera were already in the United States and letting coaches know that there were more of us – just as fast – back home. Along with Adolphe, Kwizera talked to me about the possibility of going to school in the States. By twelfth grade, I had just about given up on the idea of attending university in Burundi. Tulane University seemed to be the most interested in me, and depending on how I did on our national exams and other entrance examinations (only later did I learn more about the TOEFL – Test of English as a Foreign Language), I would be offered a scholarship to compete at an NCAA Division I school.

The days of my secondary education took on a familiar rhythm and pattern. I ran every day and at every opportunity. I kept scrupulous notes on my workouts. I put my Casio digital wristwatch to good use as a stopwatch. I *loved* that watch and used it for years. My experiences at the national camp further separated me from my classmates and friends. They were so focused on getting to university in Burundi they couldn't understand why I was spending valuable study time running. Even though I tried to explain to them that I could earn a scholarship to a university in the States by running and not just by studying, they shook their heads and asked, "Why would you want to go to the U.S.?"

To be honest, I didn't have a ready answer. We all knew the United States was a wealthy and powerful nation, but most of what we knew about daily life there came from television and films. On weekends at Kibimba we enjoyed watching movies in the cafeteria or the gymnasium, using a television and VCR that we could wheel into either spot. We got to see actual Hollywood movies – a far cry from the religious films that were the only fare available to us in primary school. We didn't have a wide selection, but we took full advantage of the opportunity to watch anything, even if it meant that the dialogue became imprinted in our brains. As a student representative on the school's board, I was selected to go into the city to rent the movies. Since we were a religious school and we had younger students, someone had to screen the movies to make sure they were acceptable. This task fell to me. As a country boy, I was supposed to have purer and less suspect morals than the city kids who'd been exposed to so much more than I had been.

Little did the faculty know that my tastes ran to the films of Sylvester Stallone and anything that Chuck Norris ever starred in. I usually brought back two movies – one appropriate for the younger students, the other for the older students. Quite often, the faculty joined us in watching these violent films. No one ever complained or got into trouble for allowing the corrupting influence of mainstream Hollywood to enter the school.

If I had to point to one thing that I liked about boarding school, it was the opportunity to get to know the faculty members as people. We still had a great deal of respect for our professors, and the line demarking their roles and ours was clear. That said, one of the Lycée Kibimba's missions was to teach students to become leaders.

Consequently, in addition to being on the student governance board, I was also a member of the drumming team's board and selected and trained new members. I was already the unofficial coach of the runners and the library monitor, and I helped oversee one of the lower school's boys' dormitories. My headmaster placed a lot of trust in me, and I tried as hard as I could to honor that trust. For the last three years of my secondary education, I did not have to pay tuition in recognition of my contributions and athletic performance.

Our other weekend diversion was dancing. Because they wanted us to stay on campus so we wouldn't be tempted to sneak off to the city and get into trouble, the administration provided us with a sound system and an allowance for cassette tapes and CDs. Since we were a coeducational school, we didn't have to import girls from a neighbouring campus. By the time I was in eleventh grade, I'd had a series of "girlfriends." These relationships were really little more than flirtations that blossomed into us becoming study partners. We would sit together in the cafeteria and go to the dances together, but we never really went on official dates. Everyone knew everyone else's business, so privacy was at a premium. Each time one of these relationships ended and another began, the school was abuzz with gossip and recriminations. I didn't like these dramas and tried to stay above them, but I fell victim to them as both a participant and spectator.

The dances served as a catalyst for rumours and as a kind of red-carpet walk at which the newly matched pairs could let the rest of the student body know they had coupled up. When I'd first gone to Kibimba, I was shy. Though I loved music and dancing, I was too timid to ask girls to dance with me. The dances weren't designed to be events for couples; and they evolved through practice into three distinct stages.

After we'd finished cleaning up the cafeteria, the older students would return to the dorms, where we would change our clothes and freshen up. I had acquired a bottle of Brut cologne as a result of one of my track victories, and I applied it liberally, fending off the entreaties of my friends Anatole and Severin, who wanted to splash themselves with my love potion. The younger students went straight to the dance hall, where they took seats along the walls. For the most part, they would remain there. The deejay, usually one of the year-thirteen students, would play rock-and-roll or reggae songs, since no one was really dancing at that point. One of my favorite artists was Bob Marley, and reggae often provided a transition from the listening phase to the dancing phase. At this point, stage two began. As the older students filtered in, they started to dance en masse. No one really paired off, and we danced to all kinds of African music. After everyone was sweaty and the younger kids exhausted, the couples would dance together in the last stage of the evening.

One night in 1992, just before the end of my first twelfth-grade semester, I was taking a break as the group-dance portion of the evening wound down. I was standing just outside the pulsating mass of my classmates when I spotted a girl walking toward me. This was odd. Usually after the group dance the girls would cluster together and, like electrons, spin around outside the circle of boys playing hard to get.

Her name was Suavis, and she was a Tutsi who had just transferred to the school at the beginning of the year. I knew her a little bit because she was a shotputter on the track team. Tall and broad, she was also on the basketball team and had earned a reputation as a physical player who would not be intimidated. She had told me earlier in the week between classes that she wanted to dance with me one day. I was, of course, flattered, but I wasn't used to girls being so forward. When I saw her coming toward me, I fought back a smile of pleasure. Suavis stood in front of me, looked me straight in the eye, and held my gaze. When I didn't take a step toward her, I saw her eyes scan the room and a flicker of doubt and embarrassment cloud her normally expressive face.

I don't know exactly what transpired in that moment, but her revelation of insecurity was endearing in a way that her bravado was not. A *zouk béton* song was playing, something furious and irresistible that I had to dance to. I stepped toward her, and we joined the others on the floor dancing to a song by Jocelyne Beroard and her female trio, Zouk Machine. Zouk music has its roots in Africa and such native instruments as drums and gourds, but most draws on rhythms from the French West Indies and Latin America and employs electronic synthesizers. I was mesmerized by Suavis, by her undulating hips and her gyrating head. She was a great dancer, and I was smitten. On the dance floor, whatever self-consciousness she had momentarily experienced was gone. The music captivated and transported her, and she took me with her.

I couldn't let her know that, however. Though I was a country boy at heart, I had learned a thing or two about women in my years at Lycée Kibimba. After the song ended, I immediately left the dance hall. My friend Gabriel Butoyi trailed after me and I told him that I was hot (I was – the air in the dance hall was stifling) and was going to the library to cool off. I let us in with my key and we sat and talked for few minutes. Gabriel commented on how well Suavis and I danced together. Pleased that he noticed, I nodded noncommittally. After a few minutes of sitting in silence, I got back up and returned to the dance hall.

My heart leapt into my throat when I saw that Suavis was dancing with another boy. Regret heated my blood. Maybe I shouldn't have walked out on her so quickly. Regret turned to pleasure a moment later when she noticed me standing there and immediately walked over to me, her eyes sparkling. She took my hand and led me out onto the floor. When the music slowed, we stayed out there with the real couples and continued dancing.

I was feeling that giddy excitement that only a new relationship can produce. I wish I could have figured out a way to bottle it – I would have guarded it even more zealously than my cologne. Eventually, my infatuation with her would turn to love. Suavis was from a very good family from near the Mwaro military camp where my brother was stationed. I got to visit her there and to meet her family. Unfortunately, she didn't pass a major exam her tenth-grade year (she was one year behind me in school) and she had to transfer to a medical training school in Bujumbura. When I had to say goodbye to her at the end of the school year, I felt terrible. We vowed to write each other, and we hoped when I was in Bujumbura training with Adolphe that she would be able to take some time away from her family to come to the capital early. Sadly, she couldn't.

We wrote to each other that summer and into the autumn. I seldom have cried in my life, and I didn't when we last saw each other. At least not until we were even more cruelly separated. I was steadfastly loyal to her and she to me, but sometimes the universe or fate or whatever you care to call it chooses not to reward our fidelity.

But before that final parting in October 1993, she brought great joy to my life. Though she seemed so fiercely competitive on the sports field, Suavis was by nature a sweet and gentle person. She enjoyed my successes and was one of the few people who understood my ambition to get to the United States on a scholarship. When I was with her, I was proud of our union. She bolstered my confidence because I saw her as a young woman who set her sights on a worthy target and devoted herself to attaining it. I was one of her goals, and I was very grateful she had the courage to let me know in no uncertain terms that I was important enough to her that she would risk being considered too forward (a very real fear among African women) by her peers.

If I have any regrets about the years that led up to my final year at Lycée Kibimba, it's that I didn't always succeed in remaining a humble victor. I revelled in the attention I received and the perquisites that came with being a champion. I remember a photograph that appeared in one of the school yearbooks (little more than hand-printed, unbound pamphlets). In it, I stand in the doorway of one of the school buildings with twenty-seven medals around my neck. I am beaming, and as I recall it, my erect carriage and the tilt of my head reveals a certain defiance and arrogance. I don't know if this part was really there or if in the intervening years I have invented it, but I remember that the door behind me is open and no light penetrates the opening. In that dark chasm is a pair of eyes. Is someone there watching over me? Stalking me? I will never be able to verify whether this remembered image was a phantasm or reality. Like most things I had in my possession at Kibimba, the photograph is lost to me.

While I still can, I want to recall one last moment of glory before that dark chasm inhales me.

The best athletes in the country were in the military, and they trained at Mwaro Camp. Toward the end of twelfth grade, Lycée Kibimba ran a dual meet against the Mwaro soldiers. We loaded the team into the back of the Toyota pickup truck, and I led us in song the forty kilometres to the camp. I was in high spirits. My brother would be at the meet, as would Suavis and her family, and I was going to have a chance to prove myself against some of the best runners in Burundi. I wanted to make a good impression on the soldiers. I knew they were aware of me because of my relation to Dieudonné, and I wanted him to be proud of me. I also knew that the results would be broadcast across the country, as they usually were, and I could enter my last year in secondary school with an even stronger reputation.

Like Lycée Kibimba, the army camp had a dirt track. In fact, the only time I ran on a composite track was at the national training facility and at the nationals. I was one of the few runners who had a number of different choices to make in selecting the right length of spikes to use in my shoes. I don't know if that was the major difference in my success that day, but I won the eight-hundred-metre race, besting a muscular soldier whose wailing exhalations made me want to get as far from him as possible. The crowd was pro-military, and my victory in the four hundred silenced them. That we were even close in the competition was somewhat miraculous. After all, even though the men we were running against (some were my age as well) were technically soldiers, in reality they trained as runners all day every day. They didn't have to attend classes as we did, worry about tests and the like. For some reason, maybe because of our relative proximity, a fierce rivalry existed between the school and the soldiers.

After running two races in the span of half an hour, I was a bit tired. When Headmaster Ntibazonkiza approached me as I sat in the infield trying to rest, I knew it must be for something important. He and I had such great respect and affection for each other, I knew he would never ask anything of me that didn't a matter of great deal to him. He knelt on one knee alongside me. He took off his hat, a straw boater that his brother-in-law had sent him from Jamaica, and wiped his glistening brow with his handkerchief. "How are you feeling, Gilbert? Are you feeling strong?"

"Yes."

"Honestly now, Gilbert. I need to know."

I thought about my answer for only an instant. I could tell he wanted the truth but only if it confirmed what he hoped was true. "I feel very good."

He put his hand on my shoulder. "Good. Good." He went on to explain that the camp's commander, a lieutenant colonel, had offered to bet him one cow that his guy could beat me in the four hundred. The headmaster wanted to know if I could win.

I knew that to us, a cow was a fortune. I cannot begin to give it a monetary value, but I can tell you that this was a very significant wager. The headmaster pointed over to the sidelines where the cow stood grazing. I'd never seen a cow like that one before. Our longhorns were positively skeletal in comparison. I don't know where the camp's commander had got it, but I could tell that it would be giving gallons and gallons of milk for a long time to come. I wished I was the one who could win the prize, but I was equally happy to have the chance to win it for my favourite teacher. I told him that I was ready to win, but that I needed to be in lane two or three. He nodded and walked off to make the arrangements.

In the four-hundred-metre race, all the runners must remain in their own lane for the full lap around the track. The racers are staggered at the start, with the runners on the inside lanes behind the runners on the outside lanes to equalize the difference in distance of the curves. I was in lane two, thirty-two metres behind the man I had to beat, who was in lane eight, on the outside of the track. I wanted those to be the starting positions so that I could see my opponent the entire race. I did not want someone to sneak up behind me and nip me at the finish line. I also didn't mind running the curves on the narrower portion of the track. As a somewhat smaller runner, I had a slight advantage in the curves and could easily stay to the very inside of my lane.

The entire base was on hand for the race, and word about the bet must have spread through the crowd. Nearly everyone from the school had made the trek to the race, and they were ringing the track or standing behind or on top of the vans and trucks that brought them there. Before the race, I drank a few sips of water, but it didn't sit well in my stomach. I was as nervous as I'd ever been before a race. I didn't want to let Mr. Ntibazonkiza down; I wanted to impress my brother and my girlfriend and her family. Given what has transpired since, it seems silly to put such stakes on a race, but at the time I felt it was a matter of life and death.

By the time I got to the line for the start of the race, I was wracked by doubt. My stomach was churning and the acidic taste of bile rose in my throat and mouth. I kept trying to spit, but little more than a dollop of foam came to my lips and clung there. I said a quick prayer and bowed my head just before the gun went off.

During the first few strides of a race, you try to get your legs to turn over as quickly as you possibly can. That means you must chop your stride a bit – take shorter steps initially. I don't know if it was because of the longer spikes that I used because the track had been chewed up in earlier races, but I got off to a fantastic start. I kept my eyes to my right, where my opponent was (the other six racers were of no concern to me), and it seemed as though with every stride I took a healthy bite out of his thirty-two-meter lead. By the time we reached the start of the final turn, I had nearly drawn even with him. I knew then that the race was over. Given the shorter radius I had to run, I knew that over the course of the last curve I would pull ahead of him, but then I'd have to watch out for his attack from the rear. Instead of powering through the curve, I slowed a bit to stay even with him and keep him within eyesight.

Slowing a bit gave me a reserve of energy I drew from once we got to the final straight. I did something then that most coaches would not recommend. I shortened my stride again for a few seconds to increase my turnover rate. The brief surge brought me ahead of the soldier, and for the rest of the straight, I pulled away. When I broke the tape, I thrust both my hands above my head in exultation. I could not have been happier. My teammates swarmed around me and thumped me on the back and head. What meant the most to me was seeing Headmaster Ntibazonkiza. He may have been more excited than I was, and he hugged me and told me how grateful he was for my efforts and how proud of me for rising to the challenge. This was a wonderful way to end the school year, and I was so looking forward to my final year beginning the next autumn.

I had no way of knowing this then, but there were already forces at work at my school and in my country that would make this shared joy short-lived. As I rode back to school in the truck surrounded by my classmates, other drivers serenaded us with blasts of their car horns. We were riding away from the setting sun, and though it defies the laws of nature, what I remember now is that the long shadows we cast ahead of us somehow overtook us and drenched us in an unfathomable darkness.

I could not be certain that the shadows and darkness could hide me. My footfalls sounded like beating drums to my ears. As soon as I was out of the circle of firelight, I encountered a Hutu man. Instinctively, I ducked. He swung his machete so swiftly that he could not hold up and redirect his attack. I felt the blade breeze past my head, and then I heard it enter his flesh and then his piercing scream. Though he wouldn't be able to chase after me, his cries alerted the others to my location. The rain stung my back, and I knew I was burned terribly, but I couldn't let that distract me from the task at hand. I was in pure survival mode, much like the antelope and other wildlife I'd tracked. I relied on some primeval response and not on anything rational.

I ran a few metres and saw a spot where the rain-soaked ground reflected no light. It was a hole, and I slid down into it, realising only later that the Hutus must have dug it to bury the bodies and cover up the evidence of their crimes. The wet earth and stones tore at my burned flesh, but I didn't cry out. I remembered all the races and workouts I'd done when the pain seemed unendurable but I'd pushed through. I had to focus.

Five or six Hutus ran up to the edge of the hole. I pressed myself more tightly against the side, praying the hole still looked pitch black. Their flashlights and torches played around the perimeter and into the bush but couldn't penetrate the darkness of the hole. I heard them discuss their plan of attack. The few moments I'd spent in the hole had helped me catch my breath, so I knew I couldn't be heard. The Hutus were yelling at one another and pointing in different directions. They kept shouting, "Get him! Get him!" I didn't know if they were after someone else or if they *thought they saw me moving in the darkness. Finally they decided to spread out to find me, leaving behind a lone guard. They figured if they fanned out and circled back around, they'd be able to tighten their noose around my neck and capture me. Again I thought of the tactics we used in hunting, and for the first time I felt true empathy for our prey. I had eaten of the antelope's heart, and now more than ever I needed its strength and cleverness.*

More important, though, I had to go from being prey to predator. The guard was standing right on the edge of the burial hole, and I crawled as quietly as I could, any sound I made drowned out by the ululating of the hunters as they moved through the streets and paths hoping to ensnare me. Fighting against the agonising pain in my back and legs, I stood hunched over. The lone Hutu who remained stepped away from the hole, and I could see him training his flashlight into other holes. I immediately retreated to my previous position, certain he was going to discover me. He came walking back toward the hole, and then the flashlight was flying in the air and he came tumbling down right next to me. He was on his stomach and I pounced on him. I slid one arm over his shoulder and clamped my hand over his mouth. With my palm flush against his lips to keep him from shouting, I reached my fingers across to the opposite side of his jaw. Once I had a firm hold on his jaw, I dug my fingers into his flesh and jerked my arm back with all my strength. His neck snapped with a satisfying pop, and he crumpled dead.

I had helped in the slaughter of a few animals in my time, and inspired by Sylvester Stallone and Chuck Norris I had studied karate, but I'd never done anything even remotely close to this. I could not afford to think about it. I had to consider my next move. Getting away from Kibimba was my first concern. I knew I could not stay in that hole. For the first time, I could smell myself. The

*putrid odour of my own burned flesh was nauseating, and I was
certain it would give my position away. It must have been at least
three o'clock in the morning; in a few hours daylight would come.
I decided to take my chances and flee. I stayed on the least used
paths, half crawling and half walking, more like a lower primate
than a man. Moving a few houses at a time, I hid among the
banana trees and coffee plants growing between houses. The Hutus
had not confined their slaughter to those of us at the school. I could
hear them shouting and chasing more Tutsis.*

*I also overheard them talking about me. Some thought because
I was so fast I must have been kilometres away by then, but others
swore they knew where I was and that they were very close to
capturing me. I edged closer to one of the main roads that led to
downtown Kibimba. No traffic passed on the highway, but there
were no trees or other underbrush to shield me. I knew that I would
have to time my move across this barrier well and move quickly.*

*I gathered myself for one quick burst and made a mad dash
across the highway. I slinked into a path between a house and a
small shop where I'd once bought a pair of secondhand shoes.
Crossing that barrier had a couple of immediate effects on me.
First, I was beginning to become more hopeful that I could get out
of Kibimba. Second, whatever anesthetic effect my adrenaline-
fueled escape had produced had worn off completely. I was in utter
agony. I could bear the pain of the burns on my back, but from the
calf to the hamstring on one leg was an oozing lesion of scalded
flesh. Whatever chemicals Mr. Niyonkenguruka had added to the
fire were caustic, and I didn't know whether I was suffering from
fire burns or chemical burns. Perhaps even worse, I was dehydrated.
It seemed my every cell was screaming for water. I was tempted to
break into a house if only to slake my thirst.*

Before I could do that, I set out on all fours, half walking, half crawling. I'd only gone another few hundred metres when I encountered a woman. She was a Hutu, and she was carrying and dragging what looked to be her every worldly possession. I guessed that she was afraid that the Tutsi military at Mwaro Camp would be able to break through the barricades her fellow Hutus had erected and at best arrest them all, at worst kill them. I had managed to drop down to the ground around the corner of a house without detection. She was soon joined by another Hutu woman and then several other people, men and women. From their conversation, I gathered that they had not been participants in the attacks and murders. I recognised one of the men, Cyril. My school hired him several years before to guard over our crops. I stood up and presented myself to them. Cyril didn't recognise me, or if he did, he did not speak up.

They asked me who I was and where I was going. My heart sank when I recognised another of the men. He wasn't someone I knew before, but he had been at the burning building. Before I could answer, he started telling them who I was and that I was a Tutsi. I told them that I was mixed – my father was a Hutu and my mother a Tutsi. They asked to see my feet – Tutsis tend to have longer feet and toes than Hutus do. They also examined my face and my nose. They started to argue among themselves. I could barely stand at this point, and the unreality of this debate penetrated the fog of pain and anger that settled over me like a shroud. I told them that I was from Rumonge, an area where there are no Tutsis, but their discussion raged on. Some of the men wanted to lead me away and kill me. They saw my wounds and figured that I must be a Tutsi if someone had already harmed me. Others said that they wanted no trouble if the soldiers came. They did not want to kill anyone if it meant getting caught.

Nearly ready to pass out, I asked them if they could give me *some water. The men, including Cyril, didn't want to give me any, but a kind woman went inside her house and returned with a mug of water. I wasn't certain I could trust her, so I sloshed the mug a bit so that some water splashed on the ground and on my foot – I thought I might be able to detect any poisons that way. I did not even bother to see if I felt any ill effects from the water I'd spilled before I gulped down what was left in the mug.*

It seemed the longer I stayed there, the more the women came to my defence. I was grateful that they had the good sense to know that with the military base so close by and Kibimba being such a large city, this was the first place the soldiers would come to restore order. I'd also like to think they were motivated by compassion. I have no way of knowing, nor does the why really matter – in the end they let me go.

If this confrontation did one thing, it gave me some time to think more clearly about my strategy. I was, of course, very frightened that they would turn me in or kill me themselves, but they were so involved in arguing with one another that I had time to consider my options. By that point, I was certain I needed medical care and a refuge from another attack. Having run through those streets many times, I knew Kibimba Hospital was only about a half kilometre away. I would have to cross one more main arterial roadway, but I hoped to find someone at the hospital – preferably members of the Tutsi military who would protect me and get me the medical help I needed. I had slept fitfully the night before, had been awake for nearly twenty-four hours since, and had not eaten. I didn't know how much longer I could keep focusing my mental energies. My body was breaking down, and I could not afford to let my mind slip.

I resumed my previous pattern of monkey walking and evading contact with anyone by slipping into the shadows and hiding behind any object at hand. Even at that hour, many Hutu men were still in the streets, and I could hear their laughter drifting over the housetops. Anger had been welling up in me all day, and the men's bragging and joviality were almost too much to bear. Yet as much as it pained me to hear them, their words fueled my resolve and gave me strength. I picked up my pace and managed to cross the next main road with little trouble. To the east, the sky was just beginning to lighten, going from black to deep indigo. The clouds that had brought the rain were now gone, and the indifferent stars marched along. Only then did I realise how fortunate I had been that the moon had not risen that night, and nearly an hour must have passed since I'd left behind the Hutus I'd encountered.

Even though the hospital was my main objective, once I got within sight of it I felt no real relief. I wasn't sure who would be there and what they might do to me. At times, twin impulses raged within – the desire for all of this to be over no matter the outcome, and a fierce determination to survive no matter the cost. Nearing the door to the hospital, I gathered myself and prepared to attack anyone who threatened me. My head level with the doorknob (not because I was attempting a stealthy approach but because my painful burns twisted my body), I turned the knob and eased the door open. All of the lights were on, but I didn't see anyone moving about. I crept across the cool tile floor and peered down a hallway toward one of the wards. Young women lay sprawled on the floor and on the few beds. Even from a distance, I could tell that they were both Hutu and Tutsi. Those who were awake looked dazed and in a great deal of pain.

From outside, I heard voices. I scrabbled toward a bathroom across the hallway, pushed the door open, and collapsed inside. The ceramic tile felt cool to the touch, but when I lay on my back the pain flared. The men who had been after me came into the hospital.

"Where is he?" I heard them ask. "Have you seen a young man here?"

I felt my jaw clench. I could not hear any responses. In my imagination I saw one girl, a girl I had ignored at school because of my vanity, slowly rising to her feet and pointing an accusing finger at the door I hid behind. The next thing I heard was the sound of retreating footsteps and closing of the entrance door. I nearly wept in relief. I lay with my cheek against the floor, my back and right hindquarters contorted and pointing to the ceiling. I battled sleep and counted out twenty seconds – the most time I would let myself rest before I had to get back up. In my exhausted state, I must have started and restarted my count after losing my place at least ten times. I pulled myself up to the sink and turned on the faucet. After struggling and failing, I finally managed to get my mouth underneath the spigot. I drank and drank, mindful of the need to take only small sips but powerless to tear myself away from the water. I rested my head against the porcelain, and in a minute what I feared would happen did. I retched. Still, I drank more water. I vomited. I drank again.

At least I was able to think a bit more clearly. I made my way out the door and to the ward where the girls were. I thought of Suavis and wondered if she was safe in Bujumbura. I chased the thought away, just as I chased away any thoughts of my mother and father and my siblings. I assumed that the violence was everywhere and Tutsis were all wiped out, exterminated. Recognising one of the girls as a classmate, I dragged myself to her bedside. Her name was Juliette, and she lived in town. Her eyes wide with terror, she pushed herself away from me, pressing herself against the iron bedpost. I imagined how horrible I must have looked and how I must have frightened her. I put my hand on her leg to reassure her, and she winced and began crying and shaking uncontrollably. I looked at her leg and saw that her foot was canted at an improbable angle. Her ankle was swollen to the size of a cassava and was the colour of an aubergine. At first all she could do was murmur, "No, no, no," and bury her face in her hands.

"I will not hurt you. I will not hurt you." I pushed myself away from her, and in a minute or two she calmed herself enough to tell me what had happened to her. She and the rest of the young women in the ward had all been raped. Some gang-raped, some individually. They'd had their feet clubbed or their ankles broken so that they could not escape – so that they could not report the attacks and so that they would remain there for the men to ravage them again. Only when night fell and the men drifted off were they able to limp their way to the hospital. Even there some of the girls had been raped again. Frederique, only fifteen or so, told me these things in an oddly calm and detached voice, as though she was reciting the plot of a novel she had read for our English class. I looked around the room and counted twenty-three women. I could only imagine what had happened to the others. I had seen so much violence and cruelty today, but somehow these rapes infuriated me. We were all innocent victims, but none more so than the young girls and the women. The Hutus had raped their own as well, indiscriminately exacting their revenge.

The sharp crack of rifle fire punctuated my conversation with Frederique. We knew the military had arrived, but since some soldiers had participated in the rapes, we didn't know if they would help us or destroy us. I knew I was defenceless against the soldiers. Even if I could manage to run, I could not outrun a bullet. I sat with Frederique and told her what happened at the school. She lay unmoving, her face a blank, but rivulets of tears filled her eyes and ran down her cheeks. For the first time in hours,

I prayed, asking God to watch over these women and me. I think I dozed off for a moment. The next thing I remember was the sound of boots on the tile floor. I looked up at a group of camouflage-clad soldiers standing at the ward's entrance. After a moment, they shouldered their weapons and circulated among us. I watched as they eyed the girls and looked back at one another. I retched again.

The sound caught their attention, and they all trained their eyes on me. I wanted to shout at them, berate them for what I thought they were considering, but before I could form the words, I heard one of them say, "Tuhabonyemana." He smiled, stepped over a few of the women on the floor, and knelt by my side. He lifted his beret and I saw his face clearly.

It had been years since I'd seen him, but Manirakiza looked much the same as he did when the two of us had run and played together at Rumeza Primary School.

He screwed up his face in disgust when he smelled and saw my wounds. "We will take you from here." I heard him explaining to the other soldiers who I was and how we knew each other. Most of them had heard of me or my brother; they agreed to take me to Mwaro Camp. I wanted them to take the girls with us, but they could not bring them onto the camp grounds. Eugene also said they had limited space in the truck, but he assured me he would do what he could to keep them safe from further harm. Frederique held my hand for a minute, and we wished each other well. I had no way of knowing what would happen to her or the other young women, but I had to trust that the voice in my heart that told me I would be okay was also watching over them.

Manirakiza pulled me to my feet and, careful to not touch any of my wounds, assisted me to the truck. I had been without clothes for so long that I had forgotten about my nakedness. My skin was hurting so badly that I didn't want anything to come into contact with it. The military vehicle was a small pickup truck, and I climbed into the open back and carefully slid myself along the bed until I could rest my unburned shoulder against the cab. Now that I was feeling real hope of survival, my body attacked me with a vengeance. My nerves, long exposed, were raw, and any touch – whether it was contact with the truck, the breeze, another person's hand – sent a searing pain throughout my body. The soldiers gave me water from a canteen, and I sipped it slowly.

The forty-kilometre trip to Mwaro Camp was excruciating. The rutted roads bucked and jounced me, and I could hardly keep my balance. I felt like I was lying on my left hip alone, pivoting around trying to prevent the rest of me from touching anything else. I was so dehydrated that any exertion shot painful cramps through my muscles. Manirakiza and another soldier rode in the back of the truck with me, and they tried to talk to me to keep me distracted. We spoke of my brother and a few others from back home. I wanted to ask about what was going on in the rest of the country, but a part of me did not want to know. I assumed that my brother and I were alone in the world. I wanted to remember the names of the others, but each time I thought of them my throat constricted and tears welled in my eyes. Each hole in the road stabbed me, and I had to think positive thoughts. I concentrated on the last time I had made the journey to Mwaro Camp and how eager I was to run in front of Suavis and her family. I pictured Headmaster Ntibazonkiza and his unrestrained glee when I won the cow for him. But I was too tired to sustain those images for long. So many of my teammates and my schoolmates were now dead or had turned against me. I looked away from the soldiers and squeezed my fist in my eyes to stanch the tears that threatened to run. I took a couple of deep breaths and composed myself. By the grace of God, I was going to survive. I did not know why, and I tried to feel his grace full upon me. At times I did, but each time the truck pitched to one side and I was jolted again, the image of fellow Tutsis, their flesh peeling from their bones or severed by a machete blow, intruded. I wanted very much for this pain to end, for everything that had gone on over the last twenty-four hours to be over.

I thought of how mightily I had struggled to sleep the night before, how molality and gram molecular weight and specific gravity had seemed so freighted with import. In twenty-four hours, my understanding of the world had been savaged. I'd seen what human beings were made of in ways that I could never have imagined, in ways that neither biology nor chemistry could help explain. I had seen human beings at their worst and how we had failed the simplest of tests.

I wondered what had happened to the card that Bishop Bududira had presented me upon my confirmation. I had put it in the pocket of the trousers that had been torn from me just hours earlier. I wondered when the murdering thief who had them now would find that card, what meaning he would find in its message, "Always love people and God."

CHAPTER SIX

RECOVERY AND REFLECTION

I was fortunate to be alive; I was the sole survivor of the fiery attack on Lycée Kibimba in October 1993. When you consider yourself lucky to have only been beaten and burned, you know that the situation elsewhere is dire. Over the next several years, hundreds of thousands of others in Burundi would be killed. In the weeks following the attack on my school, I would come to understand in better detail what had catalyzed the Hutus. Early on the morning of October 21, 1993, Tutsi paratroopers had stormed the president's residence and taken him hostage.

The coup was the fifth since Burundi had been granted independence in 1962. None of the previous coups had led to the level of violence that followed Ndadaye's assassination. Eventually, more than 200,000 would die and a million refugees would flee the country to escape the violence. The 1972 violence, during which my two uncles were killed, resulted in a nearly equal loss of life. The October rebellion was just another chapter in the story of coups and violence. In the wake of the 1972 events, Micombero got a constitutional amendment passed that named him president and prime minister. Tutsis were particularly upset that Micombero's political party, UPRONA, was also legally declared the only official political party in the country. As a result, Micombero faced opposition from both his own Tutsi group and Hutu. In 1976 an army coup led by Colonel Jean-Baptiste Bagaza overthrew Micombero. In 1977 Bagaza-led reforms resulted in a return to civilian rule, the implementation of a plan to eliminate corruption, and the promotion of Hutus to government positions. Bagaza seemed to have the country on the right track, and he continued to make sweeping changes.

In 1978 the post of prime minister was abolished, and in 1981 a new constitution, providing for a representative national assembly, was adopted. Bagaza was reelected in 1984 but was deposed in a military coup in September 1987, his government being replaced by the Military Council for National Redemption, headed by Major Pierre Buyoya, another Tutsi. In August 1988 the Tutsi-controlled Burundian army massacred thousands of Hutus, and despite Buyoya's pledges to end interethnic violence, this was seen by many as a continuation of the strife that began after the aborted Hutu rebellion in 1972. From 1987 until the attack in 1993, sporadic violence had occurred.

The 1993 elections had promised to put an end to the violence, and when Ndadaye was elected and the Hutus swept into most assembly positions, it seemed as though the Tutsis' long domination had ended. Bagaza's coup would collapse fairly quickly, but the violence it engendered would not.

While I lay in bed in a makeshift triage centre in a conference room of the Mwaro Camp, the violence remained widespread and deadly. The landscape was littered with bodies and the burned-out hulks of homes and businesses. Hutu rebels and the

Tutsi military clashed with civilians daily, and as the death toll mounted, we seemed powerless to stop the avalanche of retribution and revenge. Though all the deaths were needless, countless more died as a result of inadequate health care. While I was fortunate to be safe at Mwaro, the military did not have a doctor on staff. Instead, I was treated by a corpsman, or medic, who had never seen burns like mine. Mostly he had treated soldiers who had headaches or intestinal troubles and the odd minor injury. Whenever he came over to me, his face contorted in disgust at the sight of my blistered and raw skin. My treatment mainly consisted of drinking fluids to keep my strength up. They brought me as much milk as I could consume, and I drank it with great relish.

That first day, I lay curled like a shrimp on a mattress, canted on my good hip and shoulder, my head propped on stacked blankets. I asked about Dieudonné but was told he was away from the camp when the attacks began and had not yet returned. My brother was in a southern province (the Bururi camp) and Mwaro is a central province. I saw my brother a week later and Lucy was taking care of me. At three o'clock on October 22, I heard a familiar voice coming from the hallway. A moment later Dieudonné was at my bedside. I could tell he wanted to come close to me and hold me, but he stood at the foot of the bed shaking his head. His eyes were red-rimmed and weary, and I wondered about what things he had witnessed in the last twenty-four hours. He must have read my mind because the first words he spoke were "Our mother is alive. Our sisters are well, as is Grandmother Pauline."

We were truly blessed. Once again, Bururi had been relatively unaffected by the violence. While I was in secondary school, Beatrice had married and gone to live with her husband's family near Kivumu. Francine was in her final year of school in the capital studying to be a teacher.

I expected Dieudonné to go on to report on our father, but he did not.

"What about our father?"

"Everything is okay. All's well. What about you, Gilbert? How are you? We have to get you out of here. We're not trained to save lives, you know."

His weak attempt at a joke fell flat. I looked away from him and stared at the intersection of the cinder blocks. I heard him exhale and mutter something under his breath. "We have to get you well, Gilbert. Thinking of those bad things out there won't help."

I knew he was right of course. I was worried about his safety.

"Don't worry about me, Brother," he said. "They won't send me away from here, otherwise they won't eat." He laughed. As a quartermaster, he was responsible for getting all the provisions into the camp.

I smiled briefly before guilt overtook me. What right did I have to smile when so many others had suffered and lost far worse than me? Dieudonné must have sensed my discomfort.

"I'm going to go now. I'm going to speak to the commander about getting you to a hospital."

When he left, I was gripped by panic. I lay there feeling very vulnerable. What was to prevent a Hutu soldier from coming into the room and shooting me? Or smothering me with one of the blankets or a pillow? Every time someone in the room stirred, I felt an electric charge of energy surge through my body. I couldn't rest. Trust no one at all, I told myself. I barely slept.

The army was overwhelmed by what they discovered in

Kibimba. In addition to me, about thirty other patients were in the camp, all of us crammed into one room or spilled out into the hallway. Most of the others were more severely wounded than I was. The stench of our putrefying flesh, blood, urine, and excrement was horrendous. About all the medic could do was to change a few dressings each day. After the first day, he was joined by a couple of nurses, but without the supplies they needed, they were essentially helpless. Each day, one or more of the wounded died. All day and all night I lay there listening to the chorus of moans, the shuddering inhalations and exhalations, and the final heaving sighs of the dying.

All of the victims in the hospital were Tutsis, but a few of the soldiers were Hutus. A couple of them came by to apologize to me for what happened. As a gesture of reconciliation, they brought me bottles of Fanta orange soda to drink. Because the bottles were sealed from the plant, I drank them. I could not get enough liquids into my system. Water, milk, Fanta—once I was sure they weren't poisoned, I poured them all down my throat indiscriminately in great quantity. My wounds oozed a thickly clotted mass of brown blood, water, and pus. After the first day, the medic, Andrew, received a shipment of antibiotics. He knew enough about burns to understand that burn patients often succumbed to secondary infections once the skin's surface was breached. He also used Dettol, an alcohol-based cleanser, on the wounds. As painful as my burns had been initially, nothing was worse than these cleanings. I don't know if you have ever had a small cut treated with anything containing even the tiniest fraction of alcohol, but try to imagine what it would be like to have this applied to roughly 40 percent of your body.

I'd like to think that I am a strong person, but I could not contain my agonized screams whenever the liquid was applied in those first fews days at Mwaro Camp. Only later, after my brother was finally able to arrange for my transfer to a hospital in Bururi, did I learn that my pain could have been lessened. In his ignorance, Andrew used the Dettol at full strength. He should have diluted it with water so that it was only 50 percent alcohol. Even so, in the months of treatment that would follow, each time my dressings were changed and the wound sites cleaned, I experienced a nearly intolerable pain. Each time it felt as though I was being dipped in acid, and I could feel the nearly corrosive effect of the chemicals devouring my skin. I would have gladly done anything to avoid those treatments.

There were a few bright spots; the sister of a guy I had grown up with named Domithilel Deo came to see me and brought me potatoes to eat. When Lucy heard on the radio about the attack at Lycée Kibimba, she lived in a camp. She was married and lived inside the camp, but she grew up in my area. There, she learned that I had survived and that I'd been taken to Mwaro. Her kindness meant a great deal to me. I enjoyed the potatoes immensely, but having someone else knowing that I was alive meant a lot more to me. Talking to Lucy, I felt some doubt regarding what Dieudonné told me about my parents. She told me that she'd heard about the attack on the radio and immediately left for Kibimba. She didn't know what happened to my mother and father, but she told me that things were bad in Kayanza Province. I wondered again if maybe Dieudonné was keeping the truth from me until I had recovered more.

Nightmares plagued my sleep. I could not get the image of my burned classmates out of my mind. Sometimes I would stare at the palm of my hand, the one that had clutched the bone I used to break the window, and shudder at the horror of what I had seen and done. My conscience was clear about taking the life of the Hutu man. He and his companions clearly meant to kill me, and I had only done what I could to save my life. I was glad that my interest in Chuck Norris had led me to take karate lessons in school. They literally saved me. I wished that circumstances could have been otherwise, but killing another man had been unavoidable.

I wished I could have avoided taking another ride on Burundi's rough roads, but I couldn't. Four days after I arrived at Mwaro Camp, I was loaded into a military ambulance for the long trip to Bururi and a hospital there. Several other vehicles escorted us in a convoy. The soldiers were well aware that the Hutu rebels would do whatever they could to end my life. As a witness to the atrocities, I would remain a target. For the entire time I was in the hospital, the military kept a guard outside my door to protect me or sent one with me whenever I went out. Even so, I remained constantly vigilant and grew tired of the fear.

At the hospital in Bururi, I would be able to receive better medical treatment. Unfortunately for me, the doctor whose care I ended up in, Dr. Canesius, was a general practitioner and had limited experience with burns, and none with burns as severe as mine. Given the instability in the country and the number of refugees fleeing, that I had a doctor at all bordered on the miraculous.

A thin, serious man who wore enormous glasses he had to constantly slide back up his broad and mottled nose, Dr. Canesius did the best he could with the limited resources at hand. As before, my wounds had to be cleaned. But now the burned areas also had to be stripped of the dead layers of skin. Every second day, Dr. Canesius used a forceps and a scalpel to scrape and slice away layers of damaged tissue. The procedure took nearly an hour, and I howled in agony or bit down so hard on my bedsheet I thought I might crack my teeth. In addition, the nurses injected me with antibiotics, often directly into the wounds, to ward off infection. I was particularly sensitive in the area of my lower back and upper hip, and none of the treatments grew easier to endure over time. I made certain the nurses showed me the sealed bottles of antibiotics before they injected me. Though they chided me about being paranoid and unnecessarily cautious, I felt I couldn't be too careful.

What I was most grateful for was my cousin Bernard coming to stay with me in the hospital. He was my guard at night. For the three months I was there, Bernard seldom left my side. He buoyed my spirits just by being with me and always made sure I was safe. I don't know if I can ever repay him for all his help. I really needed him the first few days following my transfer.

At first I was placed in a room with a Hutu who'd been wounded. He had a few lacerations and bruises but was for the most part okay. We never spoke to each other. I could not stand the sight of him, but because I had to remain on my hip I had to stare straight at his bed. I don't know if he knew who I was, and he didn't remain my roommate long enough to find out. After a day he was moved to another room. The staff knew the chances of us attacking each other were too great to risk keeping us together. Bernard was only fourteen at the time, but I have no doubt he would have done whatever necessary to keep me safe. Another Tutsi was moved into my room, and over the course of the next three months I was in the hospital a succession of Tutsis shared my room with me, so many that the parade of them blurs in my memory.

What I recall most clearly was the day my mother came to

visit me. Dieudonné had arranged for her to come, but it took a week for her to be able to make the trip. For the first six days after the attack, violence raged and it was not safe for her to leave home. I was forewarned that she would be coming. For the most part, I lay in the hospital wearing nothing but a pair of running shorts. It made no sense to wear a gown – the burns on my back, shoulders, hips, and legs were covered with bandages. I was grateful my face wasn't injured at all – I could pull up the sheet and cover my wounded areas so my mother wouldn't have to see them. The morning she came to visit, she stood in the doorway looking as frightened as I'd ever seen her. My brother and cousin had informed her that I was burned, and she had no idea what I might look like.

When I smiled and said, "Hi, Mom!" her face transformed – every worried crease relaxed. She still didn't want to come near me, so I told her, "I'm okay. Please come closer."

She edged into the room and then made her way to the bed, her lips quaking. I reached out and took her hand and pulled her down to me and hugged her. My heart was bursting, and I felt her hot tears on my neck and shoulders. I wanted to do anything I could in that moment to relieve her pain. While we embraced, I kept saying over and over to her, "I'm okay. I'm all right. I survived."

After a few minutes, she composed herself enough so that she could sit on the edge of the bed and look at me, but still her tears rained down. Finally she spoke. "Do you remember why I named you Tuhabonyemana? Because you are a son of God!" She erupted into shoulder-shaking sobs, and I pulled her down to me again.

"Don't cry. Let's talk. How are you? Let's visit, Mom. How are the cows? And the chickens? How is the land?"

She kept crying and I kept trying to distract her with questions, and between her sobs she managed to answer most of them. She told me that Grandma Pauline was coming to see me the next day. She had just turned eighty, but she still ruled our family's land with a firm command. I was eager to see her. I had spent so much time with her growing up, and I missed her very much when I was at school. I was ashamed that I had got so wrapped up in my own life that I had failed to write to her regularly or spend much time with her when I was home. All my sins seemed to be on parade those days in the hospital.

My mother managed to calm herself, and we ended up having a nice visit. I told her that I was well and feeling strong, and she said the same was true of her. As it turned out, we were both lying. I was sad but grateful to see her leave. I knew that seeing me in my condition had hurt her. She promised to visit me once a week, and she did. After the initial shock of seeing me, she recovered and we both took great pleasure and comfort in the time we spent together.

Not surprisingly, Grandma Pauline demonstrated a great deal of strength. She came into the room immediately, sat down on the edge of the bed, and hugged and kissed me. We talked for a few minutes, and then she began to sing the song I'd loved to hear as a child:

O victory in Jesus, my Saviour forever
He saved me and I love him
All my love is due to him
He suffered for me at Calvary
And shed his redeeming blood

As I sat there with her, I thought of the only prayer I had made when I was in the fire. I kept asking Jesus to forgive me. In the fire, I saw that I had drifted from God. I'd succumbed to vanity, and my lack of humility was regrettable in the extreme. In the days immediately following the attack, I had not thought much about my hatred of the Hutus; instead, I had thought of all the ways that I had sinned and how the attack was my punishment. In his infinite mercy, God had forgiven me and let me live. I had been blessed with a second chance, and I was not going to lapse back into my old ways. Grandma Pauline's song reminded me of my duty, and I regretted that the minutes I spent with her were over far too soon. I knew it was difficult for her to travel to Bururi, and I would not likely see her again in the hospital. That would have to wait until I went back home to Fuku Mountain. It felt good to think about the future again, and it was with those hopeful thoughts in my heart that I said goodbye to her.

Visitors gave me an enormous boost. I don't know if I could have healed without my family coming to see me. I also do not know if I could have endured what I did in the hospital if it were not for the nurses. In the hospital, much of your dignity and privacy is lost. It was bad enough I had to expose myself when my wounds were being treated, but all the necessary biological functions became a public matter as well. While I drank a lot of fluids and eliminated them easily, the same is not true for my eating habits. Even in the hospital we did not have toilets. We had to use a latrine, and the first couple of times I had a bowel movement, I was absolutely miserable. I had to squat down so low that I thought I was going to tear apart every cell of my skin. For that reason, I stopped eating a good diet. I would have bread and milk for breakfast and a potato for lunch, but I avoided roughage at all costs. Eventually, I would give in to the temptation and eat pottage, but only rarely. I became painfully constipated and often went a week or two without a bowel movement. My doctor wasn't pleased about this, but he was so overwhelmed with other patients to care for that he didn't probe into the reasons why. He was also so busy trying to get topical treatments for my burns from France that my irregularity was the least of his concerns.

Another of my great concerns was a terrible burning rash that developed around my genitals. When I lay on my side and the Dettol was applied to my other wounds, it dripped down into my groin area and burned this highly sensitive spot. After a while, it also began to emit a foul odour. Worse, I was worried that it would render me impotent. Nothing in our culture could be worse than not being fertile. Everything that was happening to me was humiliating and a bit dehumanizing, and I tried to balance that with my gratitude at being alive. A nurse named Beatrice helped to put things in better perspective.

Beatrice and I had grown up together and spent a number of summers in each other's company. She was wickedly funny back then, and she kept that sense of humour into early adulthood. She had an ample bosom and the air of a haughty princess. She kept trying to get me to eat more and was the source of the pottage that so tempted me. One day she came into my room and paused, sniffing the air. "You stink, Gilbert!" She held her nose and waved a hand in front of her face. "This can't be good."

I avoided her eyes. The odour was the first sign of infection, and I knew the staff were vigilant about keeping my wounds clean and me infection-free. I had to confess to her that the odour's source was somewhere other than my wounds.

"So where is the stink coming from, then?" She stood with her hands on her hips and her head tilted to one side.

I glanced over at the next bed, where my roommate sat watching us. Beatrice's eyes followed mine. "Don't mind that fellow. He's got troubles of his own."

I gestured vaguely at some point that could have been my feet.

"Speak up, Gilbert." A smile ambled across her lips, and her eyebrows stood to get a better view of what was going on.

Eventually she wore me down, and I had to tell her that it was coming from "near my thing." She burst into laughter and then recovered. "Your 'thing,' you say. Might that thing be your penis?"

She had me pull my shorts down so she could inspect the area, and she returned a few minutes later with a soft sponge and an antiseptic cleaner. I asked her if Bernard could do it. At first Beatrice refused, but after she took care of the washing a few times, she left the cleaner and a sponge by my bedside so either Bernard or I could take care of it. In a few days the rash was cleared up. I was glad that I knew Beatrice from before. I don't think I could have spoken as freely or submitted so meekly to another nurse's care.

I continued to ask Bernard and my mother and brother about the rest of my family generally and my father in particular. Finally, after I'd been in the hospital for two weeks, Dieudonné told me that he had been killed. My father, a close family friend whom we all called Uncle Buzosi, and two other men were in a Land Rover, along with a doctor. They were on their way back to Honga Mountain from Rumonge, loaded with supplies. Some Hutus flagged them down, and when the truck stopped, they killed everyone and stole the truck and the goods. My mother learned of the deaths because two other Hutu men came and reported the incident to her, just as in 1972 when her brothers were killed. It may seem odd to you, but we were grateful to the Hutu men for telling us these things and we held no resentment against Hutus generally. I knew that my mother was greatly upset by what happened and her reaction upon seeing me made a lot of sense, but even after I learned of my father's death, she and I did not discuss it in any detail. I told her that I knew and I was very sorry he was gone, and she said what hundreds of thousands of African women must have said over the long course of the violence in our country: "What can we do now? We must move forward." I don't know if you would call that insensitive or optimistic or realistic. In some ways it is a reflection of the harsh reality of the turbulence in our country and the equally harsh realities of being farmers. If you collapsed at every crisis, you would not survive. I knew that I would miss my father, but I remained grateful that none of my uncles were harmed.

I was eventually able to understand and forgive those who did these things to us, but I would never be able to trust people as I had before. The hospital's staff was a mix of Tutsi and Hutu, and I worried about their allegiance. In time, I asked for and was granted the opportunity to supervise my own medication and injections. I feared that someone might poison me, and while I trusted Beatrice and a few of the other nurses (I insisted that they all be Tutsis), I had to remain vigilant. If Beatrice or one of the other Tutsi nurses wasn't available to go to the dispensary to retrieve my medication, I'd wait until they were or until a bottle was brought to me and I'd select the pill myself. I also made certain that every syringe was filled in front of me, so I could be sure what I was being injected with. To this day, I'm far less trusting than I was before the attack. I wish that I didn't have to be so wary, but my view of reality has been so fundamentally altered that I can't conceive of what would need to transpire to restore it to what it was or shift it in a different direction.

I remained vigilant about one other part of my life – running. I peppered my doctors (after a while Dr. Canesius was joined by others) with questions about whether or not I'd be able to run again. Their answer was invariable: I should stop thinking about running and think instead about getting better. Clearly these doctors were not psychologists. To me the two things were one and the same. What was the point of getting better if I couldn't run? The weeks of inactivity were getting to me. I could play cards and dominoes with Bernard and others, but just lying in bed was impossible to tolerate. Since the doctors wouldn't cooperate with me, I decided to undertake my own physical regimen. After the first few weeks in the hospital, I started to get out of bed to walk every day. My leg was still bent like a chicken's wing, but with crutches or Bernard's assistance, I could hobble around on my good leg. The benefits of even this limited movement were enormous. I began to envision what my life would be like after the doctors discharged me. For weeks, I had been cocooned in my injuries. Getting out of the hospital to sit in the sunshine and fresh air lightened my spirits.

Though the violence continued, Burundi continued to function. Bagaza had established minimal control over the government in the first week, and he moved quickly to distance himself from the violence. The speaker of the Parliament was to have succeeded Ndadaye, but he was killed as well. Into this void of leadership stepped Sylvie Kinigi, Ndadaye's appointed prime minister and the first woman to hold that position in

Burundi's history. She was of mixed descent – a Tutsi who married a Hutu. Some fifty thousand Hutus marched in support of the slain president's government, and she took control. In the first days following the coup Kinigi and other government ministers had sought refuge in the French embassy, and on the 26th of October she delivered a nationwide address refusing to grant a general amnesty and promising "severe punishment" for anyone involved in the coup and the subsequent violence.

By the 11th of November, just a few days after I'd been moved to Bururi, she had announced that she was forming a commission to hold new elections. Things began to settle down, though the flow of refugees continued and hot spots flared up occasionally. At night sporadic gunfire and grenade explosions shattered the silence. By morning all was quiet again, as though the night's eruptions had been a nightmare brought on by a meal that did not sit well in the stomach. At first I didn't dare venture out beyond the hospital and never went anywhere unescorted. I wanted to know what was going on in the world, and I'd tired of relying on others for information. Venturing out to the shops to hear and to see what was going on in the world outside the hospital was a very important kind of physical and psychological therapy. I did not enter into the many conversations I overheard about politics and the "incident." I wanted to soak up every bit of news I could, but my heightened awareness of my vulnerability and the wounds clearly marking me as a victim distanced me from fellow Burundians. The violence was intense in Kayanza, Ruyigi, Gitega, and Ngozi, but not Bururi Province; that is why I chose to go to Bururi.

Many students were in the streets due to the school year being interrupted. Even so, I received a lot of visits from schoolchildren. When classes resumed in early December, a number of teachers brought their students to see me. The students were wide-eyed with wonder and asked me all kinds of questions about my wounds and how I felt. They also brought me gifts – cards, candy, chewing gum. I was touched by their kindness. Children weren't the only ones who treated me with such thoughtfulness and deference. It seemed as though nearly everyone had heard of my plight and wanted to do what they could to restore my faith in others. Everyone who saw me asked me if there was anything they could do for me. That is typical of the generosity of my countrymen and women, and seeing that quality on display in the midst of the violence was an important step in helping me to eventually forgive my attackers and move on with my life.

Forgiveness came slowly. The process was aided by Beatrice and another nurse, named Marta. These two young women took me to the hospital's chapel and sometimes to the church they attended in a nearby neighborhood. Being able to enjoy this fellowship and be in the presence of God helped me heal and forgive. The bishop of the Bururi Diocese also came to talk to me. He got the local Catholic church to organize a prayer session every Wednesday night at the hospital. I attended every one of those meetings for the duration of my stay. I remain grateful to everyone who extended some kindness to me. I wish that I could remember them all and their names. Over time, I came to realize that for every one of those Hutus who had attacked our school and whose faces I'd thought would be indelibly imprinted in my brain, another two or three faces of goodwill replaced them. Though the faces of my attackers faded, the visages of those killed did not. I was less troubled by nightmares, but the images of my friends, classmates, and fellow Tutsi sufferers never leave me. I know covetousness is a sin, but

I guard those memories and images zealously. My body bears traces of the events of the 21st of October, 1993, and even though my scars fade, they still bear silent witness to what was done to us.

Reading the Bible and going to church helped me enormously. I understood that what had been done to me was evil. Even though I was slowly coming to terms with all the hypocrisy I encountered – how could the same people who had once cheered me or nodded to me and smiled in church have poured gasoline on me and my classmates? – I remained very angry for a long time. I thought of Severin, the boy who had mocked me and run his finger across his throat. He was the same boy who ran a relay with me and who, because he did not have his own running spikes, would wear mine and then swap them back in time for me to run the anchor leg. Though my body was starting to heal, some wounds ran very deep.

Two other people played an important part in my early rehabilitation. In mid-November Dieudonné Kwizera and Aloise Nizigama, two of the better runners Burundi had ever produced, came to visit me. Nizigama brought me a jersey from his club or team as a way to motivate me, along with a pair of running shoes and Mizumo gear. I was overjoyed to see them and to receive those gifts. They were a reminder of what I had been working so hard for prior to the attack. They hung the jersey and the shoes on the wall across from my bed, and I spent many hours staring at them.

In the days following their visit, a depression settled over me. Now, instead of serving as a reminder of what I had to look forward to, those tokens reminded me of what I had lost. I was so close to finishing school and getting a scholarship that would take me from Burundi and offer me a limitless future. I had been a focused individual my entire life. I had had my priorities straight. I had listened to everything my father and my uncles had told me about the rewards of hard work. I had ignored their hypocrisy and how nearly every holiday when they gave me the speech, they walked away from me and drank themselves into a stupor. I never drank like that. I'd have a single beer, and generally only my mother's excellent sorghum beer. I'd been to a bar maybe three or four times in my life, always with one of my uncles. I had sweated and sacrificed and laboured hard, and now I was left with this life? Had I strayed so far from God's word, had I lost my humility and craved success so strongly, that I needed to be punished to return to the right path?

I cannot fully explain why going to the United States was so important to me. We all knew that it offered great opportunity and was the wealthiest country in the world, but our chances of getting there seemed as remote as travelling to Pluto. Why was I so drawn to it? I'd had to memorise the names of all its states and its rivers in my early days of secondary school, but what really appealled to me was the unknown. I'd seen movies and loved the night shots of the big cities. How did people live all stacked up on top of one another? How did the people in New York and Los Angeles eat? Where did their food come from? As soon as other people heard about my desire to go to the States, they immediately told me about all the horrible things that could happen to me. I could get shot in New York. They didn't like Africans there at all. But as I'd come to learn, we didn't seem to like one another very much. I fantasised about going to Harvard or Yale. I wanted to walk the same steps as many of the presidents, but now the chance seemed lost. I'd always looked different from everyone else in my family, and I'd grown so accustomed to being teased about that fact that I never mentioned it to anyone. Now was I getting paid back for having dreamed of too much glory? Was it wrong for me to want to experience another culture and another world?

I didn't sink too far into this morass of self-pity. Not more than a week after Kwizera came to visit me, I got a letter from Tulane University. In it, they expressed again their desire to offer me a scholarship upon completion of my secondary-school education and a good score on the TOEFL. They didn't know about what had happened to me, and I was not about to write them a letter explaining that all I could do these days was hobble around on crutches or hop on one foot. The letter helped to pull me out of the hole I was in. I remembered how excited I was. My tongue wrapped itself around the French syllables – *Nouvelle Orléans!* It all sounded so good to me, far better than the harsher-sounding Boise State.

A week later, a friend came to visit. I'd known Renovat for a few years. He'd gone to Lycée Kibimba with me from grades seven to ten, and now he was in school in Bururi. We were sitting on a bench just outside the hospital. Renovat was studying to become a lawyer, and he wanted to talk to Beatrice and a couple of the doctors. I told him I'd wait outside for him and watch his bicycle. I leaned back against the wall and closed my eyes, enjoying the feeling of the sun on my face. The rains had been heavy for the previous few days, and I was basking in the warmth and the fragrant clean air. A moment later, I hobbled over to Renovat's Peugeot bicycle. I clambered aboard it, and with one hand on the wall to support me, I straightened the bike from its leaning position. I had no thought beyond this

– I was more comfortable sitting on the bike's seat than I had been on the bench. With my one good leg, I spun the pedals backward. It felt good to be moving, and I smiled at the pleasure it brought.

I leaned forward and put my left hand on the handlebars. My damaged left leg dangled, but I managed to put it on the pedal in the twelve o'clock position. I shut my eyes and, ignoring the pain that tore through me, put every ounce of strength I had into straightening my burned leg to crank that pedal. The next thing I knew, my body took over; my right leg did its thing, and I used my left hand to force my left leg through the pedal stroke again. I wobbled unsteadily, but after a few moments I was moving fast enough to stabilise. The feeling was awesome. Even though my leg was throbbing and my atrophied muscles groaned in protest, I was able to ride the bike around the block. By the time I got back, Renovat was standing just outside the hospital's door. Seeing me, his mouth agape, he ran toward me. I squeezed the hand brakes at the same time he grabbed the handlebars. Straddling the front wheel, he helped keep the bike – and me – upright.

I don't know who was more shocked, but I do know I was more pleased. Renovat and I shouted and laughed at each other, and the sound of our voices drew a small crowd. Beatrice came out and stared disapprovingly, her arms folded. She thought Renovat and I had staged the whole thing just to tease her, but when I spun the pedals backward using both legs, she brought her hands to her face and yelped in delight. Dr. Canesius was not so pleased. He brought me back inside to check the dressing on my leg wounds. As soon as he pulled away the bandage, a fluid as dark as chocolate pudding ran down my leg, but I wasn't in great pain. "You're a very lucky young man," he told me.

"You haven't shredded that skin. Had you fallen – " His statement hovered in the air like a hummingbird and just as quickly darted out of my mind.

That same day, against doctors' advice I got out of bed every hour or so to stretch and straighten my injured leg. I'd also sit on the edge of the bed and raise my foot parallel to the ground to help strengthen my quadriceps muscle. The leg had atrophied, and it looked like a gnarled tree root. Being able to walk on both legs again was a thrill. I promised to take things slowly, and I made good on that vow. Each day I lengthened my walk by a few metres, still using crutches, until I was ranging a kilometre or so from the hospital – always accompanied by someone to protect me. Being mobile again did wonders for my attitude. I was finally able to sleep through the night, and even something as simple as being able to shower made me feel like my life was returning to normal.

More than anything else, what I longed for was a return to normality. Everyone had gone back to school, and while I wasn't quite ready for that physically or emotionally, I had long since grown tired of the hospital and was eager to shed my identity as a victim. It's not that I didn't enjoy the attention lavished on me – not to mention the gifts and money some pressed into my hand – but I knew that sooner or later I was going to have to interact with people outside of the very small and very protective circle I'd had surrounding me since the attack. Here again, Marta and Beatrice played a key role. In addition to taking me to their respective churches, they also invited me to go with them to Paramedical Bururi, where they were continuing their nursing education. In particular, they wanted me to attend the weekend dances. Beatrice kept telling me that I spent too much time cooped up in my room and not enough time with people my own age.

I was reluctant to go with them, first because I couldn't really dance while I was on crutches, and second because I wasn't sure I should ever dance anymore. I still wanted to understand why the attack had happened. I've already spoken of my lack of humility and focus, and I wondered whether God had wanted me to experience these things because I had become too frivolous. What was I thinking by getting only passing grades on my exams and spending a lot of my time with Suavis or other girls at dances and watching movies and joking around? In my imagination, I had become like a rock star. Everywhere I went people knew me and made demands on my time, and I had revelled in the attention, the favours, the privileges I was given. And I took all of it for granted. While being given the key to the library may not sound like much, in the world of Lycée Kibimba it was a huge matter. I'd had my head turned, and as much as I wanted to believe that my focusing on my running and my desire to get to the United States was a legitimate and real possibility, I wondered if God had another plan for me. Maybe my dreams were exactly that – *my* dreams and not the fate that had been laid out for me.

In early December, after schools had reopened, one of my excuses to stay away from the dances ran out. I was no longer on crutches. Beatrice demanded satisfaction, and I saw no sense in arguing with her. "I'll go with you," I said. "But you cannot make me dance."

She nodded solemnly and then laughed uproariously. This did not bode well.

Only later was I able to identify the real source of my inner conflict – I did not know if I deserved to have fun and to laugh again. I could take pleasure in things such as being able to walk, but enjoying myself purely for the sake of enjoying myself seemed far too selfish an act. God had spared me; did he want me to spend the time he'd granted me at a dance? I see now that I was feeling guilty for having survived when so many had perished and at the same time even more proud than I had been before. Who was I to think that I was God's chosen instrument who had to live with the seriousness of a saint? I think back on the saints I read about as a child, and how their lives were reduced to a simplistic formula of prayer, good works, and suffering. I've since come to believe this: a good and holy life lived in the context of a full and rich human life is even more of a challenge and perhaps offers a greater reward than one lived in solitude, introspection, and self-flagellation.

At the dance, I wasn't thinking of such things. But by the time the first song was over, and my foot began tapping in time to the music and I remembered the joy drumming had brought me, I was inclined to think that a loving and merciful God wanted me to enjoy every moment.

Perhaps my dark view of God was a result of my reading the Bible from start to finish. A group of secondary-school students had visited me in the middle of November when I was still essentially bedridden. They filed solemnly past me one by one and whispered, "God bless you." One young woman handed me a pocket-sized Bible with a green cover. That night, after they left, I started to read, beginning with the book of Genesis. By the time Beatrice was hectoring me to go to the dances with her and Marta, I was still in the Old Testament. My outlook may have been influenced by all the smiting and retribution I read about in those pages. If that did not contribute to my decision to deny myself pleasure, it simply may have been that I missed

Suavis. I had not heard from her, and I made no effort to write to her again. She was a part of that less serious side of me that I wanted to reform yet still revel in. I am a kind of reverse romantic, I suppose. I imagined myself the lover cruelly torn by fate from the woman he loved. I don't mean to trivialise what happened to me or my relationship with Suavis. I simply have always had a somewhat overactive imagination, and recasting those events in any light other than the horrible truth still appeals to me.

Even with my powers of fantasy, however, I could not have imagined then that I had already met the woman who would help me fulfil my lifelong dreams and would eventually share her life with me.

CHAPTER SEVEN

THE ROAD BACK

To succeed at anything in this life, you must believe in yourself and surround yourself with others who do likewise. A mutually supportive environment is like a nutrient-rich soil that feeds a crop, which in turn feeds the livestock, who provide you with food and also fertilise the land, thus replacing the nutrients that had been withdrawn. While I enjoyed that kind of environment to a degree at home and at school, it wasn't until after the attack that I was really able to evaluate how people felt about my aspirations of getting to the United States to run. I knew even then that those who were not supportive meant me no malice. Quite the opposite in fact, especially following the attack – the naysayers were concerned about my well-being. My doctors in Bururi did not believe that it would be possible for me to run again. My mother's not wanting me to begin running again was rooted in her concern about my health and also the possibility that I would be in public again as a target and my safety could be jeopardised. If I had raised the question of returning to my former level and earning a track or cross-country scholarship in the United States, I would have been dismissed as crazy.

I spent the holidays at the hospital in Bururi. My mother, Dieudonné, Grandma Pauline, and Francine came to visit. I missed having the usual large family gathering, but it was impossible for Uncle Eliphaz to make it to Bururi Hospital from Bujumbura safely. With my father gone, Christmas was a somewhat somber day. We all went to church, and I sat in our pew growing angrier and angrier. How could all these people who claimed to be Christians have participated in the violence? Whether they themselves hurt someone or not, why had they done nothing to stop it? All the beautiful words about the baby Jesus's birth bringing great joy and love into the world sounded hollow to me. In years past, I had so looked forward to the new year, and though I should have wanted 1993 to end so that I could put it behind me, I was reluctant to let it go. I did little to mark its passing except to vow to somehow discover the truth about my faith, about other faiths, and what road my future would take.

I also hoped to see Adolphe. He knew I had survived the attack, but he was not able to leave Bujumbura to visit me. He did call me to wish me well. I had continued my walking routine, and by the first of the year I was moving around fairly well. My doctors were now more concerned about scarring than about infection or anything else, and they had ordered an ointment that would help reduce it. The burns also itched terribly, and I constantly felt like I wanted to tear at my skin to relieve it. Also, I was very self-conscious about the scars, and I tried to keep them covered as best I could. I would have had to wear a long-sleeve shirt all the time to hide the ones on the back of my arm, but since I lived in sub-Saharan Africa, that wasn't a practical choice. I hated the idea of people pointing at me and asking, "What happened to him?"

The salve from France was delivered to Bujumbura. An army escort took me there to pick up a two-month supply. I called Adolphe to let him know I would be in the capital, and we agreed to meet at a café. Seeing him again saddened me. Adolphe had always seemed one of the most fit, healthy, and optimistic people I had ever met. He still wore the same red Adidas tracksuit he always did, and the same gold bracelet dangled from his right wrist, but the suit seemed to sag on his frame. Worry lines creased his face, and his formerly bright and dancing eyes were now downcast. It seemed as though the weight of recent events had diminished him and extinguished some of his enthusiasm.

We spoke about the others – how Dieudonné Kwizera, Vénuste, and Aloise had done in the autumn and what their hopes were for the spring. That seemed to resurrect the old Adolphe, but his expression darkened when I mentioned my desire to resume running. His voice choked with emotion, and he spoke into his cup rather than looking at me. "You know I respect you, Gilbert. That's why I tell you this. Forget about the scholarships. Forget about the running. You must focus on getting healthy, on getting better."

I didn't know how to reply. I could not understand why he didn't believe I could resume the pursuit of my dream. I had too much respect for him to challenge him, but in my heart I vowed I would one day again be in his good graces and be back on the track under his guidance. I also understood what had passed unspoken between us – he feared for my safety. When it was time for us to part, I held out my hand to him, and he shook it very formally and then pulled me to him. He whispered "God bless you" in my ear and then stepped past the soldiers who had accompanied me. I watched him walk into the bright sunlight. His gait was constricted, and he kept his arms close to his sides; as he strode away he kept looking from side to side before trotting across the street. I watched until the traffic swallowed him.

At that point in my life, I was numb to disappointment. I wasn't happy to hear his muted response, but I didn't dwell on it. Perhaps my reaction was evidence of my maturity and resiliency or had I simply adapted to the less idealised version of what Burundi meant to me? More likely, I knew in my heart that I would be working with Adolphe again and he would champion my cause.

By the end of February 1994 I was ready to return to my schooling. I had missed nearly three months of my final year, and if I was going to get the scholarship to Tulane, I was going to have to graduate. Much of the thirteenth year is a review period for the state final exam, so I hadn't missed much new material. I was confident that I could make up the lost time. What I was far less certain of was whether I'd be able to handle being in a classroom surrounded by strangers. My mother wanted me to come back home to go to school near her, but I wanted to still have the military near me as a support. The best option for me was to attend a Swedish Protestant school in Kiremba. The religious programs there closely resembled Anglican teachings. I was not so much interested in the faith aspects of the school as I was in the security it could provide. The headmaster agreed to let me live off campus, and I moved back into Bururi Camp and lived there for the first month, with the military shuttling me back and forth each day. Eventually, I would stay in the dormitory during the week and spend my weekends at Bururi.

I was as nervous as I had ever been in my life the first day I went back to school. My bladder burned, and I could barely control my fidgeting. My first class was chemistry, and I was grateful for that – despite my persistent and horrific memories of Mr. Niyonkenguruka. I knew the chemistry teacher, Aloise, from near my home. He took me aside before the start of classes and talked to me, reassuring me that I would be safe. He was a devout Christian and a man I respected, and he treated me so well. I cannot imagine what might have happened had he not been with me the first day. Aloise introduced me to the class and told them what had happened to me and that they should go out of their way to be nice to me.

I went to my assigned seat and sat down. Seated to my right was a girl I vaguely recognised. She smiled shyly, and I smiled back. After class, she stood and asked me if she could be of any help. I shuffled my folders and notebooks, looked up at her, and shrugged. "If you'd like, I can share my notes with you," she said, holding out a notebook.

"Thank you," I said, taking it. I lingered in my seat a few moments before I got up to leave. Eventually, I learned that her name was Triphine Butoyi. Her name meant "the youngest," and she had a twin sister. The next day when I sat down again in chemistry class, I handed her notebook back to her and she shook her head. "Keep it for now. I have another and I will take notes for us both." Triphine had no way of knowing this about me, but I had always hated taking notes. I mostly relied on my memory and listening skills. Yet as good as my memory was, I couldn't recall why this girl seemed so familiar to me. Halfway through that second day of chemistry I remembered – Triphine Butoyi was the same girl who had visited me in the hospital and given me the Bible I still read daily. At the end of the class, she stood and prepared to walk out. Still a bit unsteady on my injured leg, I scrambled after her. When I came up beside her in the hallway, I reached in my pants pocket and produced the Bible. I held it out to her, and she dipped her chin and smiled.

"I know. I remember you, Gilbert."

I took our meeting again as a sign, and even though she was dating someone else at the time, I began to talk to her a lot outside of class. I was immediately drawn to her soft-spoken ways and her tremulous and trilling voice. She was so different from Suavis and a lot of the other more forward girls I had been attracted to in what I came to think of as "before this." Even at Lycée Kiremba, many of the girls asked me to dance, and though I accepted their invitation, I never considered them as possible girlfriends. A few months after I'd met her, Triphine asked me why I didn't have a girlfriend, and I told her about my past and all the girls I had dated. I told her I was through with frivolous dating. I was nineteen years old, and it was time for me to become more serious. Since the attack, I had become more careful. She sat looking at her hands, turning them over and over in her lap.

"That's what I want also. I'm not interested in dating just to date someone."

From that point forward, we became a couple. Triphine was a serious and intelligent young woman, but those traits paled in comparison with her generous spirit. From the beginning, when she first presented me with the Bible, to her kind offer to assist me in any way she could with my schoolwork, she never expected anything in return. She offered these gifts freely and without attachment. She has never wavered from this belief in true charity, and she puts it into practice daily. I believe the one we choose for our mate is a reflection of the best self we aspire to become. Triphine's spirit set an example for me, and I wanted to be more like her. I don't fully understand why, in the wake of all the turbulence behind me, I chose to trust her and open myself up to her. Intimacy takes many forms, and the first time I exposed my burns to her so she could smooth the salve on my scarred flesh, she helped me heal in ways I cannot express. When her tears flowed, they flowed not because of the horrific sight before her or the pain she knew I endured, but because she saw in those gnarled and twisted folds of my flesh a physical manifestation of the evil humans are capable of. In those tears and in her tender ministrations, I saw all the good humans can do for one another.

Together, Triphine and I erected a fortress, one that offered us solace and respite. Even more, we established a place from which we could defend ourselves and take action against those who would do us harm. As the school year wore on, I heard whispered recriminations about me. Gilbert is crazy. The guy got attacked, but he will not do anything about it. He could be a living symbol to the Tutsis, become a leader and rally us to attack the Hutus. Even when I moved into the dormitory and lived with three other Tutsi guys, I still heard these things. We were living together so we could defend ourselves, but behind my back they were talking about me.

One night in May 1994, Triphine and I were in the library studying together. Ever since the coup, Hutu students had marched in protests in the capital and elsewhere. As the violence abated, the students' agitation rose. Jean-Paul, one of Triphine's friends, came to us and told us the latest rumour – the Hutus were planning an attack on Lycée Kiremba. Before I had spent so much time with Triphine and learned another kind of courage, I would have likely dismissed Renovat's words, not wanting to risk getting involved; instead, I got up from the table and walked back to the boys' dormitory. I sought out Domitien Bamvuginyumvira, the Hutu student leader on campus. He was in a small anteroom off the main dormitory talking with a couple of friends. They quickly dispersed, leaving the two of us alone. Domitien sat at a table. He was short and squat, with a powerful neck and shoulders. As I stood above him it seemed as though his body was in the process of swallowing his head. He refused to look up at me, even after I started to speak.

"I came here to warn you. You should be very careful. I just want you to know that whatever you do" – I paused and lowered my voice – "it will come back to you."

He looked up at me and I read the fear in his eyes. Louder this time, I repeated, "It will come back to *you*."

There was no attack, and every time I saw Domitien, he steered a wide course around me. I did not know, nor did I care, whether he feared that the Tutsis would come back and get him or that God would punish him. He did not need to know that I meant only the latter. Having stood up to him made me feel strong and powerful. I was going to heal.

The remainder of the school year eased into a routine of classes and studying. Kibimba had prepared me well for the national exams and the final polish at Lycée Kiremba was all I really needed. Triphine and I studied together a great deal. Though I did not sleep much the night before the exams, the tests proved easier than I had imagined. Since the school year had been interrupted, I did not have to wait as long as I had before in order to get the results. I took the test in early August 1994 and was soon packing my things and saying goodbye to Triphine to begin my first year of university in Bujumbura. Triph and I were the same age, but she had not passed the exam and had to repeat her final year at secondary school. We were sad to be separated, but in our hearts we were already committed to each other. Our separation would be brief – or so we thought.

Burundi University had a student body of five thousand. I was among the twelve hundred or so who entered the first year in September 1994. Though I was the first in my father's family to attend university, we had little time or inclination to celebrate. We had a small party at my mother's house, and I got to see the cows again. Grandma Pauline was thrilled, but an undercurrent of worry unsettled us all. Bujumbura, as the political capital of the country, had been the site of much of the violence. If I wanted to go to university, and I needed to at that point if I still hoped to get to the United States, I had no choice but to go to school there. Tulane University still expressed interest in me, but I had not contacted them to let them know about the attack. I knew if they learned I was injured, they'd lose interest in me immediately.

Our fears about the political climate were offset by one fact. I would be able to live with family while attending school. My cousin Stany Niyonkuru, the son of my mother's sister, was returning to Burundi after a four-year absence. Stany had completed a four-year undergraduate degree in Algeria, where he'd been sent on a government scholarship, and the government had offered him a job as a civil engineer. By September 1994, "government" still meant interim rule. Prime Minister Sylvie Kinigi acted as president until February of that year, when the

Parliament elected the Hutu Cyprien Ntaryamira, the thirty-eight-year-old livestock minister to the position. Of course, this being Burundi, not all went well with that choice. The Hutu representatives had, only hours before naming him president, pushed through a constitutional amendment to make this type of non-participatory election possible.

In what amounted to a civilian coup, the two Tutsis who had shared leadership after the coup, Bagaza and Pierre Buyoya, were ousted, and Ntaryamira was officially the president. Kinigi was replaced as prime minister. Unrest followed and would continue for years, but Burundi had not heard the last from Buyoya.

Stany and his wife had bought a condominium blocks from the university campus. Uncle Eliphaz still had his place in Bujumbura, but it was too far from the campus for me to walk – still a dangerous proposition regardless of the distance – and I felt safer in Stany's neighborhood. In addition, Stany really wanted me to live with him. He was the first on my mother's side to go to college. That similarity as well as our bond of kinship made my decision easy.

Unlike colleges or universities in the States, Burundi University was highly regimented. All undergraduate students attended classes each day from seven in the morning until five in the evening. Because of the disruption the previous year, we also attended classes on Saturday. Since I was on the science track, my first-semester curriculum consisted of chemistry (organic and inorganic combined), physics, biology, and inorganic biology. I was well used to the rigours of our education system, and most of my classes were held in large lecture halls where we sat anonymously, listened to the professors, and took notes. I had little interaction with the instructors, and I kept myself apart from the other students. I spoke on the phone regularly with Triphine, went to classes, and studied. Whatever time I had away from school in the first month I spent with Stany and his wife, Gertrude Habarugira.

By November I added another component to that routine – running. I began with a very slow jog each morning, and little by little I progressed. I ran relatively pain-free, but I was still troubled by my scars, which bubbled up and hardened on my skin like cooled lava. Running became for me a kind of therapy. Once I was able to move, once I no longer felt so solidly rooted in Burundi, I could look to the future again. Since I was now literally moving forward at a pace I was accustomed to, I realised it was time to move on psychologically as well. I gradually got over the feeling that I had experienced something no one else could relate to. I had been so self-centered, and when I looked beyond my own nose, I recognised that thousands and thousands of others had gone through something similar. I was not alone. I was given a second chance, not to continue to suffer, but to make something of my life and my gifts. I had to use the talents that God had given me, and the one he'd given me in abundance was my ability to run. Before this, I had been running for personal glory. I had decided that I needed to change. I had to be a better person, a better Christian. I had to use my running skills to spread God's message.

Running helped me out in this regard as well – waking up every day and knowing I had a goal to accomplish, whether it was a half-hour run or a tempo run, gave me purpose and focused my mind. I did not have time for revenge. Triphine and running taught me so many things in the year after the attack. I did not mark the one-year anniversary in any special manner. It was simply one more day to help me put distance between who I was then and who I wanted to ultimately become. A few months ago, I was speaking to a psychologist in a casual conversation, and he asked me if I thought I had been in denial in the years immediately after the attack. He was wondering if maybe I was suffering from post-traumatic stress disorder. I didn't know how to answer his question. If what he meant by denial was me dealing with the problem by finding a source of joy in my life, then I was in denial and glad to be there. My relationship with God was better than it had ever been. I prayed all the time but especially whenever I felt myself slipping beneath the waters, and always God buoyed me. To be honest, even though I was baptised in the Catholic Church, my faith is not in a denomination but in God. I believe in the Word of God as it is written in the Bible. Whatever house of worship I find that book in – wherever I find it outside – matters far less to me than what is found in the Bible itself.

I also know that my faith made it possible for me to run again. How else can I explain that in a few months after I started running again, I was ready to approach Adolphe to begin training in earnest? Fire ate down to the bones in my right shin and calf, and I should have remained crippled for life. Somehow, no permanent structural damage was done to tendons and ligaments. Had I waited longer to heal before riding Renovat's bicycle, who knows whether I would have been able to overcome the lingering effects of my prolonged layoff from running? My passion for running had flickered but never dimmed. I was on the road to recovery and beyond. I had not heard from any American schools in a while, but I had faith my dream would still come true. One evening in late November, I was out for a run around the neighbourhood. I heard a few distant rumbles of thunder, and I looked over at my friend Emanuel and shrugged. Whether it was gunfire or a rainstorm did not matter to me. I was going to keep going. When the rain came, it pelted us with cold hard drops as large and nearly as heavy as coins. We were instantly soaked, but instead of going in for the day, we took a right turn away from campus. We laughed and splashed like two children, kicked our way through puddles, and endured the stares of onlookers. Then I did something I had not done in a while. I started to sing. At first uncertainly and then with a voice grown stronger in faith, I sang Grandma Pauline's song, and I knew then that I was well along the road to healing.

The university had a school-sponsored drum team and football team but no track team. Once I was feeling like I could come close to the times I had run before this, I went to see Adolphe. I surprised him in his office. I wore a loose-fitting long-sleeved shirt and a pair of warm-up pants. Adolphe assumed that my visit was a social one. We exchanged greetings and he kept telling me how well I looked. I sat down and rolled up the right leg of my pants. I showed him the blackened scar tissue and ran my hand over its pebbled surface. I smiled and said, "They work far better than they look."

I don't know if Adolphe had heard through the grapevine that I was back running, but as was his custom, he got up from his desk, snatched up his clipboard and his stopwatch, and walked outside. I followed him to the track and stripped off my warm-up clothes. I saw his eyes surveying the relief map of my scars. Better to get this over with immediately. I stretched my arms over my head and waited for instruction.

"You know what to do."

After a few warm-up laps, I was in the infield stretching and then doing form running under Adolphe's watchful gaze. I detected no note of sympathy or letup in his assessments. He hounded me as he always had before. When I finally hit the track again for a few time trials, I was loose and feeling good. Bujumbura's sauna like heat threatened to draw every molecule of moisture out of my body, but as soon as he raised his arm for me to get into my starting position, I blocked out any thought of the weather. After I did two hundreds, four hundreds, and eight hundreds, a dozen total, Adolphe waved me over to where he stood in the infield. His arms folded across his chest shielding the clipboard where he had recorded my times, he issued his pronouncements. "Have you forgotten the metronome?"

I shook my head. How could I forget the metaphor he used all the time to describe our arm swing and the relentlessly consistent tempo he wanted it to have?

"No, sir. I haven't forgotten."

"Gilbert, I can't find the words to tell you how glad I am to see you running again. It brings me joy. Tomorrow."

The last was more a statement than a question, but I detected a note of uncertainty in his voice I had never heard before.

"I will be here. Will you?"

I waited to see his reaction, but none came for a moment. Then a slow, thoughtful nod confirmed what I'd already suspected.

By May 1995, I was ready for my first major international meet, in Kenya. I had never flown before, so I was both nervous and excited when Stany and Gertrude dropped me off at Bujumbura International Airport. The building was a single floor, no larger than most small-town American bus stations, and it had one runway. By the time I climbed aboard the Sabena

Airlines jet for the flight to Nairobi, I was sweating nervously. Adolphe had made all the arrangements, got me a passport, and told me what to expect when I got to Nairobi, but all his words flew out of my head the moment I put my foot on the first step climbing into the jet's cabin. I was with two other runners, eight-hundred and fifteen-hundred-metre specialist Gilbert Mvuyekure and Phydia Inamahoro, who ran the women's one hundred and two hundred metres. I thought of the few times I'd come to the airport to watch the planes take off and land. I had always wondered what it would be like to be inside and how it would feel to climb so steeply above the surrounding mountains. I was soon to find out. Of course, the three of us argued over who would get the window seat, and I won. That was a battle I soon regretted winning. Once the plane was airborne and banked east to follow the route to Nairobi, we passed over Kibimba. Phydia was in the centre seat, and she leaned over to see what I was staring at so intently, a scarred spot on the landscape that to most was little different from the rest of the land. She nudged Mvuyekure, and they both started reassuring me about Kibimba, letting me know I was far away from that place.

The airport in Nairobi was a far cry from the single gate at Bujumbura. As soon as we got off the plane, we heard announcements in English and Swahili. While I understood a little of both languages, this amplified mishmash of the two, combined with the crowd noise, came out sounding like an overly excited Bugs Bunny speaking backwards at double speed. We were trying to find the person who was to take us to the Utari Hotel. As much as I tried to remain humble, I felt like a big deal. I had a pocketful of American dollars, a per diem paid to me by the Burundi athletic association. I was in one of

Africa's largest cities, and in addition to the track meet, we were to go on a couple of tours, including a visit to a national park, where I would see lions.

Unfortunately, language proved a problem during the meet. I had never seen so many runners gathered together in one spot. There were multiple heats for every event, many different divisions of competition, and I thought I heard my name being called to the start of the four hundred heat I was scheduled to run. I was wrong. The announcements were all in English, and I misunderstood which race was being called. I got in a four hundred heat that was open to all runners and not just university students. I finished a distant fourth and did not qualify for the finals. I had no complaints. I had got to fly for the first time, leave Burundi for the first time, and be exposed to the ins and outs of travel and international meets. I was probably most pleased that I was able to buy Dieudonné a good pair of Asics running shoes, and buy the sheets that Stany and Gertrude had asked me to get.

Triphine was thrilled for me but also worried for my safety – and not just because of the flight. I had a brief taste of what it would be like to be a competitive athlete and experience a bit of what Kwizera and the others had. To be honest, I was hooked immediately. I felt more comfortable outside of Burundi than I did inside its borders. I liked the anonymity I could enjoy there. I wasn't the runner who survived the horrible fire, I was the runner from Burundi. I had no real name or reputation, good or bad. No one was targeting me on the track as the one to beat, and no one was targeting me off the track.

My professors were not pleased that I had to miss classes, and I worked hard to make up any labs I skipped. But now, as had happened at Lycée Kibimba, school seemed more a means to an end than an end in itself. I was in school hoping to run and earn credits that would transfer to an American university. I needed more exposure, more chances for U.S. coaches to see me. Adolphe knew this as well, and so did a few other Burundian runners already in the States.

Fukuoka, Japan, held the 1995 World University Games, and just a few short days before the games were to begin, the dean of students learned that money had been freed for the school to send three people. Of course, he could not pass up the opportunity, so he went along with the two Gilberts. Once again I was to enter the four hundred and the eight hundred, and Gilbert M. was to compete in the eight hundred and the fifteen hundred.

I had enjoyed the trip to Nairobi, but now I was going to experience true international travel taking me halfway across the globe. Everything was arranged so last-minute, so I didn't have the opportunity to call my mother or Triphine. I found out a few days ahead of time, but I didn't want to tell them I was going and then have it prove not be true; that would have shamed me. They heard on the radio that I was going to Japan, but by that time I was somewhere between Bujumbura, Nairobi, Belgium, London, Tokyo, and Fukuoka. We crossed time zones, cultures, and cities, sometimes dashing from one airport gate to another only to sit and wait hours for the next flight. It took more than forty-eight hours for us to finally arrive. By that time, I'd discovered I had lost my wallet with the six hundred dollars that was to be my allowance for the next seventeen days. Fortunately, my two travelling companions helped me out when I wanted to buy gifts for family and friends. The rest of the time, I ate in the dormitory together with athletes from universities around the world. That year

162 nations sent athletes (the most ever) to the biannual event. I knew a little about Japan but only enough to assume I would be able to speak French once I got there – my English was still not very good.

When we got off the plane, I was groggy and in a near stupor, but not even those factors could explain the sense of dislocation I felt. We were greeted by people who looked like no one I had ever seen. I had seen a few *muzungus* in Africa and many more on television, but most of them had been westerners. When a bowing and very pale young woman dressed in traditional Japanese garb – what looked to me like ceremonial pyjamas – handed me a flower and said, *"Konnichiwa,"* I nearly fainted. Over the course of the next few weeks, thanks to the unfailing friendliness and politeness of our host families, the organising committee representatives, and the people of Japan themselves, I was completely won over by what seemed to me the cleanest and most orderly country possible.

The three of us stayed in a dorm room. On either side of us were the delegations from Malta and Brazil, and our wing of the dormitory housed runners from many other African nations. One of the highlights of the trip off the track was getting to interact with so many athletes from so many countries. I also loved getting to know about the different cultures through their food. The Japanese had hired chefs from around the world to prepare the native cuisine from each country. We lived together, ate together, and trained together. I also spent a lot of time with the family who sponsored the Burundi team. A translator helped us to communicate. They gave me a lovely Seiko watch and made up for my loss of allowance.

The opening ceremony was especially memorable. I carried

our flag in the parade of athletes and marched around the stadium in front of sixty thousand people. I was enormously honoured, and despite all the troubles in Burundi, my chest swelled with pride when I watched its red, green, and white colours furling and unfurling against Fukuoka's brilliant blue skies. I had not trained well for the four hundred, and I didn't make it out of my opening-round heat – they only took the top two finishers from each preliminary round. I did learn something from that race, though, and from watching many of the others. They were far more tactical than what I was used to. By that I mean the races were often won by guile and not sheer speed. The pace would be slow, and then someone would kick into gear, or the pace would be strong at the start and you had to decide whether to stay with it or attack at the end.

I enjoyed greater success in the eight hundred. I was less nervous. When I went to the blocks, I spent far less time looking around and soaking in the atmosphere and checking out my opponents than I had in my first heat. Adolphe's admonition to focus, run my race, and dictate to others paid off. I made it through two rounds, and then in the semifinals I missed out on qualifying for the finals by less than a quarter of a second. When I crossed the line and saw that I had finished fifth, just one place away from the finals, I covered my face with my hands and folded at the waist. A runner from Namibia who had finished just in front me and who I'd told my story to draped his arm over my shoulders. Together we walked off the track and he held up my arm in victory.

In many ways, simply getting to the event had been a victory. I don't simply mean overcoming my injuries. Burundi is a very poor country and doesn't have the kind of infrastructure to support its amateur athletes the way so many so-called developed countries do. We often have to rely on the generosity and support of larger bodies (like the International Olympic Committee) or corporate sponsors (Nike, Adidas, Asics, and the like) to help fund us. I was so grateful for the opportunity to run in my first truly international meet. I made friends from South Africa, Kenya, Morocco, and nations outside of Africa. I still keep in touch with many of them. Being among athletes and outside of Burundi and not having a military presence near me helped me drop my defences and enjoy myself. Because I shared a deep and abiding passion with these athletes, I trusted them. Many were curious about my scars, but they instantly accepted me as one of them. The truth was, I felt more like one of them – an athlete or sportsman as many called themselves – than I did a Burundian. More than anything else, this trip confirmed my desire to go to the United States. One of the reasons Adolphe wanted me to compete internationally was to draw the attention of the U.S. coaches. I did not get the opportunity to speak to them, and my performance did not merit their attention. However, when I returned home (fully laden with gifts for everyone), I had a packet waiting for me from Tulane University with an application, a course catalogue, and other materials.

I was excited about the opportunity, but I still had coursework to complete and training to do, so the package sat on my desk at Stany's place gathering dust. I don't know why I was reluctant to fill it out and send it in, but in the long run my reluctance paid big dividends.

For every amateur athlete, the Olympics are the pinnacle of achievement. No stage is more grand, and no honour is greater than to be an Olympic Gold Medalist. Running in the Olympics is the goal that motivates most of us, and though I fell short of that goal, I did get to have my own amazing Olympic experience nonetheless.

Prior to the Atlanta Games in 1996, the International Olympic Committee set up an Olympic development training camp in La Grange, Georgia. There, athletes from developing nations could send their athletes to live and to train prior to the games. The hope was that by exposing these athletes to top-notch facilities, coaches, and training methods, the economic playing field could be levelled. To be honest, I didn't think of the larger implications and consequences of the IOC's policies and programmes. All I knew was that I was going to get a chance to go to the United States.

I could barely contain my excitement. From the moment I heard in January 1996 that I was one of the eight male athletes from Burundi who would be attending the development camp, everything else in my life paled in importance. My studies were effectively ended. From that point forward I was going to train in hopes of qualifying for the fifteen hundred metres. Though the Atlanta Games weren't going to start until August, we were scheduled to leave Burundi at the beginning of April. I counted down the days. My name was on the radio constantly with announcements about who was going to the Olympics. I would later regret this inaccuracy, but in the moment I revelled in the knowledge that everyone who knew me as the boy who had been attacked would now know that I had fully recovered. At that time I used the massacre as a source of strength. These people had done their best to kill me, but it was not enough. The strength of the Lord was greater than theirs.

When the plane touched down on American soil on the 8th of April, 1996, I had no way of knowing that I would not be going back to Burundi for a very long time. Like my arrival in

Japan, my arrival in Atlanta produced culture shock. Though I had studied English for so long in secondary school, it had been several years since I'd used it much. Language barriers are one thing, but the other cultural barriers are another. Americans look funny, dress funny, and sound funny. Their cars are strange, their music strange, their food an abomination. (What is the fascination with the hamburger all about?) They live in homes that look like boxes stacked atop one another, on plots of land that seemed to be stamped from a press. I could go on, but you get the point. Everything here was new to me.

When we were picked up at the airport by Jim Manhattan, head of the La Grange Track Club and one of the chief organisers of the development camp, we climbed into a huge twelve-passenger van and made our way through a maze of roads to exit the airport. In what I later learned was a deliberate attempt to introduce us immediately to American culture, and an experience they introduced every foreign athlete to, we stopped a little while later at a McDonald's. We had been given a few dollars upon arrival, and we were now left to fend for ourselves. Herded through the door, we faced the gleaming expanse of the counter and the gaudy display above the workers' heads. I came alone and Justine came two months later. Justine Nahimana, the lone woman in our group, was from the city originally and had travelled and studied in Europe before. She quickly assumed the role of guide and instructed us. With a few simple pointing gestures and a mumbled order, we got our food. That is all I will say about McDonald's – except to say that I did "enjoy" the bread and the pickle.

The rest of the trip to La Grange Community College, where we were to spend the next five months, was a whirlwind of concrete and tarmac, an endless stream of traffic, and lush greenery sectioned off into sharply divided rectangles and squares. Even flying over the country I noticed as we came farther east that the rectangles and squares below us grew gradually smaller and smaller. I wondered why everything seemed so divided and orderly. Our farmland tended to meander, and one crop sometimes spilled over into another, just as it did in nature. It would take me some time to get used to the rigidity of space and time Americans impose on themselves. Our schedule at the camp was segmented and precise. If the schedule called for us to be at an event that began at nine o'clock, you can be sure that at nine o'clock it began. Eventually, I heard Africans who were veterans in the United States talking about how the Americans teased us for living on "African time," and I wondered what they would think of some of my countrymen who were athletes. We were the most disciplined people I knew.

Our days were filled with training and social activities. One of the coaches at the camp, Abdi Bile, was a Somalian runner, and he took us into the city of La Grange and elsewhere to visit the local shops. We were all nearly overcome by the experience of an American shopping mall, but we quickly recovered. I had never seen so many items in one store, and then to have store after store after store stuffed to overflowing with them – well, it was hard not to believe the stories we had all heard about how wealthy most Americans are. People in the streets would regard us with curiosity, but they were unfailingly nice to us. I did notice that some of the African Americans we met, not all but enough to notice, seemed a bit distant and less likely to approach us or to engage us in conversation. In some ways, I think they found us to be more strange than the whites did.

I grew to really like and admire Abdi Bile. In 1996 he was

thirty-seven years old, on the downhill side of a career in which he had been a world champion in the fifteen hundred. He came to La Grange to coach but also to compete. He knew what he was talking about, and I picked up some very good training and racing tips from him. He was amazing to watch. He came into the training centre with a best time that year in the fifteen hundred of 3:45. The A Olympic qualifying standard was 3:36. He needed to knock off nine seconds to qualify for the Olympics, and by the end of the camp, he had done it. Amazing.

To provide us with opportunities to run times that qualified us for the Olympics, various meets were held. I should explain to you about the Olympics and qualifying. Just because you are the fastest runner in your country at a certain distance, say, the fifteen hundred metres, doesn't mean you can race in the Olympics. (Bile won the 1987 world championship and holds an NCAA record, both in the fifteen hundred.) You must run an officially sanctioned race and meet or exceed the standard established. I wish that it was as simple as that, but some runners do get to compete in the Olympics without having run that qualifying time. The IOC wants to give runners (and athletes in other events) from countries with less-developed programmes an opportunity to have an Olympic experience, so some spots are filled with athletes who meet a B standard. Sometimes athletes who do not meet either standard are allowed to compete. I will get to those special circumstances later on.

I did get to compete in a triangular meet among Burundi, Rwanda, and Brazil. We beat everyone except the Brazilian 4-by-100 metre relay team, which would later earn a Bronze in the games. Unfortunately for me, I ran a 3:46 in the fifteen hundred, missing the qualifying standard by five seconds. I was disappointed, but I had been mostly running the four hundred and the eight hundred metres, and I just was not as strong in the fifteen hundred as I needed to be. I took some consolation in being the second-fastest fifteen-hundred runner in Burundi. The athletes from Burundi who had qualified were Charles Nkazamyanpi, Vénuste Niyongabo, Aloise Nizigama, Justine Nahimana, Arthémon Hatungimana, and Tharcisse Gashaka –an impressive number for a country like ours.

One honour you do not have to qualify for is carrying the Olympic torch in the relay prior to the games. I was chosen to carry the torch in Birmingham, Alabama. I travelled by bus from Atlanta to Birmingham and ran through the streets of Birmingham for a quarter of a mile. The symbolism and irony of the torch ceremony were not lost on me. As I ran along with the torch flames flaring just above my head, I felt a chill. I was glad to have had the opportunity, and equally glad to pass the torch on to the next person in line. Birmingham was an important trip in another way. I got to go to the National Civil Rights Museum there and was greatly inspired by seeing the exhibits dedicated to Martin Luther King, Jr. I had read much about him, and like most Africans I greatly admired that man of peace.

As the games drew closer, more athletes arrived. Though we did not live in the Olympic village with all of them, our status as part of the developmental camp allowed us access to all the Olympic venues as well as the village itself. I got to meet and work out with some of the most famous and fastest runners in the world. One of the guys I really liked because he was probably the most famous runner in the world at the time and had the most pressure on him to succeed was the Moroccan Hicham el-Guerrouj. Known as "King of the Mile," he holds the world record in the fifteen hundred, the two thousand, and the mile. Since we both spoke French, we were able to communicate.

What impressed me the most about him was how normal he seemed. The guy was recognised around the world as perhaps the greatest middle-distance runner ever, and you would have never known it by how he carried himself. Just to show you what kind of guy he is, the same year as the Atlanta Games, the International Association of Athletics Federations honoured him for his humanitarian efforts, and he remains a UNICEF ambassador. Along with Guerrouj, I got to know Frankie Fredericks of Namibia, Driss Mazouse, also from Morocco, and a host of other medal winners.

The highlights of the Olympics for me were attending the opening ceremonies and being in the stands when Vénuste won the Gold Medal in the five thousand metres. It was awesome! He was in the middle of the pack with six hundred metres to go and put on a finishing kick that had him breaking the tape and winning the Gold for Burundi. It was a thrill to hear our national anthem being played in the Olympic Stadium and watching our flag rise above the Kenyan and Moroccan. Vénuste was the only winner and medalist from Burundi, though Aloise Nizigama did finish fourth in the ten thousand, narrowly missing a medal.

Being interviewed on CNN was both a highlight and a lowlight. They did a story on my experiences and wanted to interview me. At that point my English still was not very good, so I was extremely nervous. Dieudonné Kwizera was with us acting as a kind of ambassador and translator, since he had been in the States for a few years. He accompanied me, as did Jim Manhattan. When I was asked how I thought I would do in the fifteen hundred, I froze and blurted out the first thing that came to my mind. I said I thought I could win a medal. In truth, I was not even going to run. I did not have the words to explain that to the reporter. I have felt foolish about that interview and the confusion it has caused ever since. Many people mistakenly believe that I ran in the Olympics, but I did not. I could have, but I didn't.

That leads to the other major disappointment. From the very beginning Vénuste did not want to run the fifteen hundred. He simply wanted to concentrate on the five thousand, which he eventually won. Because he ran a qualifying time in the fifteen hundred, if there was ever an opening in a heat, someone from his country who had not qualified for the event could run in the race. I had the second-best time in the fifteen hundred. I did not get the opportunity to run because Dieudonné Kwizera took the spot that in all fairness should have been mine. Kwizera spoke English well and was friendly with the officials, so when a spot needed to be filled in an opening-round heat, he signed himself up.

The best part of the experience was meeting all the other runners and realising how much more work I needed to do to get to their level. While my fifteen hundred time of 3:46 was four seconds away from the qualifying standard, most of the runners in the finals were in the upper 3:20 range. I had a long way to go, and I grew more determined than ever to get there.

After the games, I remained in Georgia – first in La Grange and later in Savannah. In both places I attended small junior colleges and lived in off-campus housing. At first Jimmy Manhattan and the La Grange Track Club sponsored me, and later in Savannah, my host family at the Savannah International Training Center did. The Bossons were a great couple, extremely kind and generous with their time. On weekends they took me to movies and sometimes to church with them. They allowed me to phone home to talk to my mother and Triphine. I was in the United States on a student visa, and as long as I remained enrolled in school, I was eligible to stay. I wanted to have a more secure arrangement than that, so Bob and Susan Carlay, my host family in La Grange, helped me apply for political asylum. The process was long and tedious, but it would be worth it.

The longer I was away from Burundi, the better I felt. I realised that the stress of the violence and political upheaval was greater than I had imagined. I missed my family and Triphine terribly, but I knew I could make a better life for myself and eventually for them if I remained here. Though America had seemed so strange to me at first, and elements of life here always would, I saw that it was truly a land of great opportunity.

I was blessed to have benefited from the remarkable generosity of people like Jim Manhattan, the Carlays, the Bossons, and so many others that I can't name them all. Good fortune seemed to follow me wherever I went, and when I did a good turn for someone else, it seemed to come back to me many times over. For example, I was instrumental in helping Patrick Nduwimana join us in La Grange after our initial group had arrived. I knew Patrick from Adolphe's group, and though he was still in secondary school, he was an outstanding runner. I spoke of him to Jim, and he arranged to bring Patrick over. After the Atlanta Games, Patrick went to Sydney, Australia. There he competed in the World Junior Championship for runners under the age of twenty. He did so well that he attracted the attention of a number of American coaches. Several of them followed up with phone calls, and finally, in the autumn of 1997, he asked me to go with him to visit Arizona State in Tuscon, Abilene Christian in Texas, and the University of Georgia in Athens. I had not forgotten about Tulane University and my dream of attending an NCAA Division I school. Only one thing stood in my way – the TOEFL. The coaches there were eager for me to get out of the arrangement I had at Savannah State University, and so was I. I liked Savannah, but I was living with a group of foreign students and athletes in a wing of a nursing home. To put it bluntly, our accommodation was not good. I enjoyed living with the guys, but the arrangement was beginning to wear on me.

Eventually, Patrick and I met with the coaches of the track and cross-country teams at Abilene Christian University, Wes Kittley and Jon Murray. They offered us both a full scholarship, and I accepted but Patrick decided to go to school in Tuscon. I fell in love with Abilene as soon as I saw it, and dreams of Nouvelle-Orléans faded away. The campus was beautiful, and each day at noon the bells tolled and the students all went to chapel together. In many ways, Abilene reminded me of Burundi. I loved the hot, dry weather, so different from the humidity in Georgia. Mostly I liked the campus and how peaceful I felt there. I can't really explain my decision – it felt right, and I went there. Even the longhorn cows on the nearby ranches reminded me of home.

Abilene Christian had a long history of bringing in foreign students. Among its enrollment of five thousand were students from Algeria, Morocco, Jamaica, Zimbabwe, Russia, and Ukraine – and those are just the ones who competed in track and field. We all lived in the Center for International and Intercultural Education. Prior to enrolling at ACU, I had travelled to Marsala in Sicily to compete in my second World University Games. I was coming off a stress fracture in my foot and was not running at full speed, but once again I revelled in getting to know athletes from around the world. It seemed each time I went somewhere, I learned so much more about people, and the events of October 1993 receded further into the distance. I kept in constant communication with Triphine by phone, and the advent of e-mail and the Internet made it easier to keep up to date on what was happening around the world. It seemed I knew someone living in every far-flung region of the globe – Vénuste in Italy, Patrick in Arizona, Arthémon in France, Nizigama in Japan. In our own way, we were all refugees. We had not fled in the aftermath of the political upheaval, but we had scattered nonetheless. Adolphe was still at work patching together a team and then letting them go like seeds to drift on the wind and take root elsewhere. What was to go back to? More assassinations? The presidents of Burundi and Rwanda had been shot down in April 1994, and Rwanda's genocide was then finally being widely reported. All these events saddened me and widened the gulf I felt between my home and me.

Into that gulf rushed a wonderful series of friends, teammates, professors, and strangers soon to be great friends and benefactors. I had been in the United States for nearly two years when I enrolled at Abilene in January 1998. With each day I was becoming more American. While in La Grange and Savannah I had been able to satisfy my taste for American movies. All of us learned to speak better English from films and television. One guy from Chad I lived with in Savannah took that to the extreme by watching Jerry Springer on cable television, switching from one channel to the next in hopes of catching another broadcast. I was enamoured with the music of Tupac Shakur, Puff Daddy, and Biggie Smalls – I loved the pulsing energy of the rhythm and rhymes. Later, as my English improved and I could understand their lyrics, I stopped listening to them, but their infectious beats lingered in my mind long after the lyrics faded. One group whom I continued to listen to and admire for their positive message on all levels was Boyz II Men.

Some things took longer to grow accustomed to, but I like

a great deal. America truly was the country of equals. In Burundi if you are older or wealthier, you would think nothing of cutting to the head of the line to pay for your purchases, to go into the cinema, or to be seated at a restaurant. In America, lines are democracy in action. I can remember standing in line in the grocery store and beaming because I would pay based on where I was in line and not who I was. I also liked how the prices were set – I didn't have to engage the shopkeeper in a battle of wills and wits over my produce. And the choices! I had never seen such an array.

I didn't realise how much Americans take for granted the many privileges they have, and I learned that some did not appreciate the application of equality in all areas. Once Jimmy Manhattan took a group of us out to eat when we were at the camp, and the line was long. He told us to wait for him because he was going to speak to the hostess to get us seated more quickly. We all protested, and Jimmy gave in. He was generally a very respectful man, and once we explained our reasoning, he smiled and nodded. We adopted the same sink-or-swim techniques in dealing with new arrivals as our first host did. Every trip to the airport to retrieve a newly arrived foreign athlete included a stop on the way back at a fast-food restaurant. Nothing else we could think of would immerse you as quickly and as completely in what America was really like. Where else in the world would you find a bladder-busting beverage? I still smile when I think of all my new friends whose eyes grew wide when they toted their first carton of fast food away, the cardboard threatening to sag beyond the breaking point.

I loved the fellowship of the track and cross-country teams, as well as the student body. As a Christian school, Abilene and its faculty, staff, and students certainly put into practice what they preached. I could not imagine a more life-affirming place. The entire campus gathering in prayer at noon contributed to a collective soul-stirring energy that inspired and moved me. My classes were somewhat difficult because English was not my first language. I was majoring in agriculture and business. I dabbled a bit in computer science, and as much as I loved using computers, they were a very new presence in my life, and I was hopelessly behind others.

My adjustment to Abilene was also eased by the immediate success of our track team in both the autumn and spring seasons. Arriving in January 1998, I was only eligible to compete the next year. For autumn 1998, I was the number two man on the cross-country team. I loved running cross-country, whether in races or training. Nothing else I have done could take me back to the days I spent as a young boy running up and down Fuku Mountain and the surrounding areas. It took considerable restraint not to pull off my shoes and run barefoot as I had as a child. I did keep up one tradition – I still sang as I ran. Abilene's rolling countryside and dry air were a perfect combination, and my running flourished under the coaching of Jon Murray. For the first time in school history, we qualified as a team for the national championship in cross-country. We finished in fifth place, ending a remarkable year. I was not used to running so many races, and they took a toll on my body. Living in the dorm also contributed to my fatigue at season's end. I missed being able to cook for myself. The food, even in the Centre for International and Intercultural Education, was too much like typical college food.

After that first year, I took a job on campus with the maintenance department working as an electrician's assistant. I did everything from changing bulbs to rewiring outlets and switches. With the money I made from my twenty hours a week, I was able to pay for all my phone calls to Triphine, save a bit, and buy a car. I'd got my license in La Grange, and now I had my own wheels! A 1989 Mitsubishi Galant (I christened it Konnichiwa) may not sound like much, but to me it was a priceless and princely automobile. Having a car gave me greater freedom and access to the world outside the campus. I also was so happy I was able to get Alfred Rugema to come to Abilene from Burundi. He competed alongside me in both cross-country and track, and he brought a welcome bit of home to the Center for International and Intercultural Education. I was no longer the only athlete from Burundi to compete there – but I was still the first.

If the highlight of my secondary education was winning the JRR race at the end of seventh grade, then 1999 had to be close to the top of my list for my university days. In the spring, for the second year in a row, we won the NCAA Division II National Indoor Championship held in Indianapolis the first week in March. I captured my first national title in the eight hundred metres, and I was overjoyed to have contributed ten points to the team's victory. I was especially gratified that I could achieve such a good result in the face of many distractions. Shortly after my victory in Indianapolis, I was scheduled to fly to Washington, D.C., to meet President Bill Clinton. Along with six other recipients, I was honoured at the White House on Wednesday 7th April, as a part of National Student Athlete Day. I was to receive the Giant Steps Award from the National Consortium for Academics and Sports. One other student received the award along with me – Pam White of Adams State University, as well as Pat Summitt, the legendary women's basketball coach at Tennessee.

I had never been treated like such a celebrity. A car came to pick me up at the dorm and took me to the airport. I stayed in the D.C. area for two days, spending one of them with Burundi's ambassador to the United States, a close cousin of my mother's. The other night, I got to stay in a luxurious hotel. Besides meeting President Clinton, we got to tour the White House. For some reason, I loved the Roosevelt Room the most, but the best part was meeting the president himself. He towered over me but was impressive for another reason. He shook my hand and told me he had heard my story and was inspired by it and knew others would be too. He told me to keep working hard and demonstrating the kind of courage that earned me my award. The media back in Burundi reported that I had won an award from the president of the United States, and as hard as I tried to make everyone, including my mother and Triphine, understand otherwise, an "award" did not mean the president gave me money, as it would in Burundi. While I had done something that not even the president of Burundi had done – speak in person with the president of the United States – they still expected I had been treated the way Burundi's president would have been – with a gift of cash. I did not bother to explain to them that the president was merely honouring me for being chosen as "Courageous Student Athlete." The actual award would be presented to me in February 2000.

I had a better experience with CNN following my trip to the White House. They had heard about the attack and wanted to interview me and film me competing in a meet. After a few delays, they came out on the 14th of May, 2000. I was so excited, I cleaned up my room and arranged all my photographs of my family, friends, and the various meets I had run in chronological order. The CNN reporter who interviewed me was very nice. The only unpleasant part of the interview was having to wear makeup, but the woman who applied it was very friendly and kept making me laugh with her jokes. Later in the day when we had our meet, I was cruising along in the eight hundred in first place, feeling pretty secure I had provided a happy ending for the story, when another runner shot past me and edged me out at the finish. So much for keeping my focus. Still, the trip to Washington and the CNN story generated a lot more attention for the school and the programme. I had enjoyed my few moments of being treated like a celebrity, but soon it was back to work rewiring fixtures, going to class, and enduring the good-natured but ceaseless teasing of my friends.

We capped off a remarkable 1999 season by winning the National Outdoor Championship. Even though I had won the indoor championship, I could do no better than seventh in the nation in Emporia, Kansas. I had to be satisfied with my finish. All of the extra travel and attention had me struggling to keep up with my training and my schoolwork. No matter, I still earned all-American status as I had in cross-country in the autumn '98 season. I was looking ahead to a successful cross-country season in 1999. For the autumn, I was the number one runner on the cross-country team, and I won the conference and regional individual title, and our team won the championship as well.

Because of my performance in those two meets, I was favoured to win the national championship, to be run on a hilly course in Joplin, Missouri. The race day dawned with steady showers that would not let up, and on a muddy course I wore the wrong spikes – a very bad choice on my part, and I slipped and slid out of contention. We improved by one place to finish fourth, nothing to be ashamed of, since it was the school's highest finish ever, but it was still a letdown for me.

No account of my life or of that wonderful year would be complete without mentioning some of the many people who helped me in so many ways. In Abilene, I met Moses Osborn, an English professor who taught in the freshman transitional programme. A white man in his fifties or sixties, Moses befriended me and a number of other foreign students. A number of times he took us out to dinner to give us a break from the dormitory dreck. Moses was also good friends with Jim and Emma Gibson. At first I didn't know of their connection. Jim and Emma belonged to the same church I had been attending, Holy Family Catholic Church on Buffalo Gap Road in Abilene, since I had arrived on campus. One day after services they invited me to their home for dinner. They had settled in Abilene after Jim had served in the air force all over the United States and the world. They had three grown sons, Michael, William, and Joey, all out of the house by the time I met Jim and Emma. In some ways I think they thought of me as a kind of son. Emma was originally from Ireland, and she retained the warmth and friendliness her native country is so well known for. I spent a lot of time with them at their home or out at meals, and I got to know their sons well.

When I first got to Abilene I was also blessed by meeting Graham and Diana Guttings. My sponsor family in Savannah, Allan and Cynthia Bosson, had let them know I was in Abilene. They were devout Baptists and invited me to go with them to their services. I accepted the invitation, but it took me some time to get to the point when being in church on a Sunday from nine until two felt like anything besides a punishment. On the other hand, I loved spending time with Graham and Diana, along with their daughter Kathryn (who went to ACU also) and her brothers, Brian and Mark. Later on, Professor Michael Weingarden played a key role in my life. A marketing professor originally from Germany and married to a Canadian woman, Michael had run at ACU himself a few years before. He became a great friend and was instrumental in my later move to Austin, Texas.

If 1999 was loaded with highlights, 2000 got off to an even more auspicious start when I travelled to Disney World to receive the Courageous Student-Athlete Award from the National Consortium. We had much to celebrate before that, with ACU edging ever closer to a cross-country national championship by finishing second. The award dinner was held in Orlando, and I got to tour and enjoy the theme park, but even that exercise in experiencing illusions could not help me believe that I was actually going to meet Muhammad Ali. Ali needs no introduction, but he has loomed large in the minds of Africans ever since he came to what was then Zaire in 1974 to battle George Foreman for the heavyweight title. His presence in Africa, his later humanitarian efforts, his early dissent against the policies of the U.S. government, combined to make him a living and vital symbol of all that was possible through athletics and an indomitable spirit of giving. I had heard about Ali since I was a young boy, and the names Cassius Clay and Ali were spoken with the reverence usually accorded a deity. Whenever you won anything, you were compared to "the Greatest." Sitting there that evening at the same table with him and grasping his hand brought tears of joy to my eyes. How had a young man from Fuku Mountain traveled so far?

I did not have much time to contemplate the answer. I was still busy with work and school but had a great deal more to worry about as well. To this day, I do not like to talk about these things, but in the summer of 1999 I had gone back to Burundi to visit my family. The trip did not go well. I was still very upset and worried all the time about my safety. As much as I loved being with my family and seeing Triphine for the first time in almost five years, I could never let my mind rest. I kept hearing rumours no matter where I went that Hutus were coming to get me again. My mother wanted me to stay, but everyone else kept telling me I had to go back to the United States. I was not safe there. As if to prove their point that I should stay away and never think of going back, after I left a group of Hutus showed up at my mother's house looking for me. They also shot and killed my cousin Didace Niyukuri, and they harvested and stole all my mother's crops. As 2000 began and I was in Orlando, violence was once again escalating in Burundi.

I received some more sad news toward the end of the 2000 school year. Triphine's parents both died within a short time of each other. Her father, Epimaque Ntikarahera, a lawyer and a judge, was killed by Hutu rebels, and her mother was so distraught she died only a few weeks later. No matter what good things happened to me in the States, it seemed as though something terrible was happening in Burundi. Triphine's brothers got into a dispute over the parents' estate, and she was a wreck. She had been applying to ACU and several other schools here, and she was accepted at most of them. Once her parents were gone, I immediately proposed to her, and she accepted. I wanted so much to protect her and to shield her from all the awfulness in Burundi. I knew it was impossible to never feel any pain, but I thought if we shared it, half the burden would be better than all. On the 5th of September, 2000, I stood nervously pacing the Dallas/Fort Worth airport terminal, awaiting my future bride's arrival. I had a dozen red roses to present to her, along with a few gifts from my new extended family. When I saw her, we wrapped our arms around each other and embraced for the longest time. This was better than meeting the president and Ali combined!

I had to take a crash course in American wedding traditions courtesy of Emma and Jim, and I formally proposed to Triphine on Thanksgiving Day 2000 in front of a host of friends gathered for a traditional American dinner. Triph had no idea why I was kneeling in front of her, but she understood what the ring meant and her joyful tears were all the answer I needed. That same evening, I kept a Burundian tradition alive and called her cousin and an uncle offering them two of our family's cows as a dowry. They were very pleased. We should have been able to hold a dowry ceremony and party back in Burundi, but we could not leave because of Triph's visa situation – if she left she would not have been able to return. We also had to hold off on getting married until she had been in the States for six months. We scheduled the wedding for May – the same day I was to graduate from ACU.

With gracious financial support from so many people, some of the money Triph had saved, and my salary, we managed to find an apartment where we lived together for the rest of the school year. Jim and Emma helped take care of all the wedding arrangements and paid for nearly everything. Triph and I were so blessed to have their support and encouragement. The outpouring of generosity from our friends in Abilene was overwhelming. Triph and I completed our Pre-Cana classes at Holy Family. She and Emma picked out a gown and a cake, and we rented the church hall for the reception. Even though I had been in Abilene for only four years, I found it difficult to limit the number of guests to a hundred. I had so many friends I wanted to share my joy with and express my gratitude to. The only wedding nervousness I experienced came the night before; I hardly slept. I had no doubts about Triphine, and part of my sleeplessness was due to excitement, but I wondered how I was going to support her. I was twenty-five years old, about to graduate, and I didn't have a job.

I thought back to that sleepless night in October almost seven years earlier. I had worried so much then about exams. How different my troubles were at that moment. Then I thought about how much had happened in the intervening years, and yet how much the same my life really was. I'd loved life on Fuku Mountain because I was surrounded by a loving family. In Abilene, and everywhere I had travelled both in the United States and outside it, I had found loving people who cared for me and supported me. I don't believe our life experiences should ever be subjected to a test, but my love of science leads me to say this: if I were to place on a scale all the bad things that had happened to me and my family on one side and all the kindness and generosity on the other, the goodness in people would far outweigh the bad. I saw Burundi for what it was – not a paradise and not a hell, simply a land made imperfect by the people who inhabited it.

Graduation was a blur. All I could think about was the wedding to follow. Triph and I managed to survive saying our vows – neither of us liked to talk in front of large groups. The reception was a blast. Triphine's twin, Triphose, came from Burundi, and we managed to mix into the evening some traditions from our country. One of those was of course music. We danced all night, and later, for the last dance, we turned the lights out and Triph and I danced alone in the light cast from the candles our guests held, the shadows and the flickering flames merging on the walls, the floors, and the faces of the revellers. I looked into Triph's eyes, so warm and beautiful in that light. I glanced around the room at the faces, black and white, Catholic and Baptist, from Burundi, Jamaica, Canada, Ireland, Ukraine, and a dozen other places. There stood Jim and Emma beaming, Triphose and Alfred laughing, Graham and Diana swaying arm in arm, Michael, Joe, William, Bernard, Joseph, and Musa raising a glass to us.

For just a second I shut my eyes, and those faces faded and others emerged from the darkness. *My father. Anatole. Desirée. Sahabo. Martin. Delphine. Robert. Monique. Diomede. Leonard. Solanga Beatrice. Hubert. Brigitte Patience.*

Then I heard this voice in my heart and it told me again I was going to be okay.

I am a very, very fortunate man to have lost and to have gained so much. I am blessed to hold so many and so much in this grateful heart.

EPILOGUE

Following our wedding, blessings continued to flow. Michael Weingarden was instrumental in getting me to come to Austin, where I still make my home. He introduced me to his college roommate and former track and cross-country teammate Paul Carrozza. Paul owned a running store in Austin by the name of RunTex. To say that RunTex is a running store doesn't begin to explain how wonderful and how inspirational an organisation it is. Shortly after meeting Paul in 2000, I made the move to Austin with his help and began working at the store. RunTex *is* the Austin running community, and no other city I know of has a community like the one RunTex fosters. From organising races to insuring that runners can be hydrated properly on training runs to leading classes, RunTex, Paul Carrozza, and his staff have created an atmosphere in which people give of themselves in every way imaginable.

The people of Austin have embraced my family and me, enriched my life immeasurably, and become my new extended family. It is almost as though in running away from the troubles in Burundi, I have found my way back to Fuku Mountain. I am once again surrounded by people who care for me and nurture me. There aren't pages enough to recount all the kindnesses done to me in the five years I have been here. I would be remiss, however, if I didn't give some credit to those who were most instrumental in shaping my life here.

At first I became known in Austin as a runner, but Paul wanted me to do more than simply run. He wanted me to share my story and to do everything I could to inspire others. Through various programmes, including Marathon Kids, he got me out into the community, in front of schools and church groups, to tell my story and to actively encourage others to enjoy the fellowship of running. I continued to compete in and to win races, and through my success word of my story spread. I am particularly grateful that three women saw enough in me as a runner that they asked me to coach them: Leslie Asaka, Maeve Magner, and Anjanette Gonzalez.

I had been coaching most of my days as a runner but never officially – I simply wanted to give back to the people who had done so much for Triphine and me. When Leslie, Maeve, and Anjanette approached me following a race in Austin, I agreed to help them, but I didn't want them to pay me. They insisted that my time was valuable and I should be compensated. As time went on, they realised and made me realise how precious a commodity my time was. Working full-time and running races was taking its toll on me. They saw the kind of results I was getting and told me that if I could concentrate on running full-time, I should be able to qualify for the Olympics. To help me make that dream come true, Aida and John Dieck as well as Donna and Steve Hicks organised fund-raising events. Together with Paul, they channelled the proceeds to the RunTex

Foundation to provide me with financial support so I could stop working and train full-time. The people of Austin in their great generosity contributed close to sixty thousand dollars to help me. I am grateful to everyone who helped me with money, with a word of encouragement, with a smile.

Speaking of smiles, a new joy came into my life when Triphine gave birth to our first daughter, Emma, in Abilene. She and Triphine remain the principal source of bliss in my life, and just after I finished this we welcomed our second daughter, Grace. I could not be more thrilled.

Though injury prevented me from qualifying in the marathon for the 2004 Olympic Games, I have my sights set on 2008. I continue to train, but I am also doing something else to help spread the good news of running. In 2002 I started Gilbert's Gazelles, a training group/running club for runners of all ages. It started modestly and now has more than two hundred members. Adolphe would be proud to know that I am carrying on the tradition. The deep gratification I feel when one of the Gazelles does well is like those echoes I used to love to hear when I sang on Fuku Mountain. The more I give, the more I receive, and I have the people of Austin to thank for teaching me so much.

I try not to think too much about those days before. I read that Headmaster Niyonkenguruka was arrested, tried, and executed for his role in the attack on Lycée Kibimba. I learned that Severin, the boy who I once considered a friend, was killed in the violence. I found no pleasure in either report. Lycée Kibimba remained closed until just last year. The concrete shell of the building we were all herded into still stands – only now it serves as a memorial to the many who lost their lives.

I wish I could say the violence in Burundi has ended, but it has not. The country remains unstable. With the exception of my cousin Bernard, who now lives with me in Austin, my family remains there, but I cannot go back. There are those who still hate, who still would like to see me dead. Burundi will always be like a first lover that jilted me – I now see all its imperfections, but still . . .

Though I continue to train and have my goals, I know my life and its successes cannot be measured in minutes and seconds. When I travel around Texas telling my story to church groups and at schools, I do talk about running a bit – but I have another gospel to preach as well. That said, no matter what happens in the next two years leading up to the 2008 Olympics, I know that I will always run – it will always be a passion and joy. I am so fortunate to do for a living something I deeply love, something I feel I was born to do. I'm so happy that I can give back in some small measure through Gilbert's Gazelles.

I began this book with a saying I learned as a young boy in Burundi: it is easy to light a fire and difficult to extinguish it. I understand that much better now than I did then. Though some would rather have seen me destroyed by flames, no one can extinguish the fire inside of me. The light God placed there still burns brightly. Each day I try to honour this great gift of life with some gesture of gratitude.

I must go for a run now. This voice in my heart tells me so. It also reminds me I am a man many times blessed. I wish you peace.

GILBERT TUHABONYE
Austin, Texas